BTEC
NATIONAL

CHILDREN'S PLAY, LEARNING AND DEVELOPMENT

Student Book 2

REVISED FOR THE EARLY YEARS EDUCATOR CRITERIA

Penny Tassoni
Brenda Baker
Louise Burnham
Karen Hucker
PACEY
Editor: **Gill Squire**

ALWAYS LEARNING

PEARSON

Published by Pearson Education Limited, Edinburgh Gate, Harlow, Essex, CM20 2JE.

www.pearsonschoolsandfecolleges.co.uk

Text © Penny Tassoni, Brenda Baker, Louise Burnham, Karen Hucker and PACEY (Professional Association for Childcare and Early Years) 2014
Edited by Gill Squire
Typeset by Phoenix Photosetting, Chatham, Kent, UK
Original illustrations © Pearson Education Limited and Katie Mac/NB Illustration Ltd 2013
Cover design by Pearson Education Limited and Kath Fotheringham
Picture research by Susie Prescott
Front cover photo: Masterfile UK Ltd: Marc Vaughn
Indexing by Sophia Clapham

The rights of Penny Tassoni, Brenda Baker, Louise Burnham, Karen Hucker and PACEY to be identified as authors of this work have been asserted by them in accordance with the Copyright, Designs and Patents Act 1988.

First published 2014

18 17 16 15 14
10 9 8 7 6 5 4 3 2 1

British Library Cataloguing in Publication Data
A catalogue record for this book is available from the British Library

ISBN 978 1 447 97097 2

Printed in Italy by Lego S.p.A

Websites
There are links to relevant websites in this book. In order to ensure that the links are up to date, that the links work, and that the sites aren't inadvertently links to sites that could be considered offensive, we have made the links available on our website at www.pearsonhotlinks.co.uk. Search for the title, BTEC Level 3 National Children's Play, Learning & Development (Early Years Educator) Student Book 2 (revised edition) or ISBN 9781447970972. Weblinks in Further Reading sections have been left in place for learners to access independently.

Copies of official specifications for all Pearson qualifications may be found on the website: www.edexcel.com.

A NOTE FROM THE PUBLISHER

In order to ensure that this resource offers high-quality support for the associated BTEC qualification, it has been through a review process by the awarding organisation to confirm that it fully covers the teaching and learning content of the specification or part of a specification at which it is aimed, and demonstrates an appropriate balance between the development of subject skills, knowledge and understanding, in addition to preparation for assessment.

While the publishers have made every attempt to ensure that advice on the qualification and its assessment is accurate, the official specification and associated assessment guidance materials are the only authoritative source of information and should always be referred to for definitive guidance.

BTEC examiners have not contributed to any sections in this resource relevant to examination papers for which they have responsibility.

No material from an endorsed book will be used verbatim in any assessment set by BTEC.

Endorsement of a book does not mean that the book is required to achieve this BTEC qualification, nor does it mean that it is the only suitable material available to support the qualification, and any resource lists produced by the awarding organisation shall include this and other appropriate resources.

Contents

About this book

This book is designed to help you through your BTEC National Children's Play, Learning and Development course, and includes ten units: Units 11 to 17, plus Units 19, 21 and 25. This book builds on Units 1 to 10, which are covered in Pearson's BTEC National Children's Play, Learning and Development Student Book 1.

About your BTEC National in Children's Play, Learning and Development

Choosing to study for a BTEC National Children's Play, Learning and Development qualification is a great decision to make for lots of reasons. In recent years, there has been a growing understanding that children's earliest experiences shape their life chances and it is vital that children receive the best possible early education and care. As a future early years professional, you can play a significant part in making sure that the provision children receive is of the highest quality.

Your BTEC National Children's Play, Learning and Development qualification is a vocational or work-related qualification. This means that it will give you the opportunity to gain specific knowledge, understanding and skills that are relevant to your chosen subject or area of work. This new BTEC course is a great foundation to build your skills for employment or further study.

What will you be doing?

The BTEC Nationals in Children's Play, Learning and Development are structured into **core units** and **optional specialist units**. How many units you do and which ones you cover depend on the type of qualification you are working towards. Table 1.1 shows you how the units in this book fit into the Certificate or Diploma qualifications.

Table 1.1 Core and optional specialist units

Unit	Subsidiary Certificate	Certificate	Diploma
Unit 11: Reflective Practice	N/A	Core	Core
Unit 12: The Early Years Foundation Stage (EYFS)	Optional specialist	Core	Core
Unit 13: Research Skills	N/A	N/A	Core
Unit 14: Health, Education and Social Services for Children and Their Families	N/A	N/A	Optional specialist
Unit 15: Food and Mealtimes in the Early Years	N/A	N/A	Optional specialist
Unit 16: Working With Children Under 3 Years	N/A	N/A	Optional specialist
Unit 17: Working With Children in Home-based Care	N/A	N/A	Optional specialist
Unit 19: Working With Children Who Have Additional Needs	N/A	N/A	Optional specialist

| Unit 21: Supporting Children's Imaginative Play | N/A | N/A | Optional specialist |
| Unit 25: Promoting Children's Development Outdoors | N/A | N/A | Optional specialist |

Student Book 1, covering Units 1 to 10, is also available. You can find details about this at www.pearsonschoolsandfecolleges.co.uk or from your teacher/tutor.

About the authors

Best-selling author **Penny Tassoni** trained as an early years and primary teacher. Now working as an education consultant and trainer, she specialises in the whole spectrum of learning and play. Penny has written more than 30 books about early years and frequently writes articles for national early years magazines. In addition to this, Penny is a well-known speaker both in the UK and internationally. She has in-depth knowledge of the BTEC Nationals in Children's Play, Learning and Development, and uses her accessible and friendly style of writing to bring the information to life for learners on this course.

Brenda Baker has worked in early years settings and as a primary teacher. She then taught childcare and education in an FE college and, for a number of years, managed its Health and Social Care Department. In recent years she has contributed to textbooks and support materials for learners and teachers/tutors of early years and teaching assistant qualifications. She has extensive experience of BTEC qualifications.

Louise Burnham has worked as an early years and primary teacher and SENCO. She also led teaching assistant training and worked on childcare and teaching courses at a London FE college for a number of years. Louise has written 12 books for early years and teaching assistant qualifications, and continues to work with early years and teaching assistant students.

Karen Hucker has worked in both secondary schools and FE, teaching childcare and education and health and social care. She is currently Principal of a sixth form college, but earlier in her career she managed its Health and Social Care Department. She has been an author for a number of years, contributing to numerous textbooks and support materials. She has extensive experience of both the vocational and academic curriculum post-16.

PACEY is the Professional Association for Childcare and Early Years. The organisation promotes best practice in early years and supports its members – including childminders, nursery workers and nannies – to deliver the highest standards in care and learning for children. We are very grateful to PACEY for their contribution (Unit 17 in this book).

How to use this book

This book contains many features that will help you apply your skills and knowledge to work-related situations and assist you in getting the most from your course.

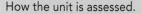

These introductions give you a snapshot of what to expect from each unit – and what you should be aiming for by the time you finish it.

How the unit is assessed.

Learning aims describe what you will be doing in the unit.

A learner or early years professional shares their experiences related to the content of the unit.

Features of this book

There are lots of features in this book to help you learn about what's included in each unit and to enable you to reflect on, or consider, key concepts. These pages show some of the features that you will come across when using the book.

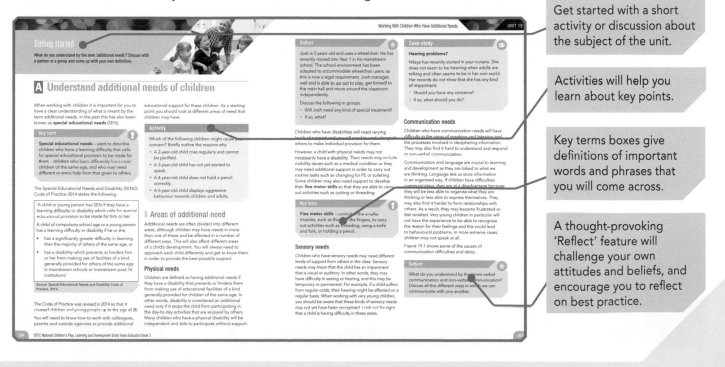

Get started with a short activity or discussion about the subject of the unit.

Activities will help you learn about key points.

Key terms boxes give definitions of important words and phrases that you will come across.

A thought-provoking 'Reflect' feature will challenge your own attitudes and beliefs, and encourage you to reflect on best practice.

Case study

Hearing problems?

Nilaya has recently started in your nursery. She does not seem to be listening when adults are talking and often seems to be in her own world. Her records do not show that she has any kind of impairment.

1 Should you have any concerns?

2 If so, what should you do?

Examples from real settings that focus on situations you could find yourself in when working in early years. These examples will make you consider how you might act in those situations and help you to improve your practice.

Assessment practice 19.3

3B.P4 | 3B.M2

Research and write a report on the emergence of the social model of disability and inclusive education, and how they have changed the way in which children with additional needs are included in mainstream schools. Refer to legislation, regulations and initiatives.

Activities that relate to the unit's assessment criteria. These activities will help you prepare for your assignments. They may include suggestions for tasks that help build towards your assignment, as well as helping you to develop your knowledge, skills and understanding.

Working With Children Who Have Additional Needs
UNIT 19

Ready for work?

Soriya Gupta Nursery worker

I have been working at the nursery for three years. I have worked with quite a few children who have had additional needs, from speech and language difficulties to Down's Syndrome and also two autistic children. It's really important to have a good understanding of how children with additional needs are looked after in different early years settings and to have a good working knowledge of the Code of Practice. This is important, as it gives us a clear document to work from alongside our own policies and procedures.

We also need to understand the whole assessment process and be able to carry out observations so that we can feedback to colleagues and parents, and be part of a whole-team approach to managing the child's needs. I have been sent on a couple of training courses on additional needs which were run through the local authority and these have given me a really good insight into the kinds of issues to look out for and also a source of additional advice if needed.

I have also had the opportunity to work with a few other professionals, including my area SENCO, the speech and language therapists, and both occupational therapists and physiotherapists. This has been really interesting for me as I have learned a lot more about what their roles involve, and it has been great to be involved in meetings with them along with parents and really feel that I am making a difference to these children.

Someone who works in early years explains how this unit of their BTEC helped them to develop as an effective practitioner. This feature gives you a chance to think more about the role that the person does, and whether you would want to follow in their footsteps once you have completed your BTEC.

Skills for practice

Effective relationships with children – supporting a child with additional needs

- Get to know as much as you can about the child from parents and other staff in the setting.
- Form a relationship with the child by finding out about them and their interests.
- Make a point of saying hello and talking to them each day.
- Find out about any additional equipment or resource they may need and learn to use it too.
- Make sure you are aware of their targets and IEP.
- Work with them on different areas of the curriculum – both indoor and outdoor – and support them where needed.

Professional relationships with adults

- Show that you can work as part of a team by supporting others in your setting.
- Be organised and prepared each day when you come to the setting. If working with a child who has additional needs, you may need to bring additional resources.
- If you are working as part of a team around a particular child, remember to keep channels of communication open and be approachable.
- Keep up to date with contact details of other agencies and individuals with whom you are working to support the child.
- Develop and nurture good relationships with parents and carers, and remain approachable and easy to contact on a daily basis.

Tips and guidance about the practical skills you need to develop in order to work with children. In some units these tips link to the **Practical Evidence Portfolio** that you will need to complete while on placement if you are taking the BTEC National Award, Subsidiary Certificate, Certificate and Diploma in Children's Play, Learning and Development.

221

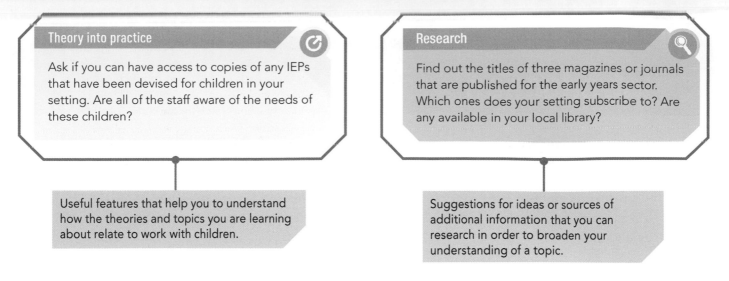

Theory into practice

Ask if you can have access to copies of any IEPs that have been devised for children in your setting. Are all of the staff aware of the needs of these children?

Research

Find out the titles of three magazines or journals that are published for the early years sector. Which ones does your setting subscribe to? Are any available in your local library?

Useful features that help you to understand how the theories and topics you are learning about relate to work with children.

Suggestions for ideas or sources of additional information that you can research in order to broaden your understanding of a topic.

BTEC Assessment Zone

You will be assessed in two different ways for your BTEC National Children's Play, Learning and Development qualification. For most units, your teacher/tutor will set assignments for you to complete. These assignments may take the form of projects where you research, plan, prepare, make and evaluate a piece of work or activity, case study or presentation. (For Units 11 and 13 these assignments are written and set by Pearson.) For Unit 1 of your BTEC (which was covered in Student Book 1), you are assessed by a paper-based exam.

The table in this BTEC Assessment Zone explains what you must do in order to achieve each of the assessment criteria.

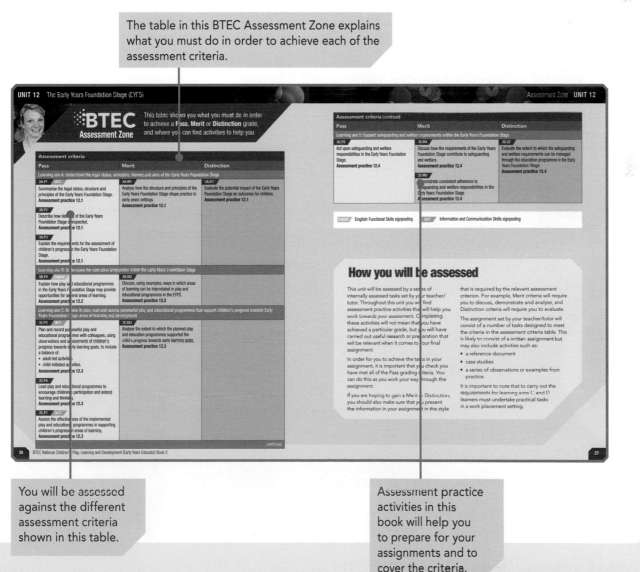

You will be assessed against the different assessment criteria shown in this table.

Assessment practice activities in this book will help you to prepare for your assignments and to cover the criteria.

Introduction

Learning to think about and question the effectiveness of your work with children is now considered an important part of being a professional. Reviewing your strengths and weaknesses and checking that your knowledge is up to date helps to ensure that you give children the best start possible. This unit is about knowing how to recognise your strengths and weaknesses and how to take steps to improve your practice especially in relation to promoting children's learning and development.

Assessment: You will be assessed by a Pearson-set assignment and by completing a Practical Evidence Portfolio containing evidence from three work placements.

Learning aims

In this unit you will:

A   understand the purpose of reflective practice in relation to working with children and developing own practice

B   understand how to develop skills of reflective practice in promoting children's learning and development

C   be able to use the skills of reflective practice in relation to promoting children's learning and development.

> When I first started working with children, I thought this reflective practice stuff was a waste of time. Now I can see that by talking about the way we work with other team members, we can make a real difference to the way we work with children. I've really enjoyed putting together my Practical Evidence Portfolio and seeing how my knowledge and skills are developing all the time.
>
> Anna, *room leader in a day-care setting*

Reflective
Practice

11

BTEC Assessment Zone

This table shows you what you must do in order to achieve a **Pass**, **Merit** or **Distinction** grade, and where you can find activities to help you.

Assessment criteria

Pass	Merit	Distinction
Learning aim A: Understand the purpose of reflective practice in relation to working with children and developing own practice		
3A.P1 English Explain the role of reflective practice in supporting children's learning and development. **Assessment practice 11.1** **3A.P2** Explain the importance of continued professional development to improve own skills and early years practice. **Assessment practice 11.1**	**3A.M1** Assess the effectiveness of reflective practice and how it contributes to work with children. **Assessment practice 11.1**	**3A.D1** Evaluate the ways that continued professional development improves own skills, practice and knowledge in supporting children's learning and development. **Assessment practice 11.1**
Learning aim B: Understand how to develop skills of reflective practice in promoting children's learning and development		
3B.P3 English I&CT Identify ways to gain information about developing own practice in promoting children's learning and development. **Assessment practice 11.2** **3B.P4** English I&CT Outline the tools that can be used to engage in and reflect on own skills, practice and knowledge. **Assessment practice 11.2**	**3B.M2** Discuss appropriate sources of information and tools used to reflect on and improve skills, practice and knowledge in supporting different areas of children's learning and development. **Assessment practice 11.2**	**3B.D2** Evaluate how improving own skills, practice and knowledge can impact on children's overall learning and development. **Assessment practice 11.2**
Learning aim C: Be able to use the skills of reflective practice in relation to promoting children's learning and development		
3C.P5 English I&CT Develop a Practical Evidence Portfolio containing evidence of developing own practice, knowledge and skills when working with children. **Assessment practice 11.3**	**3C.M3** Assess the value of developing and maintaining a Practical Evidence Portfolio in developing own continued professional development. **Assessment practice 11.3**	**3C.D3** Maths Evaluate the contribution of others in informing own Practical Evidence Portfolio and how this improves own skills, practice and knowledge. **Assessment practice 11.3**

English   English Functional Skills signposting

I&CT   Information and Communication Technology Skills signposting

Maths   Mathematics Functional Skills signposting

How you will be assessed

This unit will be assessed by an assignment that is set by Pearson. It will be marked internally by your teacher and verified by a Pearson Standards Verifier. Throughout this unit you will find assessment practice activities that will help you work towards your assessment. Completing these activities will not mean that you have achieved a particular grade, but you will have carried out useful research or preparation that will be relevant when it comes to your final assignment.

Getting started

What do you think your strengths and weaknesses are when working with children? How good are you at encouraging children's learning and development? When you have finished this unit, see whether you feel your answers to these questions are still an accurate reflection of your practice.

A Understand the purpose of reflective practice in relation to working with children and developing own practice

All adults working with babies and children are encouraged to think about the way that they work. This is known as **reflective practice** and it is considered an essential way of improving practice. In this section we will look at how reflective practice can help you to become a more effective practitioner.

The term 'reflective practice' is used to describe the process by which practitioners become aware of their limitations and gaps in their knowledge as well as their strengths and good qualities. Reflective practice should be used in all areas of your professional work with children and their families. This is shown in Figure 11.1.

> ### Key term
>
> **Reflective practice** – thinking about the way we work in order to make changes, build on strengths and stay up to date with developments.

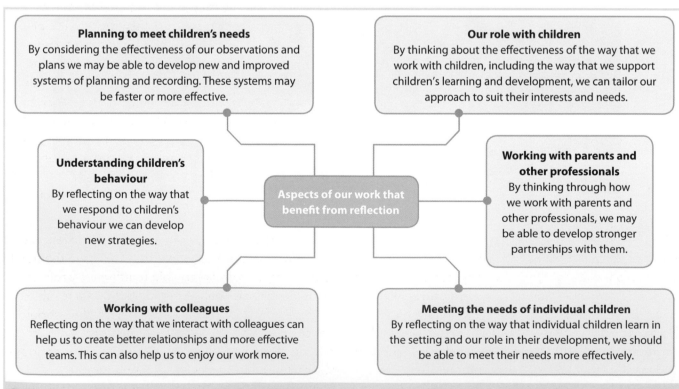

Planning to meet children's needs
By considering the effectiveness of our observations and plans we may be able to develop new and improved systems of planning and recording. These systems may be faster or more effective.

Our role with children
By thinking about the effectiveness of the way that we work with children, including the way that we support children's learning and development, we can tailor our approach to suit their interests and needs.

Understanding children's behaviour
By reflecting on the way that we respond to children's behaviour we can develop new strategies.

Aspects of our work that benefit from reflection

Working with parents and other professionals
By thinking through how we work with parents and other professionals, we may be able to develop stronger partnerships with them.

Working with colleagues
Reflecting on the way that we interact with colleagues can help us to create better relationships and more effective teams. This can also help us to enjoy our work more.

Meeting the needs of individual children
By reflecting on the way that individual children learn in the setting and our role in their development, we should be able to meet their needs more effectively.

Figure 11.1 Aspects of work that might benefit from reflection

What is meant by reflective practice?

The idea of reflective practice is relatively new to early years. It is a way of working that can improve practice considerably. For years it has been known that the quality of our work has a huge impact on children and their families, but finding ways to develop and maintain this quality was not easy. Inspections, reports by line managers and ongoing staff training have all been tried. However, today it is felt that the best person to help you work effectively with children is yourself.

A continuous cycle

The process of reflective practice can be seen as a cycle, as it is continuous and never-ending. Figure 11.2 shows this continuous cycle. Interestingly, you may find that experienced practitioners say they are still learning. This is because every child is different, every family is different and there are often changes to resources, the curriculum and approaches to early education. Reflective practice covers every aspect of your work, including your relationships with parents, colleagues and other professionals, as well as the importance of promoting children's overall learning and development.

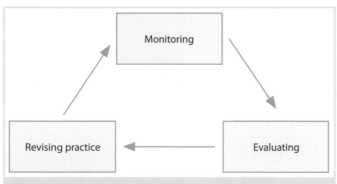

Figure 11.2 The continuous cycle of reflective practice

Monitoring

This is about being aware of what you are doing when you are with children. You may look at children's reactions or consider how children are using equipment or enjoying an activity. Monitoring is also about being aware of children's outcomes and progress, then relating this to your practice and those used in the setting. As well as self-monitoring, you can also gain feedback from a range of sources such as parents, colleagues and children.

> **Link**
>
> Go to Section C in this unit to find more information about gaining feedback from parents, colleagues and children.

Evaluation

As you monitor and gain information from a wide range of sources, you need to evaluate its significance and then consider whether any aspect of your practice requires changing.

Revising own practices

As a result of ongoing evaluation, experienced practitioners will often try out new ideas, change their practices or change the routine or equipment of the setting. In some cases, you will need to change your own behaviours or style of working with children. You may also need to change your attitudes, approaches and beliefs about how best to work with children.

The effect of behaviours, beliefs, values, attitudes and approaches on reflection

Reflective practice may lead to us changing our behaviours and attitudes. It is easy to say this but often harder to do it in practice. This is because quite often our own existing behaviours, attitudes, beliefs and values led us in the first place to use the approaches we do with children and families. Simple things, such as whether or not we encourage children to finish everything on their plate at meal times, are likely to be a result of our set of beliefs, attitudes and values, in this case those towards food, which in turn may be linked to approaches that our parents and other carers took with us.

We know that behaviours, attitudes and beliefs are powerful and this means that they can have the ability to prevent us from being able to effectively reflect on our practice and change and develop as a result. For example, if we strongly believe that children should be 'taught', it might mean that we are resistant to practices that encourage children to be independent and to learn for themselves through child-initiated play. This would mean that practice in the setting may be too formal.

As well as our own behaviours, beliefs and attitudes, we should not forget the people we work with also have their own set; and so for change to take place, we may also have to find a way of collectively changing our approach.

A good starting point when engaging in reflective practice is to understand the impact that our behaviours, beliefs, values and attitudes have on our current approach and ways of working.

Reflect

Look at the following situations. Consider what your initial reaction is likely to be. Then, think about how your approach is linked to your beliefs, values and attitudes.

- A child is bouncing on a sofa.
- A child is walking around drinking from a beaker.
- A parent is on the phone while her son is trying to tell her something.
- A child does not want to join the story time and instead is throwing beanbags at the sitting children.
- Two children are squabbling over a tricycle even though there is a spare one.

The importance of engaging in continuing professional development

Just as reflective practice is continuous, so our learning should be continuous too. As well as continuing to develop our own skills and knowledge to help us work with children, it is also important we think about any gaps in our education and try to fill them. For example, you may have disliked science at school and, therefore, may not have gained much knowledge in this subject, or you may not have had the opportunity to learn a foreign language.

Having knowledge across many subject areas is thought to be important: not only does it make us more confident but it also helps our practice with children, as we are more likely to find a wider range of learning opportunities in the environment and be able to use language more accurately.

For example, if a practitioner has some knowledge of science, they may be able to show children that a brick wall retains heat at the end of the day and give an accurate explanation of why this is.

Reflect

Look at the following subject areas.

- English
- Mathematics
- Music
- History
- Science
- Modern foreign languages
- Arts and crafts
- Cookery

1 On a scale of 1 to 5, with 1 being poor, how confident are you that you have good knowledge of the subject?
2 Consider which areas you would prioritise for improvement.

Research

Research the opportunities available to improve your subject knowledge in a particular area. Use online sources and books as well as courses offered in your local area as a starting point.

The importance of reflective practice

There are many reasons why reflective practice is important in the workplace. If you are a reflective practitioner, not only will you improve outcomes for the children you work with, but you will also develop your own skills and career.

Extending children's learning

Reflection can be used to support your personal and professional development. However, the most important reason for using reflection is to improve the quality, type and range of early learning experiences for children. These should be made as effective as possible to aid children's development.

We know that children who have sensitive and reflective adults with them are more likely to have their learning extended. These adults are likely to be more skilful at forming relationships. They are also likely to be good at recognising the best way of responding to individual children's interests and needs, and thus extending their learning. Reflective practitioners also think about trying out new ideas and approaches that might benefit individual children's needs.

Personal and professional development

When you first begin working with children, you will face a steep learning curve. You will need to adjust to working in a new environment as well as learning how to use the skills and knowledge that you acquired in your training. Being able to be a reflective practitioner and using the process that we will look at later in this unit will help you become more confident and, of course, competent.

Reflection will also help you to keep developing, as you will start to think about what new skills and areas of knowledge you would like to develop further. You may become interested in working with children who have additional needs or you may want to learn more about working with babies, for example.

Continuous quality improvement

While the basic needs of children have not changed for centuries, society and the perception of childhood are constantly changing. In addition new developments from research into children's learning have also influenced the curricula and expectations of work with children. There are also changes to the legislation in areas such as health and safety, employment and the rights of children. It is therefore important that settings and individual practitioners keep abreast of developments and are ready to reflect on, change and improve their practice. This needs to be a continuous process, which is planned and organised.

Shared understanding

In settings where reflection is built into the routine of the day, a more dynamic and interesting work environment is created. Practitioners can collaborate and discuss different options, approaches and ideas for working with children. This professional discussion can support a team's development, but also the individual development of team members. The impact on practices within the setting is usually very positive and a culture of open discussion and readiness to try out new ideas will emerge.

The importance of continuous reflection

Reflection is something that you should be doing all the time in order to carry on building your strengths and developing any ideas that have come about from your original reflections. Reflection is also important to ensure that changes in your practice are working as you had hoped.

This is particularly important because sometimes you may make changes that work well with a particular group of children or a specific child, but you may need to revise these changes at a later stage. Although children's interest levels may increase when you first introduce a new activity or resource, they are likely to decrease once children have become accustomed to them. Through the process of observation, reflection and monitoring, you can create a more dynamic environment that is keenly matched to children's interests and levels of development.

This team is reflecting on the quality of the toys in the setting.

The importance of others in supporting reflective practice and professional development

Reflective practice and continual professional development should be done with the support and feedback of others. This might include colleagues or line managers but also professionals from other agencies, such as speech and language therapists or family outreach workers. Gaining feedback, suggestions and information can help us to reflect on and improve our practice by focusing our attention on particular areas. In addition, if we attend a training course or enrol on a new qualification we will also meet other practitioners working in early years settings who have different approaches to ours. By exchanging ideas with these colleagues and learning about other approaches, we can further develop our practice.

You have been asked to give a presentation to a group of Turkish early years educators who are on an exchange visit. They are interested in finding out about the concept of reflective practice and the reasons why continued professional development is considered vital in our education system. To help the translator, you will also need to prepare detailed notes in advance of the presentation.

Your notes and presentation should include:

* an explanation of what is meant by the term 'reflective practice' and the importance of continued professional development
* the role of reflective practice and its effectiveness in supporting children's learning and development
* an evaluation of the ways in which continued professional development might improve your own skills, practice and knowledge in supporting children's learning and development.

B Understand how to develop skills of reflective practice in promoting children's learning and development

You will need to be able to use the skills of reflection in all aspects of your work with children and families. In this section, we focus on how this process might be applied specifically to promoting children's learning and development.

How to use current best practice

When reflecting on your practice you need to be aware of current best practice in relation to promoting children's learning and development. Key aspects of best practice include playfulness and play opportunities, observation, assessment and planning

as well as adult–child relationships. By being aware of current best practice, you can analyse what you and your setting are doing in each of these aspects, then compare your practice to it.

Best practice does change over time, so it is important to keep up to date. Best practice can change for a number of reasons, including government policy and changes in what is considered to be important for children's learning and development. In turn, these changes affect how the early years framework is delivered and inspected.

In earlier units in Student Book 1, we looked at what constitutes current practice (at the time of writing) in a number of areas, including the importance of the key person relationship and the need for quality adult–child relationships. Interestingly, these have not always been a focus for inspection, but they are now. In the same way, there is an ongoing debate about what type of play opportunities children need and whether there need to be more play opportunities led by adults which are not the same as child-initiated play activities.

Another area of practice that has changed over time is the extent to which planning, observation and assessment are carried out in settings and the methods used to do these. In the early years sector, long-term planning and group planning used to be used regularly, however, many settings today plan for individual children using short-term methods such as **learning journeys**.

Key term

Learning journey/learning story – a way of assessing and planning for children's development using a narrative approach that can easily be shared and constructed with parents and children.

Link

Go to Unit 9 in Student Book 1 to find more information about observation, assessment and planning and an explanation of 'learning journeys'.

The relevance of theories and philosophies in reflective practice

In earlier units, we have learned that there are many theoretical and philosophical approaches to children's learning and development. It is important to think about how these relate to your own approaches with children and which ones are most relevant. There may then be opportunities for you to attend training courses to explore the most relevant theories in more detail to support your reflective practice. A good example might be a practitioner who works in a pre-school deciding to explore in more detail the Montessori approach to children's

learning and development. By reading into the approach in more detail, attending a training course and visiting a Montessori group, the practitioner is able to reflect on whether any elements of the approach would be useful in developing the pre-school's practice.

Link

Go to Units 1, 2, 3, 7 and 10 in Student Book 1 to revisit theories and philosophies of children's learning and development.

How to gain information about promoting children's learning and development

In order to find out about best practice and how it can be applied to your own work and setting, you will need to find information, ideally from a range of sources. Examples are shown in Figure 11.3.

Figure 11.3 Where to find information to support practice

Reading articles and books

Articles and books can provide you with new information or food for thought for new activities. Magazines and professional journals can also make you aware of new developments within the sector, so it is a good idea to find the time to look through them.

Television, radio and the internet

Television, radio and the internet can be good sources of information about issues in early years or subjects or topics that link to early years. For example, you might find a radio programme that is discussing the topic of disability or a documentary on television about particular social or developmental difficulties that some families face. The internet can also be a very useful source of information, especially as there is a wide range of websites set up and run by practitioners with an interest in early childhood development. Some websites and forums can also offer an international perspective as its members come from all over the world. If you decide to use the internet, it is important you consider carefully whether the information you are reading and seeing is accurate.

Meeting other professionals

Many early years teams organise 'cluster groups', which enable practitioners from a particular area to meet up. Meeting other professionals in this way can help you to explore different ideas and reflect on your practice. Sometimes other professionals will tell you about how they have brought in a new system or piece of equipment to their setting, and their experiences can help you to explore your own ideas.

Attending training

Training courses can provide you with new ideas and thoughts about practice. Many settings will organise their own internal training sessions, either by closing for a day or as part of ongoing staff meetings. In addition, most early years advisory teams provide training courses, as do many national organisations such as Early Education. It is important to attend training in areas of your work that you feel strong in as well as those where you know your knowledge needs to be updated. This is because it is easy to become so comfortable with one way of working that you overlook other possibilities.

It is useful to write up your notes and thoughts following a training event. You can then look back at your notes and share them with colleagues.

Shadowing others

Sometimes you can reflect on the way in which you work, by noticing how other people handle situations, plan activities and relate to children. The term 'shadowing' is used to describe observing what others are doing in order to learn. Looking at how others work should not be about comparison or it can become too negative. It is about reflecting on others' and your own strengths. This can be done in your own setting with experienced colleagues or those who have particular specialisms or interests. It can be helpful, after watching others, to take the time to sit with them and talk about what you have seen. This will help you to understand the reasons behind their actions and to also learn any tips from them.

This adult is observing a colleague playing with a child.

Visiting other settings

It is also useful to watch others who are working in a similar setting in order to gain a different perspective and learn about their approaches. When visiting other settings, it is important to be respectful and polite even if you are unsure of their way of working. Interestingly, most people who visit other settings find that they come away with new thoughts or ideas.

Case study

Improving practice by visiting other settings

Joachim works at a day-care nursery but is spending the morning in a local preschool. He is particularly keen to find out more about how the preschool encourages children's communication and language development. He has been invited to the preschool as a result of making contact with the supervisor during a local network meeting. During the morning, he picks up many ideas and is interested in the different approaches that are being taken to support children who have English as an additional language. He also likes the way that the key persons spend set times with their key children. The staff are very friendly and quite open. Next week the supervisor of the preschool is due to visit his nursery.

1 Why is it important for Joachim to have an open mind during the visit?

2 How will Joachim benefit from seeing another early years setting in action?

3 How will the children in Joachim's nursery benefit from his visit to another setting?

How to gather information for continuing professional development and reflective practice

It can be hard to change practice alone. Most people benefit from having input, encouragement and feedback. There are many ways of gaining support, as Figure 11.4 shows.

Figure 11.4 Where to get the support you need to help you change your practice

Training

Training courses are valuable sources of support and information. You may go on a short course organised by your local early years team, college or national organisation. You may also decide to take a course of further study resulting in a qualification. This may be helpful in progressing your career or in allowing you to move into another area.

Websites

Websites and social media can give you support, but you must be aware of confidentiality issues and also your setting's policy in relation to social media. This means that you may not be able to share everything you are doing on a website. On the other hand, you may find suggestions for practice and information about what others have tried.

Teachers and tutors

While you are studying, your teacher or tutor will be a good source of support. They may observe you as you work and give you feedback. They may also help you to draw up an action plan and suggest ways of developing your practice a step at a time.

Supervisors

Your line manager or supervisor in the setting may be a good source of support. They may be very experienced and able to give you suggestions for how to put your ideas into practice.

They may also be able to arrange further training for you or put you in contact with other practitioners.

Sources of information to gain awareness of own practice

There are plenty of different sources of information you can use to gain awareness of your own practice.

Observation by others

Being observed by others, such as colleagues, teachers/tutors or inspectors may seem scary, but it can provide a valuable source of information. You may also find that your line manager carries out observations as part of the quality assurance process within your setting. Gathering information from others who have seen you in action is helpful because they may notice habits that you have acquired, such as saying 'okay' at the end of a sentence or not giving children sufficient time to respond. If you are being observed by colleagues, you may wish to talk to them about what you would like them to focus on. This might include your posture, tone or eye contact.

Feedback from colleagues

Listening to others can provide you with vital information that will help you to reflect on your practice. Feedback works best if you trust the people giving it and if they feel that they can give you an honest point of view. Listening to feedback carefully and avoiding being defensive is a skill in itself. It is easy to defend the reasons why you do things, but the key is to remember that the focus is on moving on and improving performance.

Feedback from children

You can gain feedback from children of all ages by simply noting down their reactions to what you do and by noticing what seems to engage them. Toddlers and older children can also tell you about activities that they enjoy and you can use photos to help them remember things that they have done with you.

Feedback from parents and carers

You can ask for feedback from parents or carers. Parents/carers may notice how their child's speech has developed and which activities or ways of working seem to have been effective.

Assessment of children's outcomes

By tracking children's progress, you can consider whether your practices are effective. If there are several children that you have responsibility for who are not making the expected progress, you may need to consider whether you need to improve opportunities for promoting their individual learning and development.

A good way to check whether children are making progress is to carry out sound recordings, as you can listen to these each month and look for progress.

Link

Go to Unit 9, Section B in Student Book 1 to find more information about making sound recordings.

Appraisals

All early years settings carry out appraisals on their staff. An appraisal is a review of both your work with children and as part of a team. An appraisal should help you to identify your strengths, weaknesses and areas for your future development. The appraisal process is usually led by the manager or deputy manager of the setting and involves feedback from your colleagues, observation of your work as well as feedback you provide about your own work. At the end of an appraisal process, a plan is drawn up that may identify targets and ways in which you can work towards them.

The skills required to evaluate your own practice

There are many skills you need in order to evaluate your own practice, but two of the most important are the ability to be objective and open-minded. If you close your mind to any information that you have gained, you will not be able to make progress. However, you also need to avoid being too self-critical and negative as this can sap your confidence. The key when evaluating your own practice is always to bear in mind that the aim of reflection is to move forward.

Factors that might affect your own practice

As part of your reflection process, you need to be able to recognise factors that might be affecting your practice. If you don't recognise them, they can sometimes lead you to be defensive about your practice or over-critical.

Experiences

Your own experiences will affect your practice. Firstly, what you have seen on placement or in your working life will be a major influence. This is one reason why it is a good idea to visit a range of settings so that you can see different approaches. In addition, past experiences of being criticised or being given feedback may also determine your immediate reactions.

Values

Your own values and beliefs about childhood and how children should behave will affect your practice. Interestingly, this often shows in the way that you manage children's behaviour. If you are aware of your own underlying values, you may find it easier to be open-minded.

Own education

Some people's own education may influence the way they work with children. A good example of this is play-based education. This is now the approach taken in all of the home countries' curricula. If your own education was more formal, it may be that your tendency is to intervene or try to structure play unnecessarily. Understanding how you were educated and comparing it to the current ways of working would be a good starting point.

These children are being taught formally. If you experienced this type of education, how might it affect your own practice?

Case study

Evaluating practice

Kay has been working with toddlers for a year. She recently attended a course about working with 2-year-olds. She realised that she had not been spending sufficient time talking to the children and that she had not been monitoring their language. At the start of the training day, she was sure that she would not learn anything new and was cross that she had to get up earlier than usual to attend.

After the training day, she returned to work upset and demotivated. Her manager noticed the change in her attitude and Kay told her that she was feeling useless and was considering resigning. Her manager explained that working with children was a learning process. Together they discussed what elements of the course could be implemented immediately and they agreed to talk about Kay's progress after a week or so.

1 How might reflection help Kay improve her practice?

2 Why might Kay's new knowledge improve the quality of outcomes for the children?

3 Why is it important for Kay to be supported by her manager?

Using tools of reflection to develop skills for effective reflection

There are a number of different tools and models that can be used to support reflective practice.

SWOT analysis

A SWOT analysis is a planning method and stands for:

S = Strengths

W = Weaknesses

O = Opportunities

T = Threats

Most SWOT analyses are used by settings and groups. However, it is possible to use the process to help you gain an overall picture of your current position.

Strengths

Consider what your overall strengths are. If you are not sure, sometimes it is easier if you ask a friend or classmate to say what they think your particular strengths are. There may be some you haven't thought of.

Weaknesses

Consider what your current weaknesses are. This can include knowledge and skills as well as working relationships that are not as strong as they should be. They might also include organisational skills such as time keeping, or gaps in your education such as spelling or writing.

Opportunities

Assuming you address your weaknesses, think about the opportunities available to you for the future. This might include career opportunities such as a promotion or moving to a different setting.

Threats

Assuming that you did not address your weaknesses, what are the possible threats to your career or work with children? For example, if you do not improve your time keeping, you will be asked to leave or if you do not pass your qualification, you may not be able to work with children.

Using a SWOT analysis

Once you have completed your SWOT analysis, you must start to think about what areas you should focus on to improve your work with children. It can be worth drawing up an action plan using your SWOT analysis and deciding on some priorities.

Action plans

When you have decided on an area of practice that you need to develop, the next step is to create an action plan. This is important because the process of drawing up a plan can help you to focus your ideas and thoughts. It also provides a framework within which you can monitor and review your progress. Many people will draw up an action plan alongside a manager, teacher/tutor or someone they trust within the setting.

Creating an action plan

There are five simple steps to take when drawing up an action plan.

1 Decide in detail about what you wish to change or develop. Base this on your evaluation. These will become your goals.

2 Break down each of your goals into smaller tasks and think about what you will need to do to complete each task. (If you have many goals and therefore many tasks, you may create an action plan for each goal.)

3 For each task, set yourself a target for when you hope to complete it.

4 Write down a date or dates when the plan will be reviewed to check on progress.

5 Provide a timescale by which all of the tasks will be completed and the goals achieved.

SMART targets

The acronym 'SMART' is often used when creating plans. The aim of SMART goals or targets is to help people focus clearly on what they want to achieve and avoid situations where goals are unrealistic. SMART stands for:

S = Specific

M = Measurable

A = Achievable

R = Realistic

T = Time bound

Specific

Try to make sure in your planning that you have thought clearly about what you need to learn, experience or develop. Phrases such as 'become better at talking to children' are too vague, but 'making eye contact and getting down to a child's level' would be better.

Measurable

Consider how you will know whether you have achieved this part of your plan. For example, you may want an individual child to approach and interact with you more frequently. You could measure how often this happens now and then set a target, such as at least five times during the day. Or you may want to support a child who uses Makaton, but not know many signs yourself. Your target in this case might be to learn 50 signs.

Achievable

When thinking about your plan, make sure that it is possible to complete each target.

Realistic

There is always a danger of being over-enthusiastic and optimistic at the start of any project. Think about how you normally cope and check that your plan will meet your needs and suit the way in which you learn and work.

Time bound

Thinking about how long each part of the plan will take is essential. Many people need a set start and end time to help them work effectively. Working out a realistic timescale will help you remain motivated.

Models of reflection proposed by others

There are a number of different models of reflection. These models can be used to help you think about your practice. There is no 'right' model, but by exploring different models, you will learn more about different ways of reflecting.

The Schön model

Donald Schön suggested that reflective practitioners can work in two ways to develop and improve their practice: reflection in action and reflection on action.

- Reflection in action

This is about how you might think about and adapt your practice at the time. This is often called 'thinking on your feet' and is likely to occur when something unexpected happens that challenges your usual way of working. A good example of this is when an activity you have done several times with children fails to gain the usual positive response from a new child. You may have to quickly consider why this might be and then test out new ways of working. You would, therefore, be learning from this.

- Reflection on action

The other method that Schön described is reflecting on what you have done afterwards. You may explore what you did and why, and decide whether it was the best way of working.

The two types of reflection are not necessarily independent of each other because if you have altered your way of working at the time (reflection in action), you may afterwards take time to consider whether there were any other strategies or approaches you could have taken (reflection on action).

The Gibbs reflective cycle model

The Gibbs reflective cycle is a way of structuring your thoughts and reflections. It is very useful to use after a particular situation, such as following an activity you felt had not worked out well. By using the cycle, you should be able to reach some conclusions to help you think how you could work differently in the future. Figure 11.5 shows this cycle.

After a situation, incident or activity (this could be either positive or negative) you need to think about what happened, your feelings about it and evaluate what was good about it or what was not good about it. You then need to go on to analyse why it occurred in the way it did. Finally, you need to draw some conclusions from the situation, incident or activity. You can include this in an action plan. Although it is possible to use Gibbs' cycle by yourself, it is often best to have a partner to do it with. Having someone else sitting with you to clarify your thoughts and ideas can make the process easier.

Figure 11.5 Gibbs' reflective cycle model

Kolb's learning cycle

Kolb's learning cycle is a useful model for reflection. It is based on the idea that we learn from experiences and then adapt our thoughts and actions accordingly. Although in theory you can start at any point of the cycle, most reflection begins with the experience as this provides a trigger for thinking. Figure 11.6 shows this cycle.

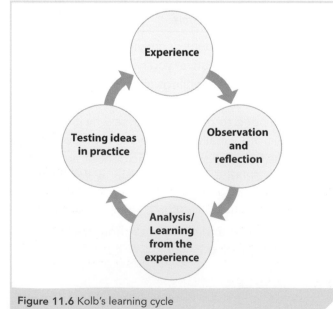

Figure 11.6 Kolb's learning cycle

We will now look at how you use the learning cycle. In this instance we will use the example of setting up an activity for children to play in a water tray.

- Experience

The learning cycle always starts with an initial experience. In this example, the children were not interested in playing in the water tray despite you having planned an activity there.

- Observe and reflect

The next stage is to reflect on the experience. Why might the children not have been interested in the water tray? Did you underestimate their age/stage of development, or were they tired?

- Analysis/Learning from the experience

Use your observations and reflections to help shape your future plans and ideas. What else could you do? Could you have chosen different materials, or a different time? This analysis will help you form new ideas to help you develop in the future.

- Testing ideas in practice

Once you have developed your new ideas, you should try to put them into action.

The next step would be to start the process all over again using the information gained from the first cycle of reflection. This ensures the process of learning and reflection is continuous.

Research

As well as the tools for reflection that we have already considered, there are others that have been created by specific organisations. An example of this is the self-evaluation form that Ofsted have on their website to help early years settings, including childminders, think about their practice. You can access this website by going to www.pearsonhotlinks.co.uk and searching for the ISBN of this title: 9781447970972.

Look at this self-evaluation form – what could you learn from completing this form? How could you use this in your setting? It is worth finding out whether your early years setting has any tools that they have developed from other sources or have been given.

One of the Turkish delegates (from Assessment practice 11.1) is in the UK for three months and will be spending time in the nursery where you work. She is keen to be shown how reflective practice is put into practice and how you use different sources of information and tools to reflect on and improve your skills. She has asked if she could shadow you as you reflect on one area of practice, draw up an action plan and then review it. You have chosen to focus on promoting children's physical development.

You should do the following so that she can see the process.

1 Based on information gathered from a range of sources, summarise your strengths and weaknesses in this area.

2 Draw up an action plan that clearly shows how you intend to improve your practice.

3 Discuss with the delegate which tools you will be using to reflect on your practice and knowledge and explain why you have chosen these.

In addition, you will need to explain to the Turkish practitioner what the barriers are when trying to reflect on own practice, the strengths and weaknesses of your plan, and how improving your own skills and knowledge could affect children's overall learning and development.

C Be able to use the skills of reflective practice in relation to promoting children's learning and development

We have considered the importance of reflection and professional development in your work with children and also the skills and tools needed to do these things. In this section, we will look at how you might put these theories into action. In order to achieve this unit, you will need to create a portfolio of evidence that shows you can reflect on your own practice, knowledge and skills. You will have been shown by your teacher/tutor the Practical Evidence Portfolio that accompanies this course and it is important you begin using it as soon as you start your work placement. It will help you to demonstrate how you have begun to build and develop the skills you need to work with children and continually improve your practice.

Tools of reflection to promote children's learning and development

One of the ways you can show evidence of reflection is through writing reflective accounts and evaluations

of your work. Later in this section we will look at how to write reflective accounts. However, the starting point is to decide which tools of reflection will work best in different situations.

Seven areas of learning are outlined in the early years curriculum in England. It is important that your practice is strong in each of them, especially as each area is reported on during inspections. If you are working in a setting outside of England, you should make sure you are familiar with the relevant curriculum.

You might like to start your reflection by considering whether you have enough knowledge about each of the areas of learning and development, and make sure that you are up to date with how the curriculum should be delivered. In terms of tools for reflection, you may like to gain information from others as well as perform a self-evaluation. You could then use this as a starting point for creating SMART targets or for carrying out a SWOT analysis.

Tools of reflection in relation to own learning and working practice

To complete this unit, you will need to show you can reflect on your own learning in many different aspects of your work with children. As most people's practice improves over time, it is worth keeping a reflective diary so you can see how far you have progressed over time in the following areas:

- your understanding of your own roles and responsibilities
- health and safety in early years
- promoting children's learning and development in different areas
- working with colleagues.

There are no set formats for a reflective diary, but it is usual to make an entry each time you have attended placement. It is worth recording briefly what you have done, how you feel it went and what you have learned. Over time, you should be able to look back on your diary and realise that you have made progress in many areas. This in turn should allow you to write a reflective account about your learning in the workplace.

In addition to keeping a reflective diary, you could also look for tools that deal with specific areas of practice. These tools might be available from your local authority or through other organisations that support early years practice. Tools may include, for example, the Eat Better, Start Better programme, which is run by the Children's Food Trust and looks at how settings can promote healthy eating.

Research

Go to the Children's Food Trust website for more information about the Eat Better, Start Better programme. You can access this website by going to www.pearsonhotlinks.co.uk and searching for the ISBN of this title: 9781447970972.

Plan and carry out activities and tasks with children

One of the areas where is it is important to reflect on our practice is in the planning and carrying out of activities and tasks with children. This is important because for activities and tasks to effectively support children's learning and development, they need to be carefully tailored to meet their individual needs. By reflecting on activities and tasks, you can find ways to be more effective in supporting and promoting the development of individual children.

We looked at observation and planning in Unit 9 and so it may be worth re-visiting this unit. While carrying out activities and tasks, you might like to try to use Schön's 'reflection in action' model to ensure they meet the needs of individual children and so promote and extend their learning and development. Here are some points you might like to bear in mind while planning and carrying out activities.

- What is the purpose of this activity?
- How will it link to children's known interests?
- What resources will be needed?
- How will children be able to participate during the activity?
- How responsive are individual children?
- What do I need to do to improve children's participation or learning?
- How might I use my reflections to adapt future activities and tasks to meet the needs and development of individual children?
- How could I adapt my plans to extend children's learning or development?

Reflect on own role in planning and carrying out activities and tasks with children

Following an activity, you should consider how well it went and what you could learn from it. Focus on all elements of the activity, including how carefully you planned, prepared and thought about the children's needs, stages of development and ages. You should also think about how your planning and activity linked to the current EYFS requirement that 'Practitioners must consider the individual needs, interests, and stage of development of each child in their care, and must use this information to plan a challenging and enjoyable experience for each child...' (Source: Statutory Framework for the EYFS, page 8, paragraph 1.6). If you are not using the EYFS, you will need to link to the learning requirements of the curriculum used in your home country.

You should also reflect on how you felt during the activity and what the positive aspects were as well as any areas for improvement. As part of your reflection, you should identify ways to improve your practice for the future.

Reflect on the effectiveness of learning and development theories and philosophies

As part of your reflective practice, you should be able to make links to theories and philosophies of learning and development. There are many ways you might do this.

Try out a new technique or approach based on a theory or philosophy

If you have adopted a theory or philosophy for the first time, you should reflect on its effectiveness. This might be in order to experiment with new ways of working with children. For example, you might use a star chart to work with a 7-year-old child to create a system of positive reinforcement.

Visit another setting

You may reflect on what you have seen when you work in a placement whose approach to extending children's learning and development is based on a particular philosophy or theory. A good example of this is if you were to visit or have a placement in a Steiner Waldorf setting and see first-hand how they work with children and the impact their approach has on children's outcomes. As part of your reflection, you would consider what elements you might try to retain, even if you are working elsewhere.

Understand how a theory or philosophy is influencing your practice

There may be times when you reflect on how a theory or philosophy is directly influencing your practice and consider how effective it is. It may be you use a lot of modelling to help children learn new concepts. You could consider for which children this proves effective and whether or not you need to adapt your way of working or use other approaches.

Reflect on own practice in working cooperatively with others

If you have strong working relationships, colleagues and other professionals are more likely to give you feedback, advice and also allow you to shadow them. They may also suggest sources of information that will help you develop further. As part of the reflection process, you need to reflect on how well you work cooperatively with others and what contribution they make to your professional development. There are many ways in which you may find out about your practice in relation to others, and we will look at two of these here.

Self-evaluation

You could observe other people's responses to you and note whether you seem to fulfil their expectations of you. The danger with this approach is you may be too subjective and not pick up on subtle cues.

Feedback

The best way to gain information in terms of your effectiveness in working with others is by asking them to evaluate your practice, either as part of a face-to-face interview or asking them to fill in a questionnaire.

Reflect on own practice in promoting diversity, equality and inclusion

Promoting diversity, equality and inclusion is an important part of the early years practitioner's role. It is, therefore, an area for reflecting on your own practice. You might like to consider the following points when reflecting on this aspect of your practice.

- How knowledgeable are you about the different issues that surround diversity, equality and inclusion?
- What sources of information could you access to help you learn more?
- In your practice how is your awareness of diversity, equality and inclusion reflected?
- How do you ensure that all children are valued as you interact with them?
- How do you ensure that families feel welcome and valued?

- How do you ensure in the planning and implementing of activities that they reflect children's interests, cultural differences and family circumstances?

Reflective accounts and Practical Evidence Portfolio (PEP)

A reflective account is a critical description and evaluation of an activity, event or situation. For this unit, you will need to write several reflective accounts showing that you can analyse, evaluate and reflect on your practice in promoting children's learning and development. The skills and experiences you need to reflect on are those within the Practical Evidence Portfolio. You also need to show you are developing your skills of reflection and professional development.

How to write a reflective account

This involves three elements:

Description

First provide a description of what happened. This sets the scene and gives the reader and yourself a chance to understand the circumstances.

Analysis

Your next step is to interpret what happened. It is useful to look at the models of reflection to help you. An analysis might include your feelings, what went well, how it linked to theory and why things did/did not go to plan. You should focus on how competently you carried out the core aspects of practice.

Evaluation

You should conclude with what you have learned from this experience and how you intend to change or develop your practice. This shows that you are able to develop your own skills of reflection. You should explain what practical steps you might take to improve or develop your practice or what you might try to do to further your learning. You should also consider how, by reflecting on your practice, you will be able to better promote children's learning and development.

Reflect on feedback received from children, colleagues and others

In your reflective accounts you should show you have been gaining a range of feedback and you are actively using it to improve your practice. You should also identify how you intend to, or how you are currently, improving your own practice. This might be, for example, by undertaking additional training, doing some of your own research or gaining some extra work experience.

Assessment practice 11.3 — 3C.P5 | 3C.M3 | 3C.D3

Your supervisor in your setting has asked you to talk to a new student, who is about to start a work placement, about the importance of reflective practice when working with children. In particular, she wants you to talk through the experience of building your Practical Evidence Portfolio. Before you meet the new student, you need to make sure your Practical Evidence Portfolio is up to date and any observations or witness testimonies which demonstrate evidence of developing your own practice, knowledge and skills in working with children have been completed. Write detailed notes to help your conversation, including:

- an assessment of the value of developing and maintaining a Practical Evidence Portfolio
- to what extent colleagues, parents/carers, teachers/tutors or other professionals have contributed to the development of your Practical Evidence Portfolio and how this has improved your own practice.

Further reading and resources

Canning, N. and Reed, M. (2009) *Reflective Practice in the Early Years*, London: SAGE Publications Ltd.

Cortvriend, V. *et al* (2008) *Advanced Early Years for Foundation Degrees & Levels 4/5* (2nd ed.), Essex: Heinemann.

Lindon, J. (2012) *Reflective Practice and Early Years Professionalism* (2nd ed.), London: Hodder Education.

Ready for work?

Ming Lee Nursery manager

We are keen to remain an outstanding setting. As a manager, I believe our success is partly down to the professional development our staff undertakes. Each staff member is regularly given opportunities to reflect on their practice and to draw up an action plan. Sometimes, we have a whole setting focusing on particular areas. This year we are looking at care routines. Next year, we will be looking at outdoor play.

To help us in improving practice, each staff member is paired with a colleague. They look at each other's work, give suggestions and help each other in drawing up an action plan. We are also part of a cluster group, and through this network staff also see what other settings are doing. This works very well and recently we have been twinned with a nursery in Finland – we are aiming to learn more about how they work with children.

What is good about having a setting where everyone is involved in continuous reflection is that we are all learning. It makes for a great atmosphere and the children really benefit from the additional stimulation.

Skills for practice

Frequently asked questions:

The training course my manager wants me to go on is on a Saturday. She will pay for the course, but not for my time.

Strictly speaking, you do not need to attend if it is not in your usual work hours. Having said that, in terms of your career, you would be making the wrong decision. First of all, you will be gaining more knowledge and ideas, which will stand you in good stead when there is a promotion opportunity in your setting. Second, if you apply for a job outside your setting, you would be able to offer particular expertise or knowledge. Finally, when you attend courses, you are likely to meet other people who may be useful contacts in the future.

You might also like to think of the children that you work with. Surely gaining additional skills and knowledge will help you to be a better practitioner?

We have a child who stammers in the setting. He is my key child. Where can I find information about stammering and what I should do?

A good starting point is to visit the British Stammering Association's website. You can access this website by going to www.pearsonhotlinks.co.uk and searching for the ISBN of this title: 9781447970972. You could also contact your local speech and language team, and they may have information that could help your practice. If you do this, remember that you cannot talk about the particular child in the setting unless you have parental consent. You could ask general questions, though.

Introduction

The Early Years Foundation Stage (EYFS) is the statutory framework for practitioners in England, which covers the curriculum, development and welfare requirements for children up to the age of 5 years. If you are working with this age group, you will need to have a firm understanding of its principles, structure and requirements, and the rationale behind each of the areas of learning. You should also know how to plan for play and activities that are both adult-directed and child-initiated and that support children's progress towards the early learning goals at the end of the EYFS. In this way, you will be able to ensure that you meet the needs of all the children in your setting and enable them to reach their full potential.

Assessment: You will be assessed by a series of assignments set by your teacher/tutor.

Learning aims

In this unit you will:

A understand the legal status, principles, themes and aims of the Early Years Foundation Stage

B understand the education programme within the Early Years Foundation Stage

C be able to plan, lead and assess purposeful play and education programmes that support children's progress towards Early Years Foundation Stage areas of learning and development

D support safeguarding and welfare requirements within the Early Years Foundation Stage.

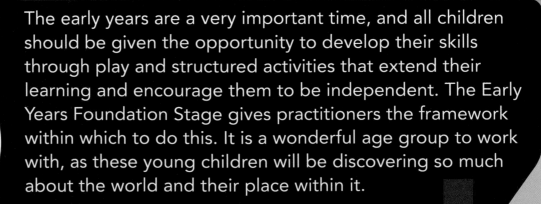

The early years are a very important time, and all children should be given the opportunity to develop their skills through play and structured activities that extend their learning and encourage them to be independent. The Early Years Foundation Stage gives practitioners the framework within which to do this. It is a wonderful age group to work with, as these young children will be discovering so much about the world and their place within it.

Anita Tempora, *nursery manager*

The Early Years
Foundation Stage
(EYFS)

12

BTEC
Assessment Zone

This table shows you what you must do in order to achieve a **Pass**, **Merit** or **Distinction** grade, and where you can find activities to help you.

Assessment criteria

Pass	Merit	Distinction
Learning aim A: Understand the legal status, principles, themes and aims of the Early Years Foundation Stage		
3A.P1 I&CT Summarise the legal status, structure and principles of the Early Years Foundation Stage. **Assessment practice 12.1**	**3A.M1** Analyse how the structure and principles of the Early Years Foundation Stage shape practice in early years settings. **Assessment practice 12.1**	**3A.D1** Evaluate the potential impact of the Early Years Foundation Stage on outcomes for children. **Assessment practice 12.1**
3A.P2 Describe how delivery of the Early Years Foundation Stage is inspected. **Assessment practice 12.1**		
3A.P3 Explain the requirements for the assessment of children's progress in the Early Years Foundation Stage. **Assessment practice 12.1**		
Learning aim B: Understand the education programme within the Early Years Foundation Stage		
3B.P4 English Explain how play and educational programmes in the Early Years Foundation Stage may provide opportunities for several areas of learning. **Assessment practice 12.2**	**3B.M2** Discuss, using examples, ways in which areas of learning can be interrelated in play and educational programmes in the EYFS. **Assessment practice 12.2**	
Learning aim C: Be able to plan, lead and assess purposeful play and educational programmes that support children's progress towards Early Years Foundation Stage areas of learning and development		
3C.P5 I&CT Plan and record purposeful play and educational programmes with colleagues, using observations and assessments of children's progress towards early learning goals, to include a balance of: • adult-led activities • child-initiated activities. **Assessment practice 12.3**	**3C.M3** Analyse the extent to which the planned play and education programmes supported the child's progress towards early learning goals. **Assessment practice 12.3**	
3C.P6 Lead play and educational programmes to encourage children's participation and extend learning and thinking. **Assessment practice 12.3**		
3C.P7 I&CT Assess the effectiveness of the implemented play and educational programmes in supporting children's progress in areas of learning. **Assessment practice 12.3**		

continued

Assessment criteria (*continued*)

Pass	Merit	Distinction
Learning aim D: Support safeguarding and welfare requirements within the Early Years Foundation Stage		
3D.P8 Act upon safeguarding and welfare responsibilities in the Early Years Foundation Stage. **Assessment practice 12.4**	**3D.M4** Discuss how the requirements of the Early Years Foundation Stage contribute to safeguarding and welfare. **Assessment practice 12.4** **3D.M5** Demonstrate consistent adherence to safeguarding and welfare responsibilities in the Early Years Foundation Stage. **Assessment practice 12.4**	**3D.D2** Evaluate the extent to which the safeguarding and welfare requirements can be managed through the education programme in the Early Years Foundation Stage. **Assessment practice 12.4**

English English Functional Skills signposting   **I&CT** Information and Communication Skills signposting

How you will be assessed

This unit will be assessed by a series of internally assessed tasks set by your teacher/tutor. Throughout this unit you will find assessment practice activities that will help you work towards your assessment. Completing these activities will not mean that you have achieved a particular grade, but you will have carried out useful research or preparation that will be relevant when it comes to your final assignment.

In order for you to achieve the tasks in your assignment, it is important that you check you have met all of the Pass grading criteria. You can do this as you work your way through the assignment.

If you are hoping to gain a Merit or Distinction, you should also make sure that you present the information in your assignment in the style that is required by the relevant assessment criterion. For example, Merit criteria will require you to discuss, demonstrate and analyse, and Distinction criteria will require you to evaluate.

The assignment set by your teacher/tutor will consist of a number of tasks designed to meet the criteria in the assessment criteria table. This is likely to consist of a written assignment but may also include activities such as:

- a reference document
- case studies
- a series of observations or examples from practice.

It is important to note that to carry out the requirements for learning aims C and D learners must undertake practical tasks in a work placement setting.

Getting started

Take a few minutes to write a brief account of what you know already about the Early Years Foundation Stage (EYFS) – why it was introduced, its structure, the curriculum itself and how and when children are assessed. Share this with a partner and compare your understanding.

A Understand the legal status, principles, themes and aims of the Early Years Foundation Stage

If you are working with children in the early years and following the EYFS, you will need to know and understand in detail its structure and scope. Taking its basis from the Childcare Act of 2006, the Early Years Foundation Stage is a statutory framework, which was introduced in 2008 with the aim of improving outcomes for children in the early years and setting the standard for all early years providers.

Scope and legal status of the EYFS

The EYFS is made up of a curriculum, which includes learning and development requirements, as well as specific safeguarding and welfare requirements. The EYFS applies to a range of settings and providers in England. This includes all those caring for children from birth to the end of the academic year in which they have their fifth birthday. This means it is very important for early years providers to understand its legal status. The EYFS documentation defines all these settings as Ofsted-registered providers on the Early Years Register. This will include childminders, nurseries and preschools, all schools in England that are attended by young children and all providers registered with an early years childminder agency.

Legislation and regulations behind the EYFS

The legal status of the EYFS is based on a number of different pieces of legislation, all of which have gradually improved the safeguarding and welfare requirements for children. The requirements mean

children have more rights and there is a greater emphasis on agencies working together for their benefit. The relevant legislation is outlined below.

Children Act 1989 and 2004

One of the key aims of the Children Act 1989 was to clarify the laws affecting children and to give a greater focus to children's welfare. It aimed to achieve a better balance and closer partnerships between authorities and parents/carers, and gave more individual rights to the child, separate from their parents/carers. The Children Act 2004, introduced after the death of Victoria Climbié, built on this and was closely linked to the publication of 'Every Child Matters', which set out to integrate services for children. Local authorities such as the police, health service and youth justice system must work together and cooperate with one another, sharing information to promote the well-being of children and young people so that their welfare is protected.

Data Protection Act 1998

This act covers the way early years settings handle information about children. Under this act, information gathered by the school or setting in the context of safeguarding and child protection must **only** be used for that purpose. If any individuals concerned, or their parents or carers, wish to know information that is held about them, they have a right to access it. There are only a few exceptions to this, which are:

- information that may cause serious harm or risk of abuse to the child or another individual
- information given to a court or in adoption or parental order records
- copies of examination scripts or marks prior to their release
- unstructured personal information, or information that is held manually and not in school or setting records.

Childcare Act 2006

This act was the first piece of legislation that focused on early childcare and early childhood services by requiring local authorities and their partners to work together. It aimed to reduce child poverty by supporting parents to get into work and to reduce inequalities and improve outcomes for all children up to the age of 5. It also introduced the Early Years Foundation Stage, which came into effect in England in 2008. This Act gives the requirements of the EYFS a legal force.

Safeguarding Vulnerable Groups Act 2006

This Act provides the legislative framework for a new vetting and barring scheme for people who work with children and vulnerable adults. Early years settings have a duty to make a referral to the Disclosure and Barring Service where a member of staff is dismissed because they have harmed a child or put a child at risk of harm.

The purpose of the new scheme is to minimise the risk of harm posed to children and vulnerable adults by those that might seek to harm them through their work (paid or unpaid).

Equality Act 2010

The Equality Act replaced nine acts of parliament over several decades. It applies to schools and early years settings and in particular the way in which they treat children and prospective pupils, so that all children have the same opportunities.

■ The overall structure of EYFS

The EYFS statutory guidance is structured so it can be broken down into three sections:

- learning and development requirements
- assessment
- safeguarding and welfare requirements.

The learning and welfare requirements are based on four overarching principles that should influence all areas of practice in early years settings. Practitioners need to bear all of these in mind when working with children so that they can ensure they adhere to them. These overarching principles are that:

- every child is unique
- children learn to be strong and independent through positive relationships
- children should be provided with a positive and enabling environment
- children learn and develop in different ways and at different rates.

Source: Statutory Framework for the EYFS, 2014, p. 6.

Learning and development requirements

The learning and development requirements cover the following three areas:

- the educational programmes and curriculum, which must cover seven areas of learning
- the early learning goals, which are a summary of the knowledge, skills and understanding that all young children should have gained by the end of the academic year in which they turn 5
- the assessment requirements, which set out how and when children's achievements and progress must be assessed and how these assessments should be reported to parents and carers.

Source: Statutory Framework for the EYFS, 2014, p. 7.

The educational programme and curriculum

The educational programme and curriculum of the EYFS are set out within a framework of seven areas of learning and development. The requirements describe how settings should promote the learning and development of children in their care, so that they are 'school ready' and able to move into reception and Year 1. Figure 12.1 shows the seven areas of learning.

Each of the seven areas will be subdivided, for example, literacy will be divided into reading and writing, and mathematics into numbers and shape, space and measures.

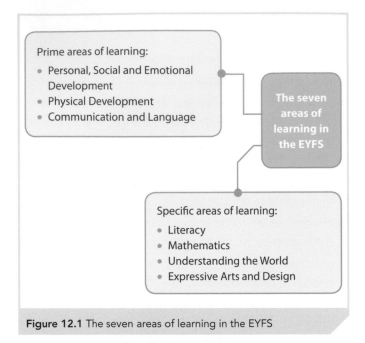

Prime areas of learning:
- Personal, Social and Emotional Development
- Physical Development
- Communication and Language

The seven areas of learning in the EYFS

Specific areas of learning:
- Literacy
- Mathematics
- Understanding the World
- Expressive Arts and Design

Figure 12.1 The seven areas of learning in the EYFS

The early learning goals

The early learning goals are designed to show where each child should be in each area of learning at the end of the Early Years Foundation Stage. For example, under reading, the early learning goal reads: 'Children read and understand simple sentences. They use phonic knowledge to decode regular words and read them aloud accurately. They also read some common irregular words. They demonstrate understanding when talking with others about what they have read.' There are 17 early learning goals in total.

Source: Statutory Framework for the EYFS, 2014, p. 11.

Assessment requirements

Assessment requirements may be ongoing (**formative assessment**) or structured (**summative assessment**). This means that assessment will take place throughout the Early Years Foundation Stage, but that children will also be assessed at two specific points, at between 2 and 3 years and again at the end of the final term of the year in which the child reaches 5 years. This is known as the Early Years Foundation Stage Profile (EYFSP). Children aged between 2 and

3 years will only be assessed in the three prime areas. The requirements for assessment will be covered in more detail later in this section.

Safeguarding and welfare requirements

Early years providers will need to take steps to ensure that all children in their care are kept safe and well. They should create settings that are welcoming, safe and stimulating so that children are able to enjoy their learning.

The areas covered under the safeguarding and welfare requirements of the EYFS include:

- safeguarding children and promoting their welfare
- promoting good health
- managing behaviour
- checking the suitability of adults who have contact with children
- checking qualifications, training, skills and knowledge of staff
- staff-to-child ratios
- key people
- before/after school care and holiday provision
- childminder agencies
- ensuring that the premises and facilities are safe and secure and meet health and safety requirements
- special educational needs
- promoting equal opportunities
- maintaining records, policies and procedures.

How settings are inspected

Providers who are registered on the Early Years or Childcare Register, whether early years or childcare providers or childminders, will need to follow the statutory framework of the Early Years Foundation Stage. This means that they must meet the legal requirements of the Childcare Act 2006 in order to remain registered, as well as the learning and development requirements.

Early years and childcare settings will be regularly inspected (every three to four years) as part of the Ofsted framework, to look at how well they meet the requirements of the Early Years or Childcare Register and the standards of the EYFS. The amount of notice of a visit given will depend on the early years setting. Group providers will normally receive no notice, whereas childminders and early years classes within primary schools are likely to receive a few days' notice.

As part of the inspection process, inspectors will ask to see the setting's **self-evaluation form**. Managers should complete this form with staff on a regular basis to ensure they are looking at the quality of provision and how well they are meeting the needs of children and improving outcomes for them.

The self-evaluation form also gives guidance on the kinds of questions inspectors will ask providers when looking at the quality of provision in the setting. Ofsted recommend that settings complete the form thoroughly as it will give them some idea about the aspects they think are working well, and those that they are working towards improving.

Inspectors will also carry out observations at the setting; look at paperwork; interview staff, parents/carers and children and assess how well the children's learning and development are progressing. They will then provide feedback on the following areas:

- how well the early years provision meets the needs of the range of children who attend
- the contribution of the early years provision to children's well-being
- the leadership and management of the early years provision.

Each of these areas will be given a grade. At the time of writing, these grades are:

- grade 1 (outstanding)
- grade 2 (good)
- grade 3 (requires improvement)
- grade 4 (inadequate).

All inspections will be published on the Ofsted website so that the process is transparent and parents, carers or others are able to view the results.

As part of the inspection process, practitioners need to provide information to Ofsted, including the type of setting, the number of children and the number of hours for which childcare is provided. Inspectors will check that settings are meeting a number of requirements including those shown in Figure 12.2.

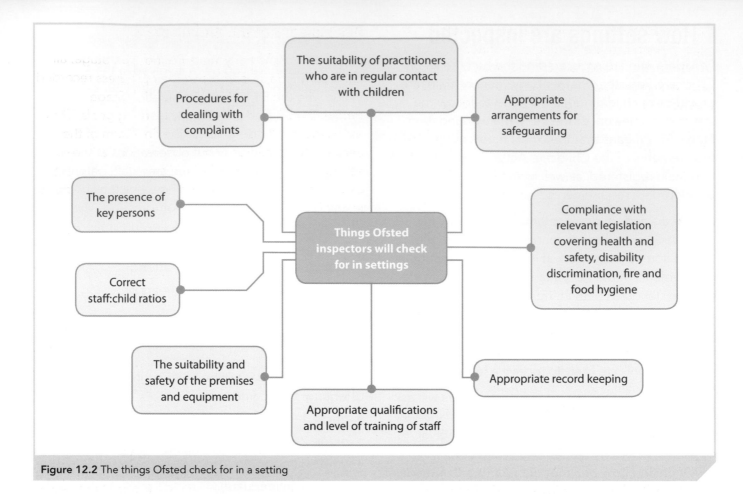

The suitability of practitioners who are in regular contact with children

Procedures for dealing with complaints

Appropriate arrangements for safeguarding

The presence of key persons

Things Ofsted inspectors will check for in settings

Compliance with relevant legislation covering health and safety, disability discrimination, fire and food hygiene

Correct staff:child ratios

The suitability and safety of the premises and equipment

Appropriate record keeping

Appropriate qualifications and level of training of staff

Figure 12.2 The things Ofsted check for in a setting

As they are legal requirements, the Ofsted inspection will assess all aspects of the setting under the headings in Figure 12.2, checking paperwork and looking at all statutory requirements. Settings can apply to have exemption from some aspects of the requirements. For example, if an individual child's family has a religious or philosophical view that is in conflict with the learning and development requirements, or if the setting is unable to meet fully the learning and development requirements due to temporary restrictions in their facilities. However, no setting may be exempted from the welfare requirements for any reason, as these requirements deal with child safety.

How and why children's development is assessed

The second part of the EYFS statutory guidance is devoted to assessment. It is important for parents and carers, healthcare practitioners and educationalists that we regularly check children's development, particularly during their earliest years. This is because it is a time of rapid growth,

physically, emotionally and in terms of general cognitive development. If there are any issues they should be picked up as early as possible so that they can be addressed. Parents and carers should work hand in hand with the setting to monitor children's development. Healthcare professionals may also liaise with providers, particularly if there is an issue that adults in the setting are able to support.

Reflect

How does your setting work with parents and carers to ensure that children are assessed and monitored throughout the Early Years Foundation Stage?

Although babies and young children will be regularly checked and monitored by healthcare professionals, issues that a baby or young child may have might not be picked up straight away, for example, any problems in hearing. It is important to look out for signs that indicate that young children may need additional support. For this reason, assessment in the early years will need to be ongoing (formative), as well as summative.

Progress check at age 2

Children's progress is assessed at 2 years. At the 2-year check, children's progress in the prime areas (personal, social and emotional development, physical development, and communication and language) will be reviewed by practitioners. Parents and carers will then be given a short summary of their child's development in these areas. They will be asked to share this with other professionals, for example, health visitors or teachers if they are moving to a school-based nursery, as it will coincide with the child's health and development review. The summary will include observations about a child's progress as well as any concerns. If there are any areas in which a child is not making expected progress, the provider should set out a plan showing how the child's future learning and development will be addressed by the setting, and showing how professionals will work together to share information. Parents and carers will also be advised on how to support their child's learning at home.

Activity

How does your setting carry out the 2-year check? What is the procedure for reporting back to parents and carers and involving other professionals if necessary?

Assessment at the end of EYFS

At the end of the Early Years Foundation Stage, all children will be assessed and their progress recorded in line with the Early Years Foundation Stage Profile (EYFSP) and the 17 early learning goals. This assessment will take place in the final term of the year in which children reach 5 years old. Early years settings must state whether children have met, are exceeding or have not yet reached the expected level of learning and development.

These profiles must be shared with, and explained to, parents and carers, and should also be shared with the child's Year 1 teacher and the local authority.

What area(s) of learning could these children be working on?

The aims of the EYFS

The EYFS sets the standards that settings must meet to make sure children learn and develop well and are kept healthy and safe. As you will be working to the EYFS, you should be clear about its aims and purpose. It aims to provide:

- quality and consistency in all early years settings, so that every child makes good progress and no child gets left behind
- a secure foundation through learning and development opportunities, which are planned around the needs and interests of each individual child and are assessed and reviewed regularly
- partnership working between practitioners and with parents and/or carers
- equality of opportunity and anti-discriminatory practice, ensuring that every child is included and supported.

Source: Statutory Framework for the EYFS, 2014, p. 5.

Terminology used in EYFS documentation

The terminology used in the EYFS documentation can be confusing. It is important that you are able to understand the terminology and know where to find information about it in the documentation so that you understand its purpose.

The statutory guidance

The statutory framework is the most important part of the documentation as it sets out the legal requirements of the EYFS and its overall structure. It is divided into:

- the learning and development requirements – these set out the different areas of learning as well as the early learning goals within each aspect
- the arrangements for assessment
- the legal requirements relating to safeguarding and welfare.

The specific legal requirements relating to safeguarding and welfare

These are part of the statutory guidance document and outline what your setting is legally required to do under the EYFS to ensure the safety and well-being of children. The requirements are specific to children. You will need to make sure that these requirements are being met at all times and in different areas. For example, the specific legal requirements for outings are that a risk assessment must be carried out prior to taking children on a trip and that they must be kept safe. As well as the safeguarding and welfare requirements, settings will also have other more general legal requirements – for example disability discrimination and so on.

The practice guidance

The practice guidance found in 'Development Matters in the Early Years Foundation Stage (EYFS)' is published by the British Association for Early Childhood Education and supported by the Department for Education to help settings implement the EYFS. It is non-statutory – that is, you do not have to follow it. However, it is useful and gives different ideas and suggestions to support practitioners in delivering the EYFS. If you look through the practice guidance, you will find that it is divided into different sections.

- The first describes the themes and principles of the EYFS and how they underpin all the guidance.
- The second section provides information on how to use the guidance to support children's learning and development and how observation, planning and assessment are linked together.
- The third section describes the characteristics of effective learning and how they run through the different areas of learning and development.
- The final section outlines the characteristics of effective learning alongside the key themes and gives useful guidance on what adults can do to support children in each area. It then goes on to do the same for the areas of learning and development.

Assessment practice 12.1 3A.P1 | 3A.P2 | 3A.P3 | 3A.M1 | 3A.D1

Create a reference document for new early years practitioners that:

1 summarises the legal status, structure and principles of the EYFS and describe how its delivery is inspected

2 explains the requirements for the assessment of children's progress

3 analyses how the structure and principles of the EYFS shape practice in early years settings, and evaluate the potential impact of the EYFS on outcomes for children.

Refer to the EYFS documentation and use examples from your work placement and case studies of individual children to help you create your reference document.

Principles and themes of the EYFS

The principles of the EYFS are designed to guide the work of all early years practitioners and influence and shape practice in early years settings. They are divided into four guiding themes, each of which has a principle behind it. They are shown in Table 12.1.

Unique child

You should be able to show that you are meeting the individual needs of children in different ways – through your role as children's **key person**, getting to know families and parents/carers and demonstrating an understanding of the needs of the child. The curriculum framework requires you to show inclusive practice and encourage the development of children's communication and language skills so that they are able to develop their understanding and self-expression. Planning should show that the setting reflects the interests and views of individual children, for example, by taking their views into consideration.

Key term

Key person – a practitioner designated to take responsibility for a child's emotional well-being by having a strong attachment with them and a good relationship with their parents.

Positive relationships

You should support children in developing positive relationships with their parents and carers as well as others. The curriculum framework requires you to do this through planning for children's personal, social and emotional development, as well as through

Table 12.1 The themes and principles of the EYFS

Theme	Principle behind the theme
A unique child	Every child is unique and is constantly learning and can be resilient, capable, confident and self-assured.
Positive relationships	Children learn to be strong and independent through positive relationships.
Enabling environment	Children learn and develop well in enabling environments, in which their experiences respond to their individual needs and where there is a strong partnership between practitioners and parents and carers.
Learning and development	Children develop and learn in different ways. The framework covers the education and care of all children in early years provision, including children with special educational needs and disabilities.

Source: © Crown copyright 2008. Adapted from the Statutory Framework for the Early Years Foundation Stage (2014).

meeting their needs on a daily basis when managing feelings and behaviour and considering the needs of others.

Do you think this child and practitioner have a positive relationship?

Enabling environment

You should ensure that relationships with those outside the setting – for example, other professionals and visitors from the community – are strong and positive, and that you act as a good role model for children. The curriculum framework requires you to ensure that the learning environment – both indoor and outdoor – is rich and varied and will support each child's development through a range of learning opportunities. You will also need to show that you plan for, assess and observe children to demonstrate that you are meeting their needs.

Learning and development

You will need to be able to plan for all areas of the Foundation Stage curriculum while being mindful of the fact that they are interrelated and should reflect children's interests. You should also take into account the importance of play, which is the key way in which children learn. The curriculum framework requires you to provide children with active learning opportunities, which allow them to make their own connections and discover things for themselves.

How the EYFS principles are reflected in the early education curriculum

It is important you think about each principle of the EYFS in relation to the children you are working with at all times. This will help you make sure that you keep the principles at the forefront of your practice. The principles should also be reflected within the early education curriculum as you carry out your work with children. Remember:

- every child is a unique child – you will need to show how individual children's progress is monitored and assessed and how you do this alongside colleagues, parents, carers and other professionals
- children learn to be strong and independent through positive relationships – you should always demonstrate good relationships with children and other adults in the setting
- children learn and develop well in enabling environments – the learning environment should be a stimulating and positive reflection of children's work and support their learning. All children should be represented
- children develop and learn in different ways and at different rates – you should make sure the curriculum is differentiated to take into account the needs of children.

The importance of applying the principles to practice

The EYFS principles are important as they are guiding themes that should shape your practice in all early years settings. You will need to show how you are applying the principles to your practice and you should have a clear idea about how they run through all of your setting's work with children. It would be a good idea to regularly look at the principles to make sure you can show how they are being applied to your practice.

You should also ensure that your setting complies with the legal requirements of the EYFS to create a stimulating, inclusive and enjoyable environment. These are set out in the statutory guidance and include:

- child protection
- suitable people
- staff qualifications
- staff:child ratios
- health
- equal opportunities
- accident or injury.

How settings can apply the principles to practice

Your setting will need to show how the EYFS principles are applied in its daily practice by:

- planning for children
- providing children with a key person
- working with parents.

Planning for children

There should be a clear structure to planning in your setting, which shows how the early years curriculum is organised as well as how it is meeting children's individual needs.

Providing children with a key person

Each child in your setting should have an adult who is their main contact. This key person should know the child well and have good relationships with them and their parents/carers so that both the child and their parent/carer knows who to go to if there are any issues. The key person should also encourage parents and carers to support their child's development at home. They should also ensure that children's learning and care is tailored to their individual needs.

Working with parents

The EYFS statutory framework places an emphasis on the importance of information sharing between parents/carers and the setting. Parents should be encouraged to share information about their child's development at home, and early years settings should provide information about:

- how the EYFS is being delivered
- staffing
- their child's key person
- all policies and procedures that are followed.

B Understand the education programme within the Early Years Foundation Stage

The education programme for the EYFS sets out a number of requirements. You will need to understand and be aware of these in your role as an early years practitioner so that you can plan effectively.

Delivering all areas of development through planned, purposeful play

The EYFS has been developed to incorporate the different areas of children's development within seven areas of learning. These areas of development must be delivered through planned, **purposeful play**. When planning activities under the EYFS, settings

will need to make sure play is a key part of the delivery. Play is essential for children's development because it:

- builds children's confidence
- encourages children to think about problems
- helps children relate to others.

Key term

Purposeful play – through play, children investigate and experience things, and 'have a go'.

The three characteristics of effective teaching and learning are:

- play and exploration
- **active learning**
- **creating and thinking critically**.

These characteristics should form the basis of child-initiated activities.

Although interconnected, children's overall development is usually considered in relation to the following prime areas:

- personal, social and emotional development – how the child relates to others and is developing emotionally, including feelings and behaviour
- physical and sensory development – how the child is developing physically, to include both fine and gross motor skills, and development of the five senses
- communication and language – how the child is developing intellectually/cognitively, or how they are learning, to include their language development.

Link

Go to Unit 2 in Student Book 1 where you will find more information about play in early years settings.

The rationale behind each area of learning in the EYFS

Table 12.2 shows the relationship between the seven areas of learning and the areas of child development. As can be seen from Table 12.2, the prime areas of

learning relate directly to the main areas of child development. These areas are considered to be those that are particularly important in building children's capacity to learn.

The specific areas of learning, which develop the breadth of children's skills in the areas of literacy, mathematics, understanding the world, and expressive arts and design, should be developed as children become more competent in the other three prime areas. If you are working with the youngest children, you should be focusing on the three prime areas, as they are the basis for subsequent, successful learning.

Table 12.2 The relationship between the seven areas of learning and the areas of child development

Area of learning and development	Area of child development
Prime areas of learning and development: - personal, social and emotional - physical development - communication and language.	The **prime** areas of learning relate directly to the main areas of child development, which are: - social and emotional development - physical and sensory development - cognitive and language development
Specific areas of learning and development: - literacy - mathematics - understanding of the world - expressive arts and design.	The **specific** areas of learning should be developed as children become more competent in the prime areas of learning.

By the time they reach the end of the Early Years Foundation Stage, children should be spending the same amount of time on each area of learning so that they continue to develop their confidence in the three prime areas while also developing in the others.

If children give cause for concern in any of the prime areas at any time during the Foundation Stage, they should be given increased support so that they are less likely to be unprepared for the start of school. In this situation, parents and/or carers would need to be informed and staff should consider whether other agencies should be involved so that the child and their family can have further support, within or outside the setting.

> ### Link
>
> Go to Unit 1 in Student Book 1 where you will find more information about how children under 5 years develop.

The scope of areas of learning and how they are interrelated

Each area of learning and development in the EYFS is expanded into two or three different strands to show the scope or breadth of what children should develop during their time in the Foundation Stage. For example, literacy is split into reading and writing, mathematics into numbers, and shape, space and measures. The personal, social and emotional development and learning goal is split into three areas, as follows. Children should be supported in each area as they progress towards the early learning goal.

- Self-confidence and self-awareness

Children are confident to try new activities, and say why they like some activities more than others. They are confident to speak in a familiar group, will talk about their ideas, and will choose the resources they need for their chosen activities. They say when they do or don't need help.

- Managing feelings and behaviour

Children can talk about how they and others show feelings, talk about their own and others' behaviour, and its consequences, and know that some behaviour is unacceptable. They work as part of a group or class, and understand and follow the rules. They adjust their behaviour to different situations, and take changes of routine in their stride.

- Making relationships

Children play cooperatively, taking turns with others. They take account of one another's ideas about how to organise their activity. They show sensitivity to others' needs and feelings, and form positive relationships with adults and other children.

Source: The Statutory Framework for the Early Years Foundation Stage, 2014, p. 11.

> ### Theory into practice
>
> Look at the statutory guidance for the EYFS 2014 to see how children will be working towards these early learning goals in the area of personal, social and emotional development. What are their expected developmental goals at 2 to 3 years and 3 to 4 years in each strand?
>
> You can access the statutory guidance by going to www.pearsonhotlinks.co.uk and searching for the ISBN of this title: 9781447970972.

As you look at each of the different areas of learning, it should be clear that they are interrelated. This means children who are learning through play will develop in more than one area. For example, a child who is playing with play-dough with a group of children will be developing their physical (fine motor) skills; their communication and language skills; their personal, social and emotional development skills; and their expressive arts skills through their imagination. They will also be developing relationships with others, exploring and learning in an active way through play. As the different areas of learning are so interrelated, planning for different areas of the EYFS is usually topic-based.

Topic-based planning has long been used as a way to introduce activities to young children, as it enables us to use ideas that are familiar to children in order to create a focus and link things together. Although it is not usually possible to cover every aspect of learning within a topic, they are a useful starting point. When you are planning, you will need to make sure you cover separately any areas that cannot be included as part of the topic.

The importance of ongoing formative assessment

When working with young children, you will always need to carry out observations, which are a type of formative assessment. These will help you look at how they are progressing on an ongoing basis. It is important to discuss observations with a range of people, such as early years practitioners, parents, carers and other professionals so that you can plan for individual children's progress. It is equally important to discuss a child's progress with these people as they may have other information to add. This helps you create a fuller picture of a child's development. Parents and/or carers, for example, should be invited to give regular feedback about children's achievements and activities at home. These may include activities such as learning to swim, baking cakes, writing their name in sand, helping to weigh fruit and vegetables in a supermarket, etc.

Observing children's development

Observations allow us to look at what children enjoy when they are carrying out child-initiated activities, as well as being a measure of how their development is progressing. They can also give us an insight into a child's thought processes if you carry out an observation when talking to a child either in a large or small group situation.

Observation is also useful if you want to find out what children already know about something before starting a new topic. You will need to note down when children say something that is unexpected, or which indicates a higher or lower level of understanding than you had anticipated. Parents and/or carers should be involved in the observation process. The EYFS requires settings to share observations with parents, and says that settings should encourage parents to share information with them too, so that a comprehensive picture of the child can be built up and plans for future activities for the child can be effectively produced.

By carrying out observations on children, you will be able to compare their progress with the expected achievements for their age group. You will need to show that you use these observations to help you plan how to progress children's development further and take their learning on to the next stage.

You will need to carry out regular observations to inform your planning.

The importance of balancing adult-led and child-initiated activities

As an early years worker, you should be aware of the importance of balancing child-initiated and adult-led activities. Much of the EYFS is based on the need for play to be part of children's learning and for adults to encourage them to develop their independence skills. However, children will also need to be guided and supported by adults as they are challenged by new concepts and ideas. As children work towards the end of the Foundation Stage, the balance of activities will gradually move more towards those that are led by adults so that children are ready for more formal learning in Year 1.

C Be able to plan, lead and assess purposeful play and education programmes that support children's progress towards EYFS areas of learning and development

As an early years worker you will need to know how to plan play and activities to support children's progress towards the EYFS outcomes, creating a balance of activities that are adult-led with those that are child-initiated.

How to plan play and activities to support children's progress

One of the key things you will need to consider when planning is that the EYFS is based around play. Children should have opportunities to play together with little adult direction or involvement (child-initiated play), as well as access to the kinds of activities where adults will give more direction or join in. It is useful to look at the different ways in which settings plan, as this can be a good way of sharing ideas to get inspiration and cutting down on paperwork.

Your plans should show how you will provide activities for each of the seven areas of learning and development within the EYFS, and include opportunities for both child-initiated and adult-directed play. These activities need to reflect the needs of individual children as well as showing that they are being given opportunities to develop in each area. You will need to have long-, medium- and short-term plans to demonstrate that what you are doing fits together with what the children have done previously and will do in the future. However, you must also remember that plans should be flexible. You will constantly need to evaluate and think about what is working or not working with children, and what will meet the needs and interests of individual children.

Link

Go to Unit 2 in Student Book 1 where you will find more information about how to plan play and activities.

Long-term plans

Long-term plans are usually used in schools or large settings where practitioners need to have plans set out well in advance – smaller settings may not need to use them. They will usually give an overview of topics or themes that will be covered over a long period, for example a year, so that resources can be shared between classes. The length of time plans cover is variable and will depend on the setting.

Medium-term plans

Medium-term plans will give more detail than long-term plans and are likely to last from a few weeks to half an academic term. They will set out what is going to be covered in each area of learning during each week. Some settings display them so that parents and carers are able to look at the different areas of focus, although they should be a working document and will need to be changed and added to as weeks progress. Figure 12.3 shows an example of a medium-term plan.

Theory into practice

Does your setting have long- or medium-term plans? What do they show, and where are they kept so that they can be referred to by staff and parents/carers?

Short-term plans

Short-term plans will be the most detailed of all. They will plan out weekly or daily activities that reflect children's interests but also build on their knowledge and skills. You will need to have a clear plan for adult-focused activities, which should indicate the learning objectives. For child-initiated activities, your setting may have a grid or provision planner to show the kinds of activities, materials and resources that will be available to children during the week. This may include opportunities for sand and water play, messy play, small-world play, role play, creative activities, construction play and so on. Remember, all settings will be different and may do this in a variety of ways.

Activity

1 Ask your setting if you can look at a short-term plan to compare it with the format used in other settings.

2 How similar are the plans?

3 What ideas can you take from them?

As well as carrying out activities that you have planned, you should also think about how you can bring learning into daily routines with children and be on the lookout for how you can involve them.

You might be able to do this, for example, when they are having a drink and biscuit, or when they are sitting around a table. You could ask, 'Do we have enough cups and chairs? How many children are here today? Let's count!', and so on. In this way, you will be developing children's awareness of how what they are doing relates to their environment.

How settings plan for children's progress within the EYFS

Although settings will all plan in different ways, they will need to include in their plans the same key information and be clear about how children are making progress towards the early learning goals of the EYFS. Planning should show:

- how children's individual needs and interests are being met and that plans are built on regular observations by staff and parents/carers
- how the seven areas of learning are being included, as well as indoor and outdoor provision
- that there is a balance of adult-led and child-initiated activities
- how children are progressing towards the early learning goals
- how observations and assessment tie in with the process
- how to plan for children's progress through working with others.

Meeting children's individual needs and interests

Your setting will need to show how it plans for children's individual needs. This may be the way in which it implements a programme for a child who has special educational needs, or through work that is carried out with parents and carers to support a child or group of children who have English as an additional language. Children's needs will change over time – for example, a child might be particularly sensitive if a family pet has just died, or if there are some issues at home due to the birth of a new sibling. All staff should be aware of these kinds of issues and in some settings a book is kept in which key workers are able to note down any issues or changes and which staff check daily.

Medium-term Planning Sheet Week 6			
Topic: Toys		Week beginning: 15/11/12	
Activities	Learning objectives	Learning outcomes	Comments
• Sort a collection of toys into old or new • Talk about characteristics of each set using adjectives, e.g. rusty, shiny, broken, dirty, ragged, clean	• How to decide whether an object is old or new • Describe characteristics of old and new objects	• Sort objects into old and new sets • Explain why they have grouped objects in a particular way	
• Discuss the meaning of words • Match adjectives to toys	• Collections of words linked to topics		
• Which would be the best paper for making a jigsaw (or a set of cards)? • What would the material need to be like? Strong? Rigid? • How could you find out which paper would be best? • Test ideas with papers. Say what you did.	• Suggest how to test an idea about whether a paper is suitable for a particular purpose	• Make a suggestion of what a paper for making a puzzle should be like • Suggest a way of testing the papers appropriate to the characteristic chosen	
• Make a paper sculpture			
• Why do games have rules? • What are they? • What would be fair or unfair?	• Recognise choices they can make and the differences between right and wrong • Agree and follow rules • Understand how rules help them		

Figure 12.3 An example of a medium-term plan

In order to meet children's interests in your planning, you could note down what children have said and then act on it, or develop a particular area that has caught their imagination. In some cases, whole topics can be built on children's ideas and interests.

Including the seven areas of learning

Your planning must include the seven areas of learning in the EYFS and you will need to show that children have opportunities for both indoor and outdoor play activities. If outdoor play needs to be timetabled for practical reasons, this should be shown in your plans.

Maintaining a balance of adult-led and child-initiated activities

Plans should be clear about which activities are adult-led and what kinds of activities are available for children to self-select or initiate themselves.

Progressing towards the early learning goals

When you are planning activities within the EYFS, you will need to ensure there are clear progression opportunities and that activities allow children to learn, building on what they have previously achieved. This means that all adult-directed activities should have clear objectives. If objectives are not specific, it will be hard to measure children's progress against them. At the end of adult-directed activities, the activity plan will need to be updated to show how children have performed. This information will then need to be transferred to the child's individual records.

Observations and assessment

Settings will need to show how observations and assessment of activities feed into their planning. For this reason, many practitioners will write evaluations on their daily plans or make notes while they are working with children to show how they are going to take children's learning forward over the coming days and weeks.

Record keeping

It is likely that your setting will have a file for each child, which will be the central source of information about their learning and development. The files may be paper-based or kept on the computer, as there are

a number of programmes available that can be used alongside the EYFS to track children's learning. Paper files are likely to show observations and summative assessments that have been carried out with children, as well as notes made by staff and parents and/or carers. Records should track children's progress towards the early learning goals.

Planning for children's progress through working with others

As part of your record-keeping process, you will need to show how you work with others, including key people, colleagues, parents and carers, to plan for children's progress within the EYFS. This may take different forms, for example, keeping records when meeting with parents and carers, and showing how you involve them in your assessment processes. You should also record any discussions with key persons or any items that are discussed as part of team meetings, if they relate to individual children.

Link

Go to Unit 9 in Student Book 1 where you will find more information about record keeping related to assessments.

How to plan an adult-directed activity

An adult-directed activity may take different forms, depending on the main area of learning it is targeting and the way in which it is being assessed.

An activity plan should show the learning intention of the activity. This should be very specific and based on the individual needs and interests of the children and what in their development needs to be addressed. The learning intention of an activity should also be closely linked to a key area of learning, although it may include, and be linked to, aspects of other areas. For example, an activity based on the topic of weight, in which children have to find out which potato is the heaviest will be linked to the mathematics area of learning (shape, space and measures), but it may also include aspects of 'Understanding the world' if children are talking about where foods come from.

Adults must be clear on what they need to do in the activity, including the vocabulary they must use and any key questions they need to ask. In some cases, adult-directed activities may be more like a lesson, in which case an adult may talk to a larger group first and then take small groups aside to continue the theme, or the activities might just be carried out with small groups or individual children throughout the day.

As well as being purposeful, adult-directed activities should be playful wherever possible, as children learn better when they are enjoying an activity.

An activity plan should also have a space for the adult to record how children have responded to the task and whether they have met the objective, so that this information can be carried over into subsequent planning.

How to balance adult-led and child-initiated activities

Your plans need to show how you balance adult-led and child-initiated activities, while allowing equal opportunities for each child to participate fully and be included. In some settings, daily plans will only show adult-directed activities – there may be a few of these each day depending on staffing – whereas

those that are child-initiated will be detailed on a separate, overarching plan for the whole week. Children should be free to self-select what they are going to do within the structure of the day – for example, if they are in the role-play area, they should be able to take resources from other areas of the room to support their play. However, it is important that all of the children in the setting have access to all of the resources; for example, if one group of children always heads for the bikes and outdoor toys, make sure that this is not preventing other children from using them. In some settings, there may be a 'wheel of activities' to prevent this from happening, so that children move to a new activity after a set amount of time. However, some practitioners do not like using this system as it interrupts the free flow of activities.

> **Reflect**
>
> How does your setting ensure that all children have a chance to use all of the resources?

How to support and extend children's learning and thinking

When planning and setting up activities for children, it is important to consider how, as an early years professional, you can support their learning and thinking as well as their development. One way of doing this is to engage in 'sustained shared thinking'. This is when practitioners support and challenge children's critical thinking skills by getting involved in their thinking process and work with them to develop and clarify their ideas and build upon their interests. Sustained shared thinking can be done on a one-to-one basis between a child and adult, or between groups of children.

A major part of supporting and extending children's learning and thinking comes in the form of talking to them about what they are doing as they are doing it, because children need to be able to make sense of what they are doing and relate it to their world. You will find that some children do this more easily and are more able to discuss and extend their ideas, whereas others may need you to question them further to stimulate more ideas.

How to lead and support children's progress in more than one area

Any activity that children are carrying out is likely to support their progress in more than one area of learning, as they are all interrelated. For planning purposes, however, it is more useful to focus on one main area that will be developed through the activity. For example, singing counting songs with children will mainly support their mathematical development, but the activity will also develop their musical skills as well as their phonemic awareness through rhyme. (If they are action rhymes they may also support children's physical development.)

Reflect

What activities have you recently carried out in your setting? How might they support more than one area of learning?

Activity

Look at the medium-term plan earlier in this section (Figure 12.3). What examples can you see of activities that will support children's progress in more than one area of learning?

How to carry out observational assessment and record children's progress

As already discussed, you and your colleagues will need to carry out regular observations on children in all contexts so you are aware of their progress towards early learning goals. Observations may take the form of sticky notes, annotated photographs or more detailed observations, as well as information on home or school achievements. The format is less important than what is being recorded; for example

What is the main area of learning that this activity is supporting?

Research

For guidance on the ways in which you might record observations, see the EYFS exemplification materials. You can access these by going to www.pearsonhotlinks. co.uk and searching for the ISBN of this title: 9781447970972.

a couple of lines on a sticky note observing that a child has been able to fasten their own coat for the first time is sufficient. You should regularly check your records to ensure you are recording observations consistently for all children and all areas of learning, as you may find some areas of learning come up more regularly than others.

How to promote diversity, equality and inclusion

Settings need to show they promote diversity, equality and inclusion in all areas of learning when they are planning, leading and assessing play and education programmes. Your setting may be in a catchment area that is diverse, or you may be working in a setting in which children are mainly from one ethnic group. In either case, your curriculum should reflect a wide range of cultures, beliefs and ethnicities, to make sure children are exposed to a true reflection of society.

So that all children are included equally in the setting, you need to make sure activities are available to all children. This can sometimes be challenging, for example, if a group of children always go to the same types of activities. You will need to be aware that this can happen and encourage all children to participate equally.

> **Assessment practice 12.3**　　3C.P5 | 3C.P6 | 3C.P7 | 3C.M3
>
> Plan, record and assess the effectiveness of a series of purposeful play and educational programmes with colleagues, using observations and assessments of children's progress towards early learning goals, to include a balance of:
>
> - adult-led activities
> - child-initiated activities.
>
> Show how you and your colleagues have encouraged children's participation and extended their learning and thinking, while supporting their progress towards the early learning goals.

D Support safeguarding and welfare requirements within the Early Years Foundation Stage

The safeguarding and welfare requirements form the third section of the statutory EYFS framework. These focus on the safety and well-being of children and set out in detail what settings must do to make sure children are able to learn in a safe and welcoming environment and the range of policies they will need to have in place to do this.

> **Reflect**
>
> Before you start to look at this section, what do you know already about safeguarding and child protection? How do you know that children in your setting are being cared for and supervised appropriately? What sort of measures do you think a setting needs to have in place?

The rationale behind the safeguarding and welfare requirements

Children are more likely to learn and do well when they are in a healthy, safe and secure environment and are cared for by adults with whom they have a positive relationship. A number of areas are covered under the safeguarding and welfare requirements in the EYFS, and practitioners are required to show how they make sure all children are cared for appropriately.

All settings will need to show they meet the requirements and practical implications for:

- child protection, including a safeguarding policy

- suitable people, to include disclosures about staff
- staff qualifications, training, support and skills
- providing a key person for each child
- staff-to-child ratios
- health and safety
- managing behaviour
- safety and suitability of premises including risk assessment
- equal opportunities
- special educational needs
- information and record keeping.

Requirements regarding children's protection

The requirements for child protection are set out in the statutory guidance and list a number of measures that settings must have in place to ensure the safeguarding of children in their care.

These must include the following measures.

- A designated safeguarding officer in the setting

This person must be responsible for safeguarding in the setting, liaising with the local children's agencies and the Local Safeguarding Children Board (LSCB), and providing ongoing support and training to staff, as well as attending a specific safeguarding course themselves.

- A policy for safeguarding

This means that all staff must be aware of the setting's policy for dealing with any safeguarding issues that arise. They will need to know how to be alert for any issues that arise in a child's life and what kinds of signs might be indicators of abuse. Policies must be in line with guidance from the LSCB and include an explanation of what will happen if there are any allegations made against members of staff. They should also include the setting's policy on the use of mobile phones and cameras.

- 'Working together to safeguard children 2013'

All settings must use this statutory guidance when addressing any safeguarding issues within the setting, and should notify agencies who have statutory responsibilities as soon as possible in this instance (local children's social care services or the police).

- Staff training

All staff must be trained to understand the policies and procedures of the setting with regard to children's protection, including the importance of recognising and recording any changes in children's behaviour. They must also have an up-to-date knowledge of safeguarding issues.

- Ofsted notification

All providers must inform Ofsted if there are any allegations of serious abuse at a setting, as well as informing them of any action taken. These notifications must be made as soon as possible, but at the latest within 14 days.

Activity

Research the signs of possible abuse and neglect. How would you follow up any of these indicators in your setting? What would you do if one of these was inappropriate behaviour by another member of staff?

Requirements regarding suitable people

In recent years there have been several high-profile cases in which people working with children and young people have been found to be unsuitable and in some cases have harmed or abused children. Legal steps have been taken to ensure this does not happen in the future. To make sure settings meet the requirements for suitable people, they will need to:

- ensure they have systems in place that allow them to check the suitability of all those who come into contact with children
- meet Ofsted requirements (or the requirements of the relevant childminder agency) for any people living on the premises or working directly with children
- ensure all staff disclose any criminal convictions, cautions and court orders that may affect their suitability to work with children through a criminal records check

- record information about staff qualifications and identity/vetting checks
- inform Ofsted or the childminder agency within 14 days if any employee is convicted or disqualified from registration
- ensure they conform to the requirements of the Safeguarding Vulnerable Groups Act 2006, by referring to the Disclosure and Barring Service (DBS) any instance of staff dismissal related to harming a child or putting a child at risk of harm.

Did you know?

Until 2002, the DBS was not in existence. It was established to reduce risks to children and vulnerable people, and was initially called the Criminal Records Bureau (CRB).

Requirements regarding staff qualifications, training, support and skills

All those working with young children and their families must have appropriate qualifications, training, support and knowledge to make sure they understand their roles and responsibilities. Early years settings must provide appropriate supervision that promotes mutual support between colleagues and opportunities to discuss issues as and when they arise. This should include regular staff appraisals and opportunities for further training if necessary.

Research

Look at the statutory guidance to find out what kind of induction training must be provided for all staff when they start at a setting.

In group settings, there must be a manager who:

- has a full and relevant Level 3 qualification
- has worked in an early years setting for at least two years (or has at least two years' other suitable experience)
- is supported by a named deputy who is able to manage the setting in their absence.

At least half of all the other staff will need to have a full and relevant Level 2 qualification. In addition, at least one person with a current paediatric first-aid certificate must be on the premises at all times and accompany children on any outings away from the setting. It is a further requirement that all staff in early years settings have a good command of English so that they are able to care for children effectively, keep records and understand policies and instructions.

Requirements regarding staff ratios and the provision of a key person for each child

All settings must provide a key person for each child so that the care meets the child's individual needs. The key person will work closely with parents and/or carers to make sure the child develops confidence and settles in well.

Link

Go to Unit 7, Section A in Student Book 1 where you will find more information about the importance of attachments and the benefits of the key person system.

In addition to this, staff-to-child ratios must be appropriate to the setting and the level of qualifications held by the staff. Only those aged 17 or over may be included in staff ratios.

Table 12.3 shows the staff-to-child ratios for different settings.

Table 12.3 Staff-to-child ratios for different settings

Provider	Age of child	Staff:child ratio	Qualifications and experience
	Under 2	1:3	• At least one member of staff to have a full and relevant Level 3 qualification. • At least half of all other staff to have a full and relevant Level 2 qualification. • At least half of all staff must have specified training in the care of babies. • Head of under-2s room must have suitable experience of working with under-2s.
	2 years	1:4	• At least one member of staff to have a full and relevant Level 3 qualification. • At least half of all other staff to have a full and relevant Level 2 qualification.
Early years setting	3 years +	1:13	• Where a person with Qualified Teacher Status, Early Years Professional Status, Early Years Teacher Status or another suitable Level 6 qualification is working directly with the children there must be at least one other member of staff with a full and relevant Level 3 qualification.
Early years setting	3 years +	1:8	• Where a person with Qualified Teacher Status, Early Years Professional Status, Early Years Teacher Status or another suitable Level 6 qualification is not working directly with the children there must be at least one member of staff with a full and relevant Level 3 qualification. • At least half of all other staff must hold a full and relevant Level 2 qualification.
Independent school	3 years +	1:30 if majority of children will reach 5 that school year 1:13 in all other classes	• Where a person with Qualified Teacher Status, Early Years Professional Status, Early Years Teacher Status or another suitable Level 6 qualification, an instructor, or another suitably qualified overseas trained teacher is working directly with the children there must be at least one other member of staff with a full and relevant Level 3 qualification.

continued

Table 12.3 (continued)

Provider	Age of child	Staff:child ratio	Qualifications and experience
Independent school	3 years +	1:8	• Where there is no person with Qualified Teacher Status, Early Years Professional Status, Early Years Teacher Status or another suitable Level 6 qualification, no instructor, and no suitably qualified overseas trained teacher working directly with the children at least one member of staff must hold a full and relevant Level 3 qualification. • At least half of all other staff must have a full and relevant Level 2 qualification.
Maintained nursery schools and nursery classes in maintained schools (not reception)	3 years +	1:13	• At least one member of staff must be a school teacher. • At least one other member of staff must hold a full and relevant Level 3 qualification.

Source: Statutory Framework for the Early Years Foundation Stage, Department for Education, 2014, pp. 22–24.

In reception classes, there must be no more than 30 children per schoolteacher. In the case of childminders, the total number of children under the age of 8 must not be more than six.

Requirements regarding the health, safety and security of children

All settings need to ensure they take steps to promote good health in children as well as ensuring their safety at all times. This includes:

- taking appropriate action if children are ill
- taking steps to prevent the spread of any infection
- having a policy for administering medicines and gaining written permission from parents and carers for doing so
- ensuring a first-aid box is accessible at all times that contains contents suitable for use with children with a written record of accidents, injuries and any first aid given
- informing Ofsted and local child protection agencies of any serious accident, illness or injury to a child while in the care of the setting, as well as the action taken, within 14 days of the incident.

It is important that all staff are aware of the setting's policies and that a written record is kept of any medication given to a child so it is available to parents/carers.

Research

Find out about the statutory requirements for the provision of food and drink in early years settings. What are the obligations of providers from a staff-training point of view?

Requirements in relation to managing behaviour

Children will need to be supported by clear and appropriate behaviour management in the setting.

The statutory guidance states that no member of staff or anyone who is in regular contact with a child in a setting where care is provided should give or threaten corporal punishment. Physical intervention should only be used if there is a possibility of danger to the child or another person.

Link

Go to Unit 7 in Student Book 1 where you will find more information about the importance of supporting children's positive behaviour and the role of the adult.

Requirements regarding the safety and suitability of the premises, environment and equipment

All early years settings must comply with requirements for keeping the environment safe for all who use it. Health and safety requirements are such that settings should have in place policies and procedures that ensure the setting is kept safe and free from hazards.

Link

Go to Unit 4 in Student Book 1 where you will find more information about health and safety practice in early years settings.

Settings must make sure the learning environment – both indoor and outdoor – as well as all equipment and furniture are safe for use by children and suitable for the ages of children and the types of activities provided for them. Specific space requirements are given in the statutory guidance. These requirements are shown in Table 12.4.

Table 12.4 Specific space requirements

Age of child	Space requirement
Under 2 years	3.5 m² per child
2 years	2.5 m² per child
3–5 years	2.3 m² per child

Source: The Statutory Framework for the Early Years Foundation Stage, 2014, pp. 27–28.

The learning environment must be safe and secure and kept clean, and settings should have a health and safety policy that outlines procedures that will be followed when identifying, reporting and dealing with accidents, hazards and any faulty equipment. Settings must show that they have procedures in place for managing safety and have appropriate equipment such as smoke detectors, fire extinguishers and fire alarms, all of which must be regularly tested.

Other specific requirements

- In settings where there are children under the age of 2, there will need to be a separate baby room (except in childminding settings), although children attending a baby room should be moved into a room with an older age group when it is appropriate to do so.
- There should be adequate toilets and hand basins available for the number of children (usually one toilet and one hand basin for every ten children over the age of 2 years). Except in childminding settings, separate toilet facilities should usually be provided for adults.
- Settings will need to provide an area for any confidential meetings or discussions.
- Settings must ensure that all entering the premises are identified. Children may not leave the setting unsupervised and parents/carers must notify the setting if other individuals are collecting their children.
- Settings need to have in place reasonable measures for managing risk. Risk assessments should identify aspects of the environment that should be checked regularly, and when and by whom this will take place. Outings must be organised, risk assessed and should include an appropriate number of adults. If vehicles are used to transport the children, the vehicles and the drivers must be insured.
- Settings must not allow smoking in or on the premises when children are present or about to be present.
- Settings must have public liability insurance.

Requirements regarding equal opportunities and challenging inappropriate attitudes and practices

All forms of prejudice and discrimination have a negative effect on children's lives. Childcare workers have a duty to protect children from discrimination and to promote respect for others. It is important that settings have a policy, procedure and practices in place to promote equality and diversity, and these should not only help everyone to engage in inclusive practice within the setting but should provide a framework for discriminatory practices to be challenged should these practices be observed.

All settings must show they support children with special educational needs and disabilities. Settings that are funded by the local authority for the provision of early education will need to comply with the Special Educational Needs and Disability (SEND) Code of Practice, which came into effect in September 2014. The code of practice is statutory guidance from the Department for Education that provides practical advice on how to carry out duties to identify, assess and make provision for children and young people with SEN. In addition, preschools are expected to identify a member of staff who will act as Special Educational Needs coordinator (SENCO).

Staff should be aware that they need to follow their legal responsibilities under the Equality Act 2010, which states all children should have equal access to facilities and activities. They should also always challenge inappropriate attitudes and practices among other children and adults, whether they are other staff or parents and/or carers.

Requirements in relation to records and the provision of information for parents or carers

As in any organisation, records will need to be kept by settings and information shared with others in order for them to run smoothly. Settings will need to show how they keep the required records and how and when information is collected, stored and shared. It is important that all staff are aware of the confidentiality of the information and the requirements of the Data Protection Act 1998, which states that information must only be used for the purpose for which it was gathered.

Information about the child

Settings will need to keep basic information about the child, which they will need to gather from parents or carers before the child starts at the setting. This should include the child's full name, address and date of birth as well as the name, address and contact details of all parents or carers who have parental responsibility. This information should be updated regularly in case of emergency.

Information for parents and carers

The setting will need to make certain information available to parents and carers. This should include:

- staffing and the name of their child's key person
- information about the EYFS and how it is delivered in the setting, including where they can access more information
- the types of activities and experiences that are provided and how they can support their child's learning
- how children with special educational needs and disabilities are supported
- policies and procedures of the setting
- information about food and drink.

All of this information will need to be easily accessible to parents and carers through different means, for example, via a website, letters, noticeboards and/or regular newsletters.

Information about the provider

As well as having a certificate of registration, the setting must keep records of the name, address and phone number of all staff working with children, as well as anyone else who will be in contact with them. They will also need to keep a register detailing when children have attended and the name of each child's key person.

Information about complaints

There must be a written procedure for dealing with any complaints as well as records kept of the outcome. All settings must investigate any written complaints within 28 days and the record of complaints must be made available to Ofsted.

As well as any direct complaints, information must be made available to parents and carers about how to contact Ofsted if they believe the setting is not meeting its obligations under the EYFS. They will also need to be given a copy of the report following an Ofsted inspection.

Changes notifiable to Ofsted

All settings will need to inform Ofsted about:

- a change of address of the premises or any changes in the premises itself that may affect the space available
- a change of the name or address of the provider, or changes in management
- any event that may affect the suitability of the provider or any person caring for children on the premises to look after children
- any proposal to change the hours of childcare
- any changes to the organisation that runs the provision, whether this is a company, charity or partnership.

Your responsibilities in relation to safeguarding and health and safety

It is important to remember that the areas of safeguarding and health and safety are not the same – these are sometimes confused in early years settings. Safeguarding relates to the welfare and protection of children from abuse and neglect. Health and safety issues relate to the general safety of **all** those in the setting. You will have a safeguarding policy in your setting and will need to be aware of health and safety procedures.

Link

Go to Unit 8 in Student Book 1 for more information about the individual responsibilities of early years practitioners in relation to safeguarding.

Your responsibilities in relation to safety and security

Your responsibilities in relation to safety and security in an early years setting will be around ensuring children are kept safe and secure while they are in your care. This means following the correct procedures for health and safety at all times and making sure you act on them, as they are the responsibility of all adults in the setting.

Activity

Outline what you would do in the situations below. What are your responsibilities?

1 You notice an unfamiliar adult in the setting and have not been told that anyone is visiting today.
2 You have found a broken item of furniture that has a sharp edge.
3 You are aware that there has not been any kind of fire practice for over a year in your setting.
4 You find a number of children's coats have not been put on pegs and are lying on the floor in a narrow part of the corridor.

Link

Go to Unit 4 in Student Book 1 to find more information about health and safety in early years settings.

How to identify and provide for children's physical welfare needs

As well as keeping children safe and secure, you have a responsibility to make sure children are well looked after and that all their needs are met. This includes making sure they have enough sleep and rest, and that they have appropriate amounts of food and drink. Very young children will not always be able to identify when they have needs in these areas and you should make sure you know the signs to look for, including ensuring they have access to toilets, rest or food and drink when necessary. As you get to know them, you will also be able to look out for signs that they are unwell and may need to support them if they are unaware of this themselves.

Link

Go to Unit 3, Section C in Student Book 1 to find more information about children's physical care needs.

How to value diversity and promote equality of opportunity and anti-discriminatory practice

As well as through the curriculum, you will need to show other ways in which you value diversity and promote equality of opportunity and anti-discriminatory practice in your setting. You should make sure you are aware of the importance of valuing and respecting others in all of your actions within the setting and model this to children.

Discrimination should always be challenged. If you ignore it, it could be assumed that you condone discriminatory language or behaviour. To be able to challenge discrimination it is essential that you have a good understanding of legislation and the policy, procedures and practice in your own setting. You should feel confident that you know what good practice is. You should also be prepared to challenge your own prejudices as these can lead to discriminatory practice. Prejudice can be overcome by undertaking training and becoming more aware of the diverse groups of people that exist in society.

How to record and manage accurate information about children

You should show you have an awareness of the importance of confidentiality when managing information about children, and that your records are accessible to those who need to see them. Be aware that staff may work different shifts or times of day, and ensure you pass information to others if they are not present at meetings. You may need to suggest additional ways of passing on information so that all staff are included.

Assessment practice 12.4　3D.P8 | 3D.M4 | 3D.M5 | 3D.D2

Discuss the different policies that are required in order for settings to meet the safeguarding and welfare requirements of the EYFS.

- How do you and your setting show that you adhere to these requirements consistently?
- Evaluate the extent to which these requirements can be managed through the EYFS education programme.
- Discuss how the requirements of the EYFS contribute to safeguarding and welfare.

▌ Further reading and resources

Department for Education (2007) *Letters and Sounds* (DFES-00281-2007) This is a government document, produced through the Primary National Strategy, which starts in the Foundation Stage and builds up through different stages. It features valuable suggestions for progression, including focused activities.

Department for Education (2014) *Statutory Framework for the Early Years Foundation Stage*.

Langston, A. and Doherty, J. (2012) *The Revised EYFS in Practice: Thinking, Reflecting and Doing!*, London: Featherstone Education.

Moylett, H. and Stewart, N. (2013) *Emerging, Expected and Exceeding: Understanding the Revised Early Years Foundation Stage*, The British Association for Early Childhood Education.

Tassoni, P. (2012) *Penny Tassoni's Practical EYFS Handbook (2nd edition)*, Essex: Pearson.

Websites

EYFS documentation: www.education.gov.uk/eyfs
Information and guidance on using the EYFS.

EYFS forum: http://eyfs.info
A useful site for resources, information and support for early years practitioners.

Early Years Educator (EYE magazine): www.magonlinelibrary.com/eye
A good source of articles and information.

Nursery World magazine: www.nurseryworld.magazine.co.uk
Useful articles, information and jobs.

Ofsted: www.ofsted.gov.uk
This website has information about EYFS Ofsted requirements.

Ready for work?

Jim Collins Nursery assistant

I have recently started working in a nursery that is attached to a large school. Previously I was working in a small church-run nursery and it has been really interesting to find out about how the two different settings do their planning and assessment. At first I found it difficult as I had thought things would be the same, and had made quite a few assumptions about how planning, staffing and activities would take place as this is only my second job. I have had to get used to a different way of working, and have learned another way of planning, which has been good. I have also been able to bring some of my own ideas to the setting and talk about things that worked well in my previous role.

One of the main differences has been that because the nursery is attached to a school we have different routines as part of our day, which spills over into our planning. For example, we share our outside area with a reception class, and at the moment this means we are only able to use it on a timetabled rota. We also have to have our breaks at set times to coincide with the school day.

It has been good for me to learn about how different settings operate and I am enjoying developing my experiences. I have made a few contacts and am trying to set up a local group for different settings to attend so that we can get together on a regular basis to look at different ways of planning and to share ideas.

Skills for practice

You can focus on the area of supporting learning but you may also like to ask at your setting whether you can organise the learning environment (either indoor or outdoor) to show how you can set up and maintain different areas and activities such as sand, water, role play and so on. You could also prepare resources such as making basic dough or gloop, or show how you have created a wall display using children's work and photographs.

If you are working with babies, you should be able to develop many skills for work with babies, for example, caring skills, preparing for play and learning, supporting play and learning, supporting literacy, and observing, assessing and planning.

Look through the skills for work in the early years settings section in the *Practical Evidence Portfolio* for more ideas.

Observe, assess and plan

- Complete five observations and assessments of children aged from 2 to 4 years using the documentation/techniques employed in the setting.
- Complete five plans relevant to the appropriate curriculum framework to meet the learning/development needs of children aged from 2 to 4 years using the documentation of the setting.

Introduction

Being able to carry out effective research is an important skill for working with young children. It will help you to draw conclusions from facts rather than assumptions. Research in early years might include observations of children, questionnaires for parents or a review of the latest theories that support childcare practice. For example, it is easy to reach assumptions about a child's behaviour and the factors that influence it without any real evidence, but using observations as a method of research provides you with first-hand evidence to be able to back up any conclusions you draw. Understanding research, and how to carry it out effectively, will help you appreciate the ways in which it can increase your understanding of children and their development, plan for their learning or even improve the setting in which you are working.

Assessment: You will be assessed by a Pearson-set assignment.

Learning aims

In this unit you will:

A   produce a research proposal related to work with young children

B   locate and present secondary research

C   carry out a small-scale research project related to work with young children

D   be able to evaluate the research project.

"Whatever childcare setting you work in, you will use research skills as part of your everyday routine. You may not realise it, but you will be gathering information, analysing it, drawing conclusions from it and taking action as a result. This is research. However, it is important that you do not draw conclusions without well-researched and analysed evidence as this can lead to mistakes. Therefore, an ability to understand how the research process works is essential.

Andrew George, *manager of a childcare setting*"

Research Skills

BTEC
Assessment Zone

This table shows you what you must do in order to achieve a **Pass**, **Merit** or **Distinction** grade, and where you can find activities to help you.

Assessment criteria

Pass	Merit	Distinction
Learning aim A: Produce a research proposal related to work with young children		
3A.P1 I&CT Present a realistic research proposal including: • objectives • selected research methods • related ethical issues. **Assessment practice 13.1** **Assessment practice 13.2**	**3A.M1** Analyse how the selected research methods informed and shaped the research proposal. **Assessment practice 13.1** **Assessment practice 13.2**	**3A.D1** Discuss research objectives in terms of feasibility and application to practice. **Assessment practice 13.1** **Assessment practice 13.2**
Learning aim B: Locate and present secondary research		
3B.P2 I&CT Be able to select secondary research appropriate for the research proposal. **Assessment practice 13.2**	**3B.M2** Discuss the reliability and relevance of the selected secondary research. **Assessment practice 13.2**	
Learning aim C: Carry out a small-scale research project related to work with young children		
3C.P3 I&CT Maths Collect and record research findings relevant to the project objectives. **Assessment practice 13.3** **3C.P4** English Maths Present research findings in a relevant format, demonstrating a good command of written English. **Assessment practice 13.3** **3C.P5** Explain the possible implications of the research findings for current practice. **Assessment practice 13.3**	**3C.M3** Produce a coherent argument and relevant conclusions based on the research findings. **Assessment practice 13.3**	
Learning aim D: Be able to evaluate the research project		
3D.P6 Describe how the research findings relate to the original research question. **Assessment practice 13.4**	**3D.M4** Review the chosen research methods in relation to the results obtained, including for any sources of bias or error. **Assessment practice 13.4** **3D.M5** Recommend possible improvements to the research, referring to any relevant implications. **Assessment practice 13.4**	**3D.D2** Evaluate the extent to which the findings from the research undertaken can be implemented. **Assessment practice 13.4**

English English Functional Skills signposting   I&CT Information and Communication Technology skills signposting

Maths Mathematics Functional Skills signposting

How you will be assessed

This unit will be assessed by an assignment that is set by Pearson. It will be marked internally by your teacher/tutor and verified by a Pearson Standards Verifier. Throughout this unit you will find assessment practice activities that will help you work towards your assessment. Completing these activities will not mean that you have achieved a particular grade, but you will have carried out useful research or preparation that will be relevant when it comes to your final assignment.

For your final assignment you will be required to carry out a small-scale research project and present your findings in a report. The research project will need to focus on a topic related to work with children that you have chosen in consultation with your teacher/tutor.

The assessment will test your ability to:

- understand the importance of research for work with children
- produce a valid research proposal
- plan a small-scale research project related to work with young children
- carry out a small-scale research project and present a report of the findings
- evaluate the processes involved in your research.

How much do you know about how research is used in early years settings? Discuss the following examples of research and explain why you think they might be useful:

- observing a child who is biting other children

- asking parents about their experiences in the setting

- researching a particular medical condition that a new child attending the nursery may have.

A Produce a research proposal related to work with young children

A good place to start is to think about why we carry out research when working with children.

The role of research

Research is an activity where we aim to find out information and/or gain knowledge about something. It is carried out in an organised way. Research can range from observations about how a child interacts with others in a setting, to a nursery carrying out a questionnaire with parents and/or carers to see how its service might be improved.

Sometimes people draw conclusions but may not have any evidence to back them up. When statements or assumptions are made about things that happen with children, research can provide the evidence to support or disprove those statements. The results of research can make people change their minds about something they may have seen, or help them decide what action to take to improve or change something, or to help a child progress.

Research within the early years field can also be used to:

- inform policy or practice

- highlight gaps in provision

- extend your knowledge and understanding

- improve outcomes for children by improving your practice

- help professionals to reflect on their work.

Research activities could cover several of these things. For example, a piece of research on how children use outdoor play areas could extend your knowledge and understanding of children's play habits and how they use outdoor play equipment. As a result it could inform policy on how outdoor areas are used in the curriculum and might also highlight gaps in terms of the facilities available for outdoor play provision. Changes that may happen as a result of these findings would lead to improving practice and, in turn, outcomes for children.

Identifying a focus for research

All research projects begin with a decision about what to investigate. The area chosen for the project needs to be focused enough to enable a detailed piece of work in the timeframe allocated. The timeframe for the project and the resources available to you will determine what you might study.

You should always study something that is of interest to you – make this the starting point for choosing your area of study. It might start off as a very broad topic, such as imaginative play, or it could be something much more focused such as the value of a communal lunchtime for children's development of social skills.

If you start with a broad area, it is important to quickly focus your thinking on an area that is manageable. If your project remains too broad, the work will not be achievable.

It is useful to have a number of areas of potential interest, which you then try to narrow down to establish the area of focus that might be available to you. At this point you need to consider the availability of sources of research, as this may impact on your final decision. You also need to make sure that your final topic area offers a realistic area for research.

You will need to formulate a title for your work. Often the best titles are written as questions as they provide a focus for the work. If you do decide to use a question, try not to write one that has a 'yes' or 'no' answer. Use a sentence stem instead, such as 'To what extent does…' or 'How far does…' as this type of question requires a detailed response. It is essential that you settle on a relevant, realistic and identifiable research question.

Discussions with your teacher/tutor

Your teacher/tutor will be a good source of ideas for your research project. They may be able to give you ideas or help you narrow down a broad idea to a more focused and manageable area of research.

You may also wish to discuss ideas with your placement supervisor. They may have ideas about a piece of research that would help them in the setting.

Observations of practice

Throughout your course, while on placement, you will be involved in observing children and how they react to each other and their environment. You will see similarities as well as differences in how children react to the same event, game or activity. Something you might have seen in this kind of situation could provide a stimulus for your research.

We look at the different types of observations that you could carry out on children later in this section.

During your placement experiences you will be working with early years professionals in different settings. You will see a range of approaches to early years work, depending on the philosophy of the setting (for example, Montessori, or the Forest School approach) and the ways that the setting is organised. You may want to look at the way that these philosophies influence the practices within the setting as part of some secondary research.

Journal articles

Throughout your course, you will have been encouraged to keep up to date with the latest thinking on early years issues. These are usually reported in journals first, rather than in textbooks, as textbooks take some time to be published. Therefore, journals could provide a source of inspiration for your area of research.

Previous research

Information you have gathered for previous assignments or even just reading around a subject might provide a stimulus for your research project. You may have read something that interested you and want to investigate further or you may have come across information outside of the work you had been doing that could provide a potential avenue for research.

Suitability of topic

Once you have decided on your chosen focus, you need to ensure that your topic is suitable. This means you need to consider any ethical issues that may impact on your ability to carry out primary research. You need to make sure that you can carry out your research without causing distress to anyone who may be involved. Consider this checklist.

- Make sure you have gained permission from your teacher/tutor and any other appropriate people, such as placement supervisors, if carrying out the work in a setting. They will need to check your work regularly to ensure you do not go wrong.
- Make sure you have asked the permission of the people you wish to involve in your project, or their parents or carers if they are children. You do not want to plan an elaborate project only to find that the people you need to be able to carry it out do not wish to be involved. Remember, you will need **informed consent**.
- Be ready to explain the purpose of your research in detail: what you are trying to find out, the research methods you want to use and how you will use the information. This will help your participants make an informed decision.

Key term

Informed consent – getting agreement from the person involved in the research, ensuring they fully understand what is happening and why.

- Ensure you are clear about confidentiality and how you will maintain this. Your participants will want reassurance before agreeing to take part, particularly if your focus is a sensitive one.

The subject of ethics is looked at in more detail later in this section.

Importance of achievable aims and objectives

Aims and objectives will help you focus your work and clearly set out the boundaries of your study. Aims are broad statements that identify what the study hopes to find out. They will further clarify the title or **hypothesis** and outline the direction of study that the project will take.

Aims will usually begin with verbs, which describe what the work hopes to achieve through the different research methods that are used. Examples include:

- to find out
- to establish
- to discuss
- to explore
- to identify.

Written well, aims will set the scope of the work and help to identify the research methods that will be used.

Objectives detail exactly what you intend to achieve within the research work. This might be linked to a specific research method or a more general outcome. Objectives are generally more specific than aims and are easier to measure in terms of whether they have been achieved successfully. An example of an aim might be 'to establish parents' views of childcare provision using a questionnaire'.

▮ Research methods

Research methods can be either quantitative or qualitative.

Quantitative research

Quantitative research methods produce data that can be statistically analysed. They usually generate large quantities of information, and **sample** sizes (the number of people studied) are big. Questionnaires and surveys are generally considered quantitative

research methods, as they aim to gather information from large numbers of people. To be able to handle the large amount of data, most researchers design questionnaires and surveys with questions that have a choice of specified answers.

The most effective way to make sense of the information is by presenting it in a manageable format – usually a graph, chart or diagram. This allows the reader to see patterns easily and analyse the results.

Qualitative research

Qualitative research methods such as interviews or observations are designed to achieve a response that has more depth. Therefore the quality of the response is more important than the number of people who respond. These methods focus on finding out attitudes, opinions and thoughts. They allow the researcher to understand a situation in more detail.

This type of information cannot be easily analysed in a mathematical way and therefore qualitative data is not usually converted into graphs or charts. This is because a lot of the quality and meaning of responses would be lost through this process. The information is used to support arguments, and is often quoted as it has been said.

Key terms

Hypothesis – an explanation for an observation or scientific problem made using limited evidence as a starting point for further investigation.

Qualitative research – exploratory research that allows us to go deeper into the research issues. Common methods to collect data include interviews and observations.

Quantitative research – research that tries to quantify the problem and uses statistics to analyse results. Common methods to collect data include questionnaires and surveys.

Sample – a section of people or data used in research.

A student and parent are engaged in a two-way conversation. What type of research method is the learner likely to be using here – quantitative or qualitative?

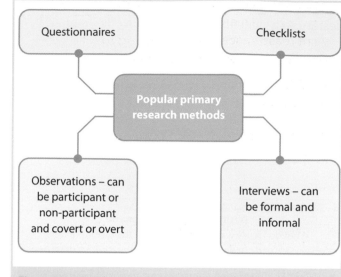

Figure 13.1 Popular primary research methods

The features of primary research

As well as being qualitative or quantitative, research can be classified as either primary or secondary. **Primary research** involves collecting your own original data using a primary research technique. Figure 13.1 shows examples of primary research methods. We will look at sources and effective use of **secondary research** in Section B of this unit.

All of the primary research methods need careful planning if they are to produce information that is **valid** and **reliable**. The primary research methods chosen will depend on the focus of the topic and what the researcher hopes to find out.

Key terms

Primary research – finding things out (new information) for yourself.

Reliable – this means that your research will produce similar information to that found by someone else using the same methods with a similar sample.

Secondary research – finding things out using material produced by others.

Valid – this means that your research produces information that is well supported, justifiable and trustworthy.

Questionnaires

A questionnaire is a list of questions, which are given to potential respondents in a written format. Questionnaires are not usually completed with a researcher present and therefore can be a cost-effective way to gather a lot of information.

Questionnaires are often used because they give breadth of information about a subject. However, they do not generally provide any depth of information – this is best gained through interviews.

A questionnaire is a piece of quantitative research as it can provide lots of responses relatively easily, and responses can be directly compared, collated and analysed. It is a good way of asking straightforward questions of a large number of people.

However, it does take time to collate and analyse the large number of responses that are gained.

Key features of a good questionnaire

To design a good questionnaire, there are a number of stages that you will need to go through to ensure it will get you the information you need. If you miss out or rush through any stage, it is likely that the finished result will not be useful or will yield unreliable or invalid results.

Figure 13.2 shows the things to think about when designing a questionnaire.

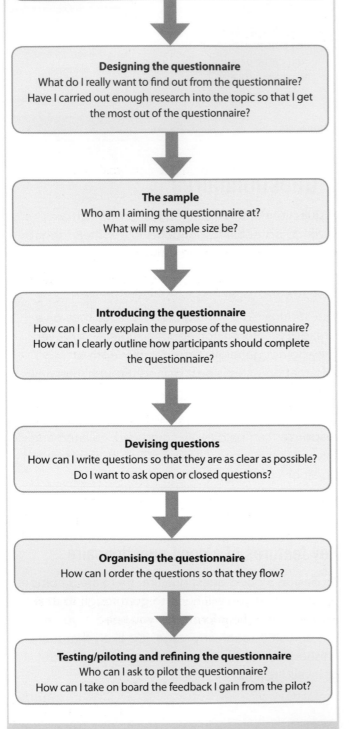

Planning the questionnaire
How long do I want the questionnaire to be?
How can I present the questionnaire so that people can answer it easily?

Designing the questionnaire
What do I really want to find out from the questionnaire?
Have I carried out enough research into the topic so that I get the most out of the questionnaire?

The sample
Who am I aiming the questionnaire at?
What will my sample size be?

Introducing the questionnaire
How can I clearly explain the purpose of the questionnaire?
How can I clearly outline how participants should complete the questionnaire?

Devising questions
How can I write questions so that they are as clear as possible?
Do I want to ask open or closed questions?

Organising the questionnaire
How can I order the questions so that they flow?

Testing/piloting and refining the questionnaire
Who can I ask to pilot the questionnaire?
How can I take on board the feedback I gain from the pilot?

Figure 13.2 Things to think about when designing a questionnaire

Planning the questionnaire

Before you start to design the questionnaire, consider the following.

- The length of the questionnaire

Long questionnaires tend to put potential respondents off and they are less likely to complete them. Keep your questionnaire as short as possible by only asking what really needs to be asked.

- The presentation of the questionnaire

People are less likely to complete a questionnaire that looks complicated, wordy or asks for information that is non-essential or too private. When designing a questionnaire, aim for an attractive layout with plenty of space around each question, as this gives the appearance of fewer words. Position the response boxes on the right, as most people are right-handed and this makes it easier for the respondent to complete.

Designing the questionnaire

You need to have a very clear idea from the outset what you want the questionnaire to find out, as this will ensure that the information you gather will be of genuine use to you in your research.

In order to do this effectively, you must research your topic well. A good questionnaire often comes from thorough research of secondary source material, such as textbooks and media articles. This research should help direct you towards what you hope to find out and will also give you something to compare your results with when you analyse them.

Sometimes the area you wish to investigate has no previously published material available. If this is the case, you will have to consider your line of enquiry even more carefully to ensure that you are clear about the purpose of your questionnaire.

Decide on your sample

To ensure your questionnaire produces valid and reliable information, it is important to consider who you will give it to, and how many people you will ask. Remember, however, that a small sample, especially a sample of less than 20, is not likely to be representative, regardless of how the sample has been chosen.

Most samples will be a balance between the ideal and what is practical. The choice is likely to be affected by cost, time and resource limitations, but as long as this is recognised in the analysis of the results, this is reasonable.

Introduction to the questionnaire

A clear, concise introduction is important as this explains the purpose of the questionnaire. It should outline what the questionnaire is trying to achieve and why, as well as how the results will be used. Mentioning confidentiality will provide reassurance and encourage more people to complete the questionnaire.

The introduction should also outline how to complete the questionnaire, the deadline and how to return it. This is particularly important, as response rates to questionnaires are typically below 30 per cent, so it is therefore important to make the questionnaire as easy to return as possible.

Activity

Devise an introduction for a questionnaire on childcare choices for working parents. How might you choose your sample for such a questionnaire?

Devising questions

Writing good questions for questionnaires is a challenge. Questions need to be clear to ensure that the respondents understand what is being asked. It is easy to write a question that you believe will gain information in a specific way, but those completing the questionnaire may interpret it completely differently. Therefore, it is worth spending some time considering your questions to ensure they are clear.

Open versus closed questions

Questions are usually open or closed. Open questions require more than a yes/no answer. They will prompt a wide range of responses and are, therefore, more difficult to analyse. For example:

---

1. What do you think is the most effective way of encouraging children to eat healthily?

However, the responses to open questions give a more personal insight into the respondents' thoughts.

Closed questions are more limiting in their possible responses for the respondent. They generally require a yes/no answer, or else there are a number of predetermined responses for the respondent to choose from. For example:

---

2. Did you ensure your child had five
   pieces of fruit or vegetables   Yes [ ]
   yesterday?   No [ ]

This question would be answered 'yes' or 'no'.

Closed questions are useful if you are covering facts or where it is reasonable to guess the range of possible responses. They are also used when you need to categorise age or time.

When using preselected responses, it is important that they have clear meanings. Avoid using words such as 'poor', 'adequate' or 'good', as each respondent will have a different interpretation of these words. Try a grading scale instead, for example, from 1 to 5, as this may bring a better response for analysis.

It is also important that each option is sufficiently distinct to allow the respondent to be able to make a clear choice.

For example, when classifying age groups there should not be any crossover in the categories. Use 20 or under, 21–35, 36–50 and so on, rather than 20, 20–35, 35–50, etc. – otherwise those who are 20 or 35 will not know which category to select.

Closed questions are easy to analyse and are also easy for the respondent to complete as often they only involve ticking a box. For example:

---

3. Meat is a good source of   a) protein   [ ]
                                b) vitamin D [ ]
                                c) vitamin C [ ]
                                d) fibre   [ ]

Multiple questions

It is easy to write a question that really asks more than one question. An example would be:

> 4. How many times a week do you read with your child for more than half an hour, and what time do you usually read?

With such questions, some respondents will only answer one aspect of the question and this will reduce the reliability of your results.

If both parts of a question are important, it is better to break the question up into parts or even make it two separate questions. Breaking up a question into separate parts will ensure that all respondents are clearly directed into answering it completely.

Other things to consider

There are several other points to bear in mind when devising questions for a questionnaire. Table 13.1 will help you avoid the potential pitfalls.

Table 13.1 Potential pitfalls when writing questionnaire questions

Potential pitfall	Factors to consider
Irrelevant questions	Questions must be relevant. Questions on age, gender and occupation are often included on questionnaires but you need to consider if this information is relevant to your study. The rule is, if the question is not relevant to the study, leave it out.
Poor choice of language	Think carefully about the language you are using and who you are hoping will complete the questionnaire. Choose words that are straightforward and that people will understand. People are less likely to answer a question if it looks complicated.
Asking too much personal information	Respondents do not like giving personal information, so only ask for it if it is necessary and relevant. If personal information is needed, use a range rather than asking for exact information, as people are more likely to answer that. Questions requesting personal information are often placed at the end of the questionnaire as the respondent is more likely to have completed most of the questionnaire before they get to that section. If the respondent chooses not to complete this part, then you still have the information from the rest of the completed questionnaire.
Asking questions that make assumptions	Always avoid questions that assume something about the opinions or actions of the respondent. This also applies to knowledge and experiences.
Asking questions that require a good memory	Most adults may be reasonably expected to remember events from the preceding year with relative accuracy. However, it is not wise to ask people for information about things that happened five or ten years ago. Where detailed information from the past is needed, interviews are probably a better research method.
Asking leading questions	It is important to devise questions that do not suggest a preferred response to the respondent. This trap can be easy to fall into if you hold a particular view yourself.

Organising the questionnaire and testing the questions

Questions need to be grouped in an ordered manner so that, where appropriate, one question leads to another. Once all the questions have been drafted, they can be written on small pieces of card or sticky notes and ordered and reordered until they flow well. This is a good way of assessing the way the final questionnaire will look before typing it up.

Piloting the questionnaire

A questionnaire must be piloted by a small number of people to see if it is effective and to highlight any areas that might have been missed. As the writer, you will not always see the errors, mistakes or confusing sections because you are so close to the work. It is always better to ask objective people with a fresh eye to look at it. Ask people to comment on such things as the clarity of the instructions and layout, time for completion, any ambiguities as well as any questions they feel are irrelevant or offensive. Use the comments to adjust the original questionnaire before sending it out to the main group of respondents.

Carry out the questionnaire

The next stage is to carry out the actual questionnaire and wait for the responses to come back.

Collate and analyse the results

Questionnaires generally produce large amounts of data that need analysing. The method of analysis chosen will depend on the way the questions have been asked. Closed questions lend themselves to graphical presentation (i.e. charts or graphs), as the data will be quantitative, whereas open questions will produce qualitative information, which is best presented in a written format.

Interviews

An interview provides more detailed information than a questionnaire. Interviews often take longer to carry out than questionnaires but they make it possible to explore issues in more depth. This is particularly useful when researching beliefs, attitudes and feelings, as these cannot be fully explored through either observations or questionnaires.

Interviews draw out reasons and explanations, due to their very structured nature. Interviews also allow people to speak directly and at length in a way that questionnaires cannot.

Interviews are a responsive method of research, as it is possible to change the questions in response to the answers the interviewee gives. This means that an interviewer can get more information than might otherwise be possible.

Interviews also have better response rates than questionnaires, as questionnaires can be easily lost or forgotten. If asked directly, people are more likely to agree to answer questions. Interviews can also be recorded. This means that the researcher can replay an interview as many times as needed to collect the information accurately.

Interviews rely on effective communication between two people. For an interview to be successful, the interaction between the interviewer and the participant is very important, as this can affect the responses. Factors such as the interviewer's appearance, gender, age and even accent can affect the answers given, as the interviewee may form an opinion about them. Interviewers can also influence responses without knowing they are doing so, through normal mannerisms such as nodding or smiling. Uttering 'mmm' or even 'yes' when someone speaks can influence the relationship. You must remain non-judgemental when interviewing to get the best outcome. A good rapport may allow you to ask questions of a sensitive or more personal nature, but it is worth remembering that interviewees may sometimes respond to questions with what they feel the interviewer wants to hear rather than their true feelings or behaviour.

Interviews are generally one-to-one and are therefore quite time consuming. They are generally used for relatively small samples.

The nature of the data collected during interviews makes it difficult to draw overall conclusions or generalisations. Such qualitative data is not generally used to produce detailed statistics.

Types of interview

There are two main approaches to interviews as a method of research.

Formal interview

A formal interview is one in which there is a standard set of questions that each participant will be asked. The interviewer can only ask these questions, whatever the responses given, and can neither adapt the wording of the questions nor change them in any way. This is a very rigid form of interviewing, similar to a questionnaire. However, using such standardised questions allows generalisations to be made. There is also less chance for the interviewer to introduce bias, as they have to ask a specific set of questions.

However, being so rigid can be problematic because opportunities for developing information may be lost, as interviewers cannot follow up on answers that may be of interest.

Informal interview

In an informal interview, the interviewer has much more control and influence over the questions that are asked. Interviewers have the freedom to develop the questions as they feel appropriate. The informal interview process is similar to a discussion, rather than just being a question-and-answer session, which can make it more unpredictable.

An interviewer usually has a list of areas or issues they wish to cover during the interview. These are often called 'trigger questions'. They are also able to follow up on responses and develop the interview more fully. This type of interview has the advantage that it can produce richer information, as interviewers can probe for thoughts and develop what might appear to be off-the-cuff comments into fuller answers. It is therefore a good source of detailed qualitative data.

You can combine both formal and informal interview techniques. This is called a semi-structured interview and enables you to benefit from the advantages of both methods.

Case studies

A case study might be used within a research project to investigate a particular aspect of the project that is based on an individual or organisation. For example, if a research project was looking into the support the voluntary sector provides for children in a particular town, a case study of a voluntary organisation would be extremely relevant. A case study may also be used if looking at a topic where you wanted to see how something applied to a child. For example, you might research why some parents do not have their children vaccinated, and a case study of a child who was not vaccinated would be a useful research method for that topic.

A case study requires an in-depth investigation where historical evidence is taken into account. Case studies look at the impact of past and present events on the topic being studied.

Most case studies will draw on a range of research methods. You might start a case study with some secondary research and then use interviews, questionnaires or observations to investigate the case study further.

Observations of children

Observations of children can be used to study all aspects of development, including physical, social, emotional and intellectual. They can be used as the main method of research as part of a longitudinal study – a study that takes place over a long period of time, perhaps six months or more, to chart developments over the period. Observations may also be used as a research method to support other methods you may have used, or as one-off pieces of work.

This practitioner is observing a child. What method of observation could she be using?

Participant and non-participant observations

There are two different types of observation – the main difference is whether or not the observer chooses to get involved with what they are observing.

- Participant observation

This is where the observer becomes part of the group they are observing. Being part of a group and observing at the same time can make recording details difficult. The observer may also influence the outcome by being involved. However, this type of observation can result in a more reflective picture of what goes on, as the observer is part of the group.

- Non-participant observation

In this type of observation, the observer is an onlooker who is not involved in the action in any way. They record only what they see and have no interaction with the person or people being observed at all. This means the observer can record a lot of detail as they can concentrate on this, rather than getting involved. They can also see things that are not immediately obvious when part of a group. The main disadvantage with this type of observation is that the observer may have an effect on what happens, as those involved know they are being watched. This may make them feel intimidated or self-conscious.

Overt or covert

In both participant and non-participant observations the observer can be overt or covert. Overt observation is where the observer does not hide the fact that they are observing or why they are observing. In covert observation, on the other hand, the observer does not inform those being observed what they are doing or why they are doing it. This type of observation is useful when observing children who are likely to behave differently when surroundings or people change. However, in some circumstances, covert observation may raise ethical issues if those being observed feel they have been misinformed when they find out.

Main types of observations

There are many different types of observations that can be used in an early years setting, depending on the focus of the work – for example, an event sample, a checklist and a time sample.

Link

Go to Unit 9, Section B in Student Book 1 where you will find more information about methods of observation.

Limitations on observations

Observation as a method of research in childcare settings can have limitations that affect the quality of the results gained. The objectivity of observation can be affected by the actions of the observer. Other factors can also affect the situation and the child or children being observed so that they behave in a way that is out of the ordinary. It is worth being aware of some of these factors.

- Knowing the environment

If the environment in which the observation is taking place is familiar, those being observed will be more relaxed and feel more comfortable. This situation is likely to result in a more accurate impression than one that takes place in unfamiliar surroundings.

- The timing of the observation

If a child is tired they may have a lower concentration span and, therefore, an observation is likely to show non-typical behaviour. This is not the best situation in which to carry out a straightforward observation. It may be, however, that observation is done deliberately at this time to look at how unknown or stressful situations affect behaviour.

- Environmental factors such as the weather

Windy or stormy weather is known to have an effect on behaviour and make children excitable. Therefore you may get observations that are outside the norm if observing in these conditions.

- Times of the year

There are certain times of the year when people traditionally act out of character because they are excited, such as Christmas, and this is likely to affect observation results.

- Changes in the immediate environment

Changes in noise levels, the organisation of the immediate environment and the people who are usually in an area (for example, a new practitioner) can all trigger changes in behaviour that will be reflected in any observation that is carried out.

An observation needs to be a true record that is not adversely affected by anything as this makes it easier to interpret. It also gives a fairer analysis of what is going on. However, due to the nature of observations, you should not use observations to prove cause and effect as they are not controlled in the way a scientific experiment would be controlled. An observation can only provide an understanding of what is happening with a particular child at that particular time.

This child is tired and irritable. How might this behaviour affect an observation?

Checklists

A checklist is a list of skills, attributes or signs being looked for or assessed during an observation. These can be used to assess against norms or expectations. Checklists can also be used to compare skill levels across different groups, such as gender, age or developmental stage.

When may a checklist be used?

A checklist may be used to assess physical development, gross and fine motor skills, social skills, levels of ability (such as reading levels) or key health indicators (such as blood pressure and heart rate).

Advantages and disadvantages

A checklist is very quick to carry out and produces clear results, which are easily interpreted. However, to be really effective, the checklist needs to be well prepared and thought through. It is important that the observer only records what they see. There may be a risk of not getting true results if the person being observed feels under pressure to perform.

Scientific experiments

Scientific experiments might be used in the early years environment to understand causal relationships. This means looking at instances where something happens (the cause) to produce a reaction (the effect). This approach is often used in psychology to look at behaviour. The plan of the experiment will involve identifying one factor that you want to change, so that you can see the effects of that change. The factor is called the **variable**. Keeping all the other factors (variables) the same will allow you to see the impact of the change you have made. Within any experiment there is always a control group where none of the variables are changed.

It is important that experiments are set up accurately and carried out with precision to get valid results. An experiment is reliable if, when repeated by another person at a later date, using the same variables, they get similar results.

Key term

Variable – an element, feature or factor in a research project that is likely to change.

Experiments could be used in a research project if you were looking at a child's cognitive development. You could use some of Jean Piaget's experiments to look at the stages of cognitive development.

Activity

Research Piaget's experiments and design your own experiment that you could use to test the stage of a child's cognitive development.

Try your experiment out and then compare your results to Piaget's theory. What conclusions can you draw?

Selecting appropriate research methods

Once you have decided on your research project title, you need to think about the research methods you might use and how you will carry these out. This can also act as a way of double-checking that your project has the potential to meet all of the assessment criteria for this unit.

To do this successfully, you should identify all the potential research methods and think about how you might apply them to your project. You should also think about how to record the results. Figure 13.3 gives you a good way to do this.

Once you have completed the table in Figure 13.3, you need to review your title and the potential research possibilities against the assessment criteria. You must be able to carry out primary research, so if the table shows that your topic only lends itself to secondary research, you need to rethink either your title or your approach.

about themselves and their decisions or thoughts. It is important that you first consider the rights of the person involved in the research. This means ensuring confidentiality, so that the people used in your research remain anonymous while still allowing you to represent them and their opinions accurately. This is an important consideration.

Ethics is all about human behaviour – it looks at whether the way something is carried out is right or wrong. It includes considering whether behaviour is morally right and the way actions affect others. When talking about ethics, we may also think about **attitudes**, beliefs and **values**. These things influence what we think is 'ethical'.

Reflect

It is better to change a project at this stage rather than spending a significant amount of time on something that has to be abandoned later. Careful planning will help ensure that your project does meet the criteria and will get you the marks you would like to achieve.

Ethical issues

Research usually involves finding out information from different people – often the information is

Key terms

Attitudes – the views or opinions of an individual about an issue or topic. These views may be positive or negative.

Ethics – the values and principles that govern the way a society operates.

Values – the principles or personal rules or standards that allow people to make decisions and choose between alternatives.

Research method	Can it be used for this project? (Yes/No)	How can the method be used?	Are there any ethical issues I need to consider?	How can the results be recorded?
Secondary research: • books • journals • magazines • newspapers				
Interviews				
Questionnaires				
Observations				
Visits				

Figure 13.3 An example of a table to help you identify a suitable research method

The beliefs held by an individual are based on the knowledge and information they have about the world around them. They are often personal opinions based on what that individual believes to be true.

Values influence behaviour, and guide people into choosing appropriate behaviour in different circumstances. Values can also encapsulate the beliefs and accepted standards of behaviour within a social grouping.

Ethics is an abstract concept and understanding exactly what it is can be difficult, as it is based on attitudes, values and beliefs that are hypothetical – that is, based on ideas or thoughts. Ethics are used as guidelines when making decisions. In some situations, ethical considerations are the basis of a Code of Practice, which individuals in a society or group should adhere to. For example, many doctors take the Hippocratic Oath, swearing to practice medicine honestly.

Every individual has a set of ethics that define what they believe is right and wrong. These may differ from person to person. Ethics are based on the values of individuals and they will influence behaviours and attitudes as well as conscience.

In every aspect of research that you carry out, you will be applying ethics. Ethics also applies to the way the information that has been gathered is used. In practice this means you need to take a responsible attitude to the work being carried out and the results obtained.

Ethical breaches

In the past, some researchers have been accused of not acting in an ethical way. A well-known example is the Milgram experiment. In 1961, an American psychologist called Stanley Milgram carried out experiments to find out to what extent people would obey orders from a figure of authority, even if the orders went against their own conscience. The people taking part in the experiments thought they were giving real, high-voltage electric shocks to people in another room. Unknown to the participants, the subjects in the other room were faking their response and the electric shocks were not real. Participants were ordered to keep on applying stronger and stronger electric currents despite believing that the victims were in pain. Milgram's study concluded that most people will follow orders to the point of causing suffering or even death, and that obedience to authority is ingrained in humans through their upbringing. The way in which Milgram deceived the people taking part in his study was considered to be immoral and even abusive, and remains controversial to this day.

Another example of an unethical project is 'The Monster Study'. This experiment focused on stuttering and involved 22 orphaned children in 1939 in Iowa, America. The study gave positive speech therapy to half the children and involved praising them for their efforts. The other half were subjected to negative speech therapy and given negative feedback about their efforts.

The outcome showed that those receiving the negative therapy suffered negative psychological effects and many retained speech problems for the rest of their lives.

Another example of a research study that was considered unethical was the Tuskegee Syphilis Study, which took place in the United States from 1932 to 1972. Find out more about the study by doing your own research. Do you think it was carried out in an unethical way?

Confidentiality of participants and the setting

Confidentiality is an important issue. Any information that is collected through different primary research methods should be confidential. Often people involved in your research will give you personal and sensitive information about something. It is important that this information is treated with respect and only used for the stated purpose. This includes respect for people's cultural and life-choice differences. Remember that different people have different opinions about what is sensitive information and what they would want repeated. Therefore, the best approach is to treat any information that is given to you in any research method as confidential. Do not repeat information to anyone in a form that can be traced back to the person who gave it. Also make sure you do not invade the privacy of those involved.

It can be very easy to forget the importance of confidentiality when chatting casually to family and friends, but you could find yourself in a difficult situation if you were overheard or if someone repeated your comments. Others will be interested in what you are doing so you should be prepared to give an overview or general findings but not to attribute comments to individuals.

Protection of data

Any data you collect must remain confidential between you and the participant. You must ensure you do not reveal any responses to others – intentionally or unintentionally. This means you must ensure all information, whether paper-based or electronic, is stored securely and safely, and cannot be linked to any individual.

Legislation, policies and procedures

When carrying out research projects that involve collecting and processing information about individuals, you need to be aware of your legal responsibilities under the Data Protection Act 1998.

The Data Protection Act is a complex legal act which must be complied with by anyone who holds information about individuals. Essentially, any data held which can be linked to an individual comes under this act. It is essential that any personal information collected as part of your research is not shared with others or used in a way which identifies the source. Also information should only be kept when there is a clear purpose for doing so.

Any data collected must only be used for the purpose stated when collecting the data. You must also ensure you avoid any invasion of privacy.

Therefore, when carrying out research it is wise to depersonalise the information as much as possible so that the source of the data cannot be identified. It is also important that you destroy any source materials

as soon as you have finished using them in order to maintain confidentiality.

Research

The website of the Information Commissioner's Office contains a lot of detail about the Data Protection Act which you may find interesting. You can access this website by going to www.pearsonhotlinks.co.uk and searching for the ISBN of this title: 9781447970972.

Did you know?

The Freedom of Information Act 2000 gives individuals the right to access information which is held by public bodies, often for a fee. This could be personal information or general data about a range of issues. There are some restrictions on the information that can be released.

Children's rights

In recent years, the importance of children's rights has been promoted. It is now recognised that the views of children should be listened to and acted on. This could influence how children are involved in research. There is a lot of debate around children's rights when it comes to being involved in research. Some people believe that children should not be part of a research activity, as they believe children cannot give informed consent. Others believe that children can be involved in research provided they are not hurt in any way as a result.

Research

The website for the Children's Rights Alliance for England (CRAE) contains a lot of information about the rights of the child, which you may find interesting. You can access this website by going to www.pearsonhotlinks.co.uk and searching for the ISBN of this title: 9781447970972.

It is important that you consider the rights of the child and all related ethical issues when using children in research.

Seeking informed consent

Anyone you ask to become involved in research has a right to know how the information that is being collected about them will be used. This means that for people to consent to taking part in research they need to understand the purpose of the research and how any information they provide may be used. Formal written permission may be needed before some information can be collected, especially if the research involves gaining information from children under 18 (in which case the consent of their parent or carer must be given) or researching in a particular organisation or establishment.

It is also worth remembering that participants have the right to withdraw from research at any point if they feel uncomfortable about the process.

The Nuremberg Code

The Nuremberg Code is a set of principles that provide the guidelines within which experiments involving humans should be carried out. The Code was developed in 1947 after the Second World War, following the Nuremberg Trials where leading Nazis were tried for their crimes, including carrying out experiments on humans in concentration camps.

The Code has ten points, the most important of which states that anyone taking part in experiments must give informed consent. This means they must understand what is happening and any potential risks. No one should be forced into taking part in experiments.

Among other things, the Code makes it clear that a subject (in other words, a person) can choose to leave an experiment at any time if they wish. It states that an experiment should be stopped if it becomes evident that it could harm humans. The Code also makes clear that the risks should not outweigh the benefits of any experiment.

Reflect

Look at the Nuremberg Code in more detail. How might the Code impact on research involving children? Can children give informed consent?

Conflicts of interest and how to avoid them

Conflicts of interest can occur when carrying out research if there is a potential that a personal consideration might impact on the judgement and objectivity of someone involved in the research. This could lead to bias which will impact on the validity of the results of the research.

Conflicts of interest cannot always be avoided but if you are aware of where potential conflict might exist, you can take steps to minimise it. You should always ask subjects if they have any conflicts which should be disclosed before you carry out any research.

Peer reviews

Peer reviews occur when an individual's work is evaluated by people of a similar competence. Peer review can lead to allegations of bias and suppression of views as reviewers can sometimes be critical of any research which contradicts their own views. This can mean that peer reviews are not as independent as you might expect.

Human subjects

Whenever you are using humans in research, their personal bias may impact on the information they give you and this can impact on your findings. Human beings may also give the answer they think you want to hear or may not give you a full answer if they do not wish to pass on certain information. It is important you bear this in mind when you are collecting information from individuals.

Mentoring

Mentoring is sometimes provided to support researchers with their work. A mentor will act as a critical friend and encourage you to reflect on your work and question yourself about the work you are doing. Good mentoring can help improve the outcome of a piece of work as it encourages the writer to really examine how successful the research is and how it could be improved. A good mentor can also support a researcher to overcome difficulties or barriers they might encounter by discussing the options and possibilities and helping to identify a solution.

Research misconduct

Research misconduct may occur when a piece of research is not carried out correctly. It can cover a number of issues including:

- fabrication or making up research findings
- plagiarism – where a researcher copies another person's work and passes it off as their own
- misreporting of research findings to present a particular picture.

You need to ensure you always carry out your research accurately and report it with integrity.

Professional distance

The term 'professional distance' refers to the manner in which you carry out your research. It is important that you maintain an appropriate relationship with your subjects and ensure it is professional at all times. These professional boundaries are important as they define the parameters in which you work.

Disclosure

When carrying out research, you may be in a position where a subject discloses sensitive information to you. Clearly confidentiality is important but if a subject discloses information which is of concern, you may need to pass this on. You will need to have strategies for dealing with this.

Whistle blowing

Whistle blowing occurs when someone suspects wrongdoing which might be illegal or which endangers someone's health or safety. Sometimes research can lead to whistleblowing.

The use and misuse of statistics

Statistics are fascinating as they can be used both to present truths but also to assert a falsehood. Statistics can be misapplied to present information in a particular way and this can influence decisions made. Claims can be made without sufficient evidence as research findings can be manipulated.

One example of this is the controversy raised around the measles, mumps and rubella (MMR) vaccinations in the late 1990s. Andrew Wakefield, a British surgeon, produced a research paper that claimed to prove a link between the MMR vaccination and the appearance of autism in children. However, his research was only carried out on 12 children and this theory was later discredited. No other medical researchers could replicate the findings.

The impact of this claim was that thousands of parents decided not to have their children vaccinated. This put them at greater risk from the illnesses the vaccine would have protected them against.

Research

Research Andrew Wakefield and the MMR vaccination research. Think about the implications for parents and children as a result of the way the research was presented to the public.

Producing a research proposal

Once you have identified the topic you want to research, you need to produce a research proposal. First, you need to consider the title or the research question you are going to explore. It is important to think carefully about the question you use and to make sure it is not one with a 'yes' or 'no' answer. For example, use the sentence stem 'to what extent…', as this will prevent you from falling into this trap.

Once you have identified your question, and your aims and objectives (which must be achievable), you can plan your research project in detail, and this will help you identify the methods you will use, the target group you are focusing on and the samples you will use for each research method you have decided to use. Producing a detailed action plan as outlined in this unit will help you organise yourself within the timeframes allocated to the work.

Once you have your plan, it is essential that you monitor and review it regularly as you progress through your project and modify it as needed. You may find that findings from a piece of research will lead you to want to explore something that you had not originally planned to at the start of the piece of work. You need to be flexible enough to be able to change your plan as you go along to ensure you produce the most effective piece of work.

All early years practitioners need to be able to carry out effective research. To do this they need to understand the importance of research methods in early years settings.

Prepare an article for an early years magazine on the importance of research in early years settings, using examples. Make sure you:

- explain the value of research when working with children

- summarise the potential ethical issues in research related to work with children

- assess the role of research in work with children

- analyse how research methods can inform and shape a research proposal

- discuss how research objectives need to be feasible and applied to practice

- evaluate the impact of research on improving outcomes for children.

B Locate and present secondary research

The sources of secondary research

There are several sources that can be used for secondary research including:

- textbooks, journals and periodicals (both printed and electronic)
- the internet
- websites of professional bodies
- research bodies
- media sources such as newspapers and magazines
- government publications or reports, including statistics.

The topic chosen will determine which type of secondary information is relevant. There will usually be some secondary source material, whatever your topic. However, for more current topics, the sources are likely to be in a professional journal or found on the internet rather than in textbooks. It can take up to a year for new information to appear in textbooks.

There are also specialist research bodies, such as the Joseph Rowntree Foundation, which support a wide range of research and development projects.

Assessing secondary sources of information is not always easy. When looking at any secondary research, think about the way in which the information has been collected. If the research methods have not been carried out thoroughly and accurately, the results will not be valid or reliable.

How to carry out a literature review

A literature review is a good place to start when you begin thinking about a research topic. At this point, you are likely to have several ideas.

Carrying out a literature review means looking at material that has already been written on the topics you are researching. This task should always come at the beginning of a piece of research, as it will give you an idea of the issues linked to your topic area as well as an understanding of any previous research that has been carried out. It may also give you some idea of the focus of the work and the primary research methods you should be using. Being able to compare your own findings with the information from the literature review will help to inform your conclusions and recommendations.

A literature review might include a range of sources such as textbooks, journals, newspapers, magazines and the internet.

Conducting electronic researches

Electronic searches are a good way to begin your research. They also provide a start to your bibliography (the list of books or journals that you will be using). An electronic search uses keywords to identify information. The number of keywords and the combination used will influence the results you get.

The internet contains a lot of information so using keywords can help you to refine your search and reduce it to a more manageable size. You can also use the advanced search option on search engines to add more information to your search and, therefore, further refine your search criteria.

Search tools and methods

You can choose from a range of general search engines, for example Google Scholar, which has a vast database of academic titles and journal articles. A more specialised database for work with children, and one that is worth checking out, is Current Educational Research UK (CERUK).

One common search method is a Boolean search. A Boolean search allows you to enlarge or narrow a search by using the terms 'and', 'or' or 'not'. For example, you can search for:

- 'childcare AND nurseries' which will provide all records containing both
- 'childcare OR nurseries' which will provide all records containing both or either
- 'childcare NOT nurseries' which will provide all records containing childcare but not nurseries.

You can also combine the search terms for a more complex search, for example:

'childcare OR early years care AND nurseries NOT nannies'

Reading academic journals

Academic journals are an important source of the most recent research in the early years field. They usually contain the most recent thinking and research long before it can be published in a textbook. Therefore, they are an essential source of information when you are researching any topic in the field. Academic journals are usually set out in a particular way, which you need to understand. The sections are:

- title – the name of the article which should indicate what the journal is about
- keywords – the important words identified in the article
- abstract – a summary of the content of the article

- methodology – the methods used to carry out the research outlined in the article
- findings – the conclusions drawn from the research
- discussion – a detailed description and explanation of the work
- conclusion – the summing up of the points made
- recommendations – a suggestion or proposal for a course of action following the findings of the research
- bibliography – a complete list of the literature drawn on to complete the article.

Reading an academic journal is different to reading a book or newspaper. You are trying to pick out the important points. Often you will not read an academic journal from beginning to end. You will find ways to be able to read the article efficiently and effectively that enable you to pick out the structure of the author's arguments. This is a difficult task but the more you do this, the better you will become at it.

Be prepared to read an article more than once, as often the contents of an academic article cannot be understood fully in one reading.

Later in this unit, in Section C, we will look at the **conventions** of article and report writing and the various components which make up an academic report in more detail.

The Harvard referencing system

Most academic journals use the Harvard system for referencing. This is explained in Section C of this unit.

Producing a bibliography and reference list

When you present your research findings, you must provide a bibliography and a reference list. You will find more information on how to do this in Section C of this unit.

Key term

Conventions – using a set of agreed characteristics, e.g. in writing we use full stops, capital letters, commas and sentences.

You need to plan a small-scale research project related to young children, with particular reference to secondary research.

- Think about different areas you might want to research and consider the opportunities for using different research methods.

- Choose one of your ideas to develop as your research project. Describe your objectives and give reasons for your choice of project. Discuss why your research objectives are feasible and how they apply to your practice. Summarise the potential ethical issues in your research

project and analyse how your selected research methods helped shape your proposal.

- Identify current reading or research relevant to your research project and explain why you have chosen these sources.

- Carry out a literature review and record your findings. Analyse how your literature review will inform and shape your research project.

- Discuss and evaluate the reliability and relevance of the secondary research you have used in your literature review.

C Carry out a small-scale research project related to work with young children

To be able to carry out a good research project, you need to combine a number of skills.

Skills required to carry out research

Figure 13.4 shows the things you will need to consider when carrying out research.

Planning your time

Planning your time effectively is as important as having a well-focused title that has the potential for good research opportunities. Even the best projects can fail as a result of poor planning and poor time management.

It is important that you plan the time you have to carry out the research project effectively. It is easy to underestimate how long research can take, particularly primary research, where you may be relying on others to return questionnaires or you may need to carry out observations over a period of time. In addition to carrying out the research, remember that it takes time to record and analyse the results.

You can design an action plan however you like, but it is important that the plan works for you.

Figure 13.4 Things to consider when carrying out research

An effective plan has a number of elements. An outline for an action plan is given in Figure 13.5. Good time management is essential if you are going

Timeframe for the research (from start to finish)	What is my overall aim?	What do I need to do?	What materials do I need?	Have I achieved my aim?	If not, what do I need to do?
12th February– 12th March	To find out how the nursery could make cooked lunch more attractive.	Plan a questionnaire to find out why parents choose a particular type of lunch for their children.	Questionnaire		

Figure 13.5 An example of an action plan

to carry out a valid research project effectively. Therefore, it is important that every research project is well planned and that you stick to that plan in order to meet the deadlines set.

Research projects often have long deadlines and it is a mistake to concentrate on work that is due in earlier to the detriment of the longer-term elements of the project.

Tips for effective time management are:

- start the project straight away
- develop a realistic plan, with timings, and stick to it
- work on the project at regular intervals
- always follow the plan you have set and monitor how you are doing at regular intervals
- if you fall behind, allocate some additional time to the work to catch up
- talk to your teacher/tutor regularly about the research project's progress – they will help to ensure you remain on schedule.

Organisational skills

Good organisational skills are essential if you want to produce a good piece of work within a given timeframe. A research project normally takes place over a longer period of time and consists of several pieces of work, so you need to be well organised to do this effectively.

In addition, the project will produce a lot of data and you will need to do written work. Therefore, you should have an effective way to organise your notes and research findings so that you can access them easily when you need to write up the results.

It is advisable to write up the work as you go along and not leave it until you have carried out all of your research methods. You may find that this written work takes longer than you think.

You need to manage your time very effectively and ensure that you do keep to your plan.

Non-judgemental practice

When carrying out research, it is important that you keep an open mind and do not make judgements about the people involved in your research, particularly if they express ideas that are different to your own. This is not always easy, as you may communicate your thoughts through your body language and facial expressions as well as through the tone of your voice and the language you use. Therefore, you need to work to ensure that you appear non-judgemental in every way. You must also remember to keep a professional distance from the people you are speaking to, and not get emotionally involved in what they are discussing.

It is also important that, as a researcher, you do not introduce bias by influencing the participants through the way you ask questions or reply to responses given. It is important to remember that it is likely that participants will have different views and ideas from your own. You must appear neutral and non-judgemental if you are to gain open responses and valid information from participants.

Carrying out the research

When you carry out your research project, you will be implementing each of the secondary and primary research methods you have chosen to use and, from this, generating your research findings. You need to make sure you carry out each research method systematically and thoroughly to get the best results you can. Good results are important, so that you are able to draw valid conclusions. Remember to carry out your research in a professional manner, especially when working with people.

It is important to follow your action plan during the research project. As projects are often carried out over a long period of time, it would be easy for you to put this to one side in favour of more immediate, short-term pieces of work. However, this would be a mistake – rushing such a detailed, demanding project will produce a poor quality end result.

You need to be strict with your time. If you are unable to carry out an activity as planned, you need to work out immediately how to get yourself back on track. You will also need to monitor your progress as you carry out your project, using the final two columns on the plan in Figure 13.5.

Think about bias or potential errors as you reflect on each research method you have carried out. It is important you address potential sources of bias as bias or errors can impact on your results and therefore the conclusions you draw from them.

It is useful to note down any thoughts you have on the process as you go through, as this will help you when you write your reports and reflect on your evaluation.

It will also be helpful to plan regular review sessions with your teacher/tutor in which you can explain what you are doing. You should set yourself goals to achieve before each of these sessions. This will give you a target to aim for and is another way to help you keep on track.

Sampling methods for small-scale research projects

Sampling is used to reduce the number of respondents in a piece of research, while still ensuring you get a representative sample of the group you are studying. A sample can be decided in a number of different ways depending on the topic being studied. Some examples of different sampling methods are outlined below.

- Random sampling

This occurs where each member of the population has an equal chance of being sampled. There is no particular selection; the sample is chosen at random. A lottery system would provide a random sample. For example, if trying to find out about after-school activities, a researcher would just select a number of students from the school roll at random. All names would have an equal chance of being selected.

- Systematic sampling

This is where a sample has a pattern to it; for example every tenth person would be a systematic sample as long as the list does not include any hidden order. This could be the tenth person on a list or the tenth person who walks by.

- Stratified sampling

This method is defined by a particular characteristic or stratum. For example, it may divide the possible sample up into different age groups and ensure the sample includes a mix from across the different groupings. The sample in each grouping needs to be large enough to ensure it is sufficiently representative of the population. For example, if surveying a school on the quality of school meals, a stratified sample would ensure that every year group is represented in proportion and that both males and females are represented in equal proportion.

Triangulation

Triangulation is an important concept in research. It involves the researcher using at least three methods to collect data on a topic – for example, secondary research, an interview and an observation. The aim of this is to show that there are similarities in the findings across the three research methods and so adding to the validity and reliability of the work. You need to think about this when considering how valid your data is.

Analysing data

Research produces a lot of information, known as **data**. This **'raw' data** is then analysed and the findings presented so that you can draw conclusions from it. Raw data may be condensed or may not be presented as part of the finished project, but it is retained for a period of time after the project is finished in case the findings are queried. Sometimes it is presented in an appendix.

Key terms

Data – the information that is produced by your research methods. It covers facts, statistics and perceptions. Data has to be interpreted.

Raw data – data as it is collected, before it has been organised, analysed or interpreted in any way.

There are a variety of methods by which you can analyse data. When a large amount of data has been collected, as well as displaying this in a table or diagram, you can work out key numerical values which summarise the information. These include the statistical averages of mean, mode or median, and measures of speed, such as range.

Statistics

Statistics can be generated by analysing the raw data that you have collected. They allow you to consolidate, interpret and present your findings in a concise way. Presenting information in this way may allow you to make comparisons, for example, with similar information from a previous year.

Here is an example.

Your research might look at how many children have a school lunch in a small primary school. If you can see a trend in the data you have collected, or the numbers of children are similar over a period of three academic years, then the school can draw conclusions about how many staff to employ to manage the demands for lunches.

Statistics need to be produced and handled with care. If your sample size is small, the statistics that can be generated from the data may not give an accurate picture of a situation overall.

For example, if ten children take a test and two of them fail, it follows that eight out of ten have passed. The pass rate can be worked out as 80 per cent. However, if 100 children then sat the same test and two fail, 98 children will have passed. The pass rate will then be 98 per cent.

So, if a school reviews the results of these two tests and concentrates on the pass rates in order to inform future decisions about the design of the test, the future test might end up being different depending on how many children sat the test originally.

To get a more accurate picture, the research would need to take place over several tests, with a consistent number of candidates sitting each test. This would allow for an overall outcome from which conclusions that inform the writing of future tests can usefully be drawn and acted upon.

Summary statistics

It is useful to summarise your data by working out a representative value and also by giving a measure of the spread of the data.

The representative value is called an average. There are three main types of statistical average. They are the mean, mode and median.

To measure the spread of the data, the range is often used.

Averages

Mean

The mean is the one that most people refer to as 'the average'. It is the figure calculated by adding up all the values in a set and dividing the total by the number of values in the set.

Here is an example.

Five children get the following marks out of ten in a test: 9, 6, 4, 4, 7.

To work out the mean, add together the individual marks.

So: 9 + 6 + 4 + 4 + 7 = 30

Then, divide by the number of children.

So: $\frac{30}{5} = 6$

The mean average mark for the test is, therefore, 6.

Mode

The mode is the most commonly appearing value, so the mode of the test results in the earlier example is 4.

The mode is a useful average when you want to know the most popular value. However, not all sets of data have a mode. Also, if there are more than two modes then the mode is not a useful average.

Median

The median is the middle value when all the values are arranged in ascending order.

The test marks in ascending order are 4, 4, 6, 7, 9. The middle value is 6, so this is the median.

Here are the marks of another group of children: 1, 6, 7, 8, 8, 10

There are two middle numbers, 7 and 8, and the median is the mean of these, i.e.: $\frac{7+8}{2}$ = 7.5

In this set, the mark of 1 is unusual.

The median is particularly useful when there are unusual or extreme values, sometimes called outliers, as the median is not unduly influenced by them.

Range

The range of a set of numbers is the difference between the highest and the lowest values, i.e. range = highest value – lowest value.

So, for the test marks 4, 4, 6, 7, 9, range = 9 – 4 = 5

For the test marks 1, 6, 7, 8, 8, 10, range = 10 – 1 = 9

The marks in the first set have the smaller range so they are less variable and more consistent.

Use of percentages

Percentages can be a useful way to analyse data as they allow you to show proportions of the 'overall' picture. For example, 65 per cent of children chose an ice cream and 35 per cent of children chose an iced lolly.

Drawing conclusions

Once you have your data, you need to draw conclusions from it. You should look for patterns or facts in the data you have found. You might look for similarities or differences between different results. You may draw conclusions from one piece of research that you are able to support with findings from another. Sometimes research may show that there is no connection or obvious conclusion to be drawn.

Make sure any conclusion you draw can be backed up by evidence from your research.

Presenting data

Presenting research findings in clear and concise formats, such as tables or diagrams, makes the information easier to read and more accessible.

Some data is best presented in certain formats, but generally the choice of presentation is down to your preference. Make sure the method you choose presents the information in the clearest manner.

Quantitative research methods generally produce a large amount of numerical data that is usually best presented using statistical diagrams. Take care not to misrepresent the data, especially when drawing diagrams.

Tables

Tables are a useful way to present information in a neat, clear format, particularly where comparisons are being made. For example, if you wanted to study information over a number of years and look for changes and trends, you might use a table.

The information in Table 13.2 shows the results of a fictional study of the number of parents using different forms of full-time childcare on a particular housing estate over a period of time. The years are shown across the top and the types of childcare down the side.

You can draw conclusions from Table 13.2 about which types of care are growing and which are declining.

Table 13.2 Forms of full-time childcare used by parents on one housing estate

Type of childcare	2007	2008	2009	2010	2011
Childminding	20	22	24	25	25
Private nurseries	18	21	24	26	28
Nanny based in own home	10	10	8	7	7
Family or friends	6	6	6	5	5

You might decide to analyse in further depth whether there is any difference in the ages of the children who attend the different types of care, for example.

A table can include a lot of information in a small area. It is therefore important that tables are clearly labelled so the reader can understand what is being depicted. Units of measurement must also be clearly stated.

Statistical diagrams

Most research projects will require you to present information in a pictorial format. Statistical diagrams, often generally referred to as 'graphs', are usually in the form of a line graph, bar chart, histogram, pie chart, pictogram or scatter graph.

There are a number of points to note when presenting information diagrammatically.

- The diagram should have a clear title.
- The source of the data should be given at the bottom of the diagram.
- Axes should be clearly labelled.
- Any units of measurement should be made very clear.
- Graphs should be presented on graph paper (not lined or plain paper).
- Pie charts should be presented on plain paper (not lined or graph paper).

Line graphs

Line graphs have horizontal and vertical axes, which must be clearly labelled. Points are then plotted on the grid.

Line graphs are particularly useful in seeing trends over time.

Figure 13.6 is a line graph illustrating Table 13.2.

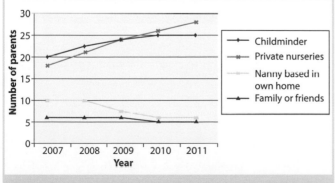

Figure 13.6 Example of a line graph showing forms of full-time childcare used by parents on one housing estate.

Bar charts

As bar charts are easy to draw and understand, they are the most common type of statistical diagram. Bar charts show information in either vertical or horizontal bars and are particularly useful for presenting data that fits descriptive categories.

Bar charts have a number of common features.

- All bars are the same width.
- Bars may be horizontal or vertical.
- The bars can be drawn next to each other or with a space between each one.
- The height (or length) of the bar indicates the frequency, (the size of the group defined by the category label).
- The other axis shows the descriptive categories – these describe the type of data being measured.
- Bar charts are often coloured to improve the presentation.

Codes may be used to label the bars as long as a clear key or legend is included to the side of the diagram to explain what they mean. This may be useful if the labels are very long. For example, you might be measuring how often a setting carries out child-initiated activities compared to adult-initiated activities, in which case you may choose to label the axis using the labels 'C-I' and 'A-I' to save space.

Figure 13.7 is a bar chart of data taken from Table 13.2 showing the types of childcare used in 2007.

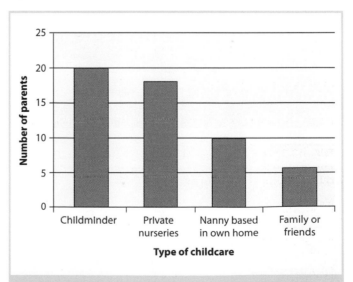

Figure 13.7 Example of a bar chart showing types of childcare used in 2007 by parents on one housing estate.

Compound bar charts are particularly useful for comparing sets of data.

Figure 13.8 is a compound bar chart to illustrate the data in Table 13.2.

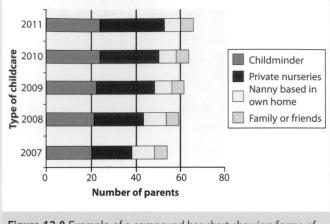

Figure 13.8 Example of a compound bar chart showing forms of childcare used by parents.

The data can also be illustrated in individual bars, as shown in Figure 13.9.

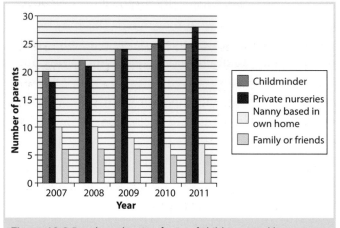

Figure 13.9 Bar chart showing forms of childcare used by parents.

Histograms

Histograms look similar to bar charts but are in fact different. Histograms have a number of common features.

- They are used for continuous data that is grouped, i.e. data that covers a band.
- They contain bars that are not always the same width – the width of the bar along the horizontal axis relates to the size of the grouped data.
- There are no gaps between the bars.
- The frequency of the class is indicated by the area of the column.

Pie charts

Pie charts are a way of presenting data according to each category's share of the total. Making one involves first converting your results into percentages. We will now look at how to do this step by step.

Imagine you have collected the data shown in Table 13.3 on how learners in three classes travel to their placements.

To work out the percentage of the different forms of travel, you need to divide the number of people who travel by a particular method by the total number of people questioned. Then, you need to multiply the answer by 100 (per cent). An example of the calculation for children travelling by car is shown below.

By car: $\frac{24}{60} = 0.4$

$0.4 \times 100 = 40\%$

Table 13.3 How learners travel to their placements

Form of travel	Number of people	Percentage	Degrees
Bus	15	25	90
Train	3	5	18
Walk	9	15	54
Car	24	40	144
Bike	6	10	36
Moped	3	5	18
Total	60	100	360

Once you have calculated the percentage, you then need to convert this into degrees so that you can construct the pie chart.

To find how much of the pie chart should be taken up by the 40 per cent of learners who travel by car, you first need to work out how big a slice of pie 1 per cent of learners would need. This will allow you to then work out how much 40 per cent would need.

There are 360 degrees in a circle, so to work this out, carry out the following sum:

$$\frac{360}{100} = 3.6 \text{ degrees}$$

To work out the degrees required for learners travelling by car, you simply multiply the answer by 40, as follows.

40 x 3.6 = 144 degrees

This is shown in Figure 13.10.

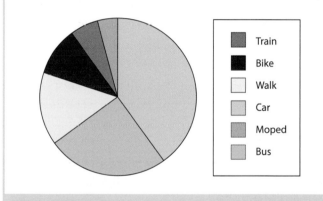

Figure 13.10 Example of a pie chart showing how learners travel to their placements.

You usually round up, but sometimes it may be necessary to round down to ensure that your total angle is 360 degrees.

If your values are not exact, leave the numbers on your calculator during the calculation and do not round until the final stage.

When drawing a pie chart, remember to:
- show any calculations you do
- colour each sector to improve the presentation
- label each sector with the percentage it represents
- provide a clear key or legend so the reader knows what each sector represents
- give the pie chart a title
- present the pie chart on plain paper.

Scatter graphs

Scatter graphs are generally used where data showing two corresponding variables needs to be presented in order to see whether there is a pattern or **correlation**, such as the relationship between blood pressure and age in a group of people.

Scatter graphs may show a positive correlation, where if one variable increases, so does the other – or a negative correlation, where if one variable increases, the other decreases. Or there may be no significant correlation.

Key term

Correlation – a relationship or connection between two things.

A pattern or correlation does not always indicate that changes in one variable cause the changes in the other variable, i.e. it does not always indicate cause and effect.

When the data has been plotted on a scatter graph, it is useful to draw a 'line of best fit'. This is where the main clustering of the data occurs. This line can be used as the starting point for a hypothesis to link the two variables and make predictions of one value given the value of the other.

Figures 13.11, 13.12 and 13.13 show scatter graphs with positive, negative and no correlation, together with a line of best fit, as appropriate.

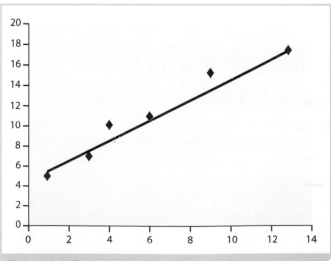

Figure 13.11 Scatter graph with positive correlation

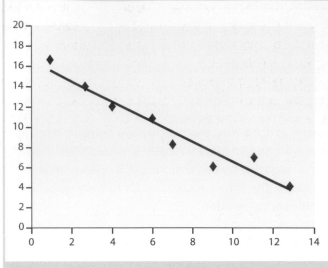

Figure 13.12 Scatter graph with negative correlation

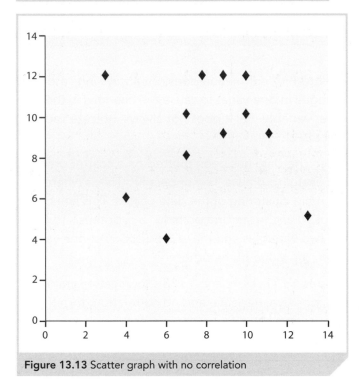

Figure 13.13 Scatter graph with no correlation

Using computers to present data

The best way to display your numerical data from methods such as questionnaires or checklists/surveys is to use a computer package such as Microsoft Excel® to present your findings. Researchers often use computer programmes to help them analyse and present their data. Computers have the advantage of being able to calculate accurately as long as the information is input correctly. Once the information is input, you can present the data in a wide range of formats at the touch of a button. This enables you to see how best to present the information with ease. You can also use the software to find the mean, mode, median or range, as well as other statistical values that may be of use.

Research

Find out more about the types of graph covered in this unit. It is useful to research their similarities and differences so that you can decide the best way to present data you have gathered. Most mathematical websites will have examples. You can access such a website by going to www.pearsonhotlinks. co.uk and searching for the ISBN of this title: 9781447970972.

Use of good English

Using good English is extremely important when carrying out and presenting your research. Firstly, when using spoken English, the correct terminology is important to ensure you are finding out the right information. You need to be able to express yourself clearly when collecting the data to ensure you gain the material you need. You need to speak confidently and with clarity.

When using written English for any aspect of your research, from questionnaires to the final write-up of the work, it is important that your spelling is correct and that you use conventions such as full stops, commas and capital letters. This lends a professional approach to your work. It also ensures that the meaning of what you are trying to communicate will come across clearly and without ambiguity, avoiding any possible misunderstandings.

The conventions of report writing

Your report will need to be written in a particular way to ensure that you can access all the assessment criteria. Below is an overview of the different elements your report should contain.

Title

You should always write the title of the project at the start of the report so that the reader is clear about what you have researched.

Contents

A list of contents is important so the reader knows what is in the report and where to find it.

Abstract or summary

An abstract or summary is a brief outline of what the project is about and the general approach that you have taken to carry out the research. It is very brief and usually no longer than half a page. It is very similar to the kind of overview that you might find on the back of a novel. It should tell the reader what the work is about but not all the details – those will be in the body of the report.

Introduction

This should briefly state the aim(s) and the research hypothesis, if this is relevant. This section should include a summary of current research findings in the field of study. You may have looked at current research as part of your secondary research at the start of your project. Providing a summary of the current research will help to give some context to your own research. Some topics will have a wealth of previous research for you to draw on. However, if you have a particularly original area of research, there may not be much written about your topic.

Methodology

This section should explain the methodology used in your study. You need to outline and justify the method of study chosen, stating clearly what was measured and how. You need to list any apparatus and measuring instruments used.

There should be a brief description of the sample of participants used (indicating size, age range, location and other factors relevant to the study) and you should state and justify the sampling method used.

As discussed earlier in the unit, ethical issues should also be covered. This section should draw the reader's attention to the specific ethical issues raised by the study, for example, temporary mild deception where a participant may not be fully aware of the reason for the research or the risk of a participant's embarrassment on performing poorly in some measure of skill.

Finally, there needs to be a description of the procedure experienced by the participant in the order in which it happened (not the process by which you planned or designed the study). It should include reference to the initial request, a detailed description of what was done to obtain the data and reference to **debriefing**, if appropriate.

Key term

Debriefing – a conversation between a researcher and participant following an experiment to inform the participant about their experience and allowing them to talk about it.

Results or findings

This should include a graphical summary of results or findings (such as a table of means, or percentages), and/or appropriate chart(s) properly labelled, as well as an analysis of the findings in relation to the aim or hypothesis.

Discussion

In this section of the report you should discuss your findings and support any conclusions you might have drawn with evidence that you have found out through your research. You might refer your reader to the appendices, where you should have presented full details of your research methods and findings.

Conclusion and recommendations

The conclusion section is where you need to draw together the findings and produce some recommendations as a result of those findings.

Appendices

This part of the report should include examples of materials used, raw data together with calculations, and a reference section, using the conventional form and giving references for all studies and authorities cited in the report. It is not useful to put in lots of notes, but do include a bibliography of the textbooks and other sources used.

The appendices should be set out in an organised manner, giving details of the work carried out. Each section of the appendix should be labelled with a letter or number. In general, each section will represent a method of research. Each appendix allows you to show off the full extent of the work you have done in each research method you have used, as you may not draw on all of it for the report itself.

| Surname, initial of author | ⟶ | Date published | ⟶ | Full title | ⟶ | Where published | ⟶ | Publisher |

Figure 13.14 The Harvard method of referencing

Referencing and writing the bibliography

There are conventions to follow for writing a bibliography. The Harvard method is commonly used (see Figure 13.14).

Below is an example of this in practice.

Tassoni, P. (2012) *Practical EYFS Handbook*, 2nd edition, Oxford: Pearson.

Generally, the title of the book is written in italics or bold, or underlined to make it stand out.

The date is the published date of the edition you have used and this should be in written in brackets.

Note the presence of commas and full stops in the reference. This punctuation should always be used.

When using a number of books, they should all be recorded in a bibliography in alphabetical order according to the author's surname.

If you refer to the books listed in the bibliography in the text of your report – for example, if you refer to the author's arguments or if you take quotes from the content – you will need to add a reference. This should be done in the main body of your report by simply writing the author's surname and the date the book was published in brackets at the end of the sentence. For example: (Tassoni 2012).

If more than one person has written a book, then the referencing is slightly different. For two or more authors, the bibliography should list all the authors. For more than two authors you can write the name of the first author followed by *et al. Et al* means 'and the others', and this form of shorthand saves you time in writing all the names out in the reference.

Magazine articles, journal articles and chapters in edited books are referenced in a different way as well, which is not as straightforward as books authored by one person.

It is important that you know how to reference articles in magazines, journals and newspapers.

Assessment practice 13.3   3C.P3 | 3C.P4 | 3C.P5 | 3C.M3

Carry out your research and present valid findings in a report based on the evidence you have collected from your primary research. What conclusions can you draw from your research findings? Present any strong arguments that come out of the work. How could your findings affect current early years practice? Explain the potential impact and implications of your research project on work with children. Finally, make sure you check your work for the quality of the English.

D Be able to evaluate the research project

Analysing the project's strengths and weaknesses

Evaluation is an important part of the research process. To evaluate your work, you need to show that you appreciate the factors that have affected the project. As you evaluate, think about each section of the research project and comment on any issues that could have affected the validity and reliability of the findings, including bias or errors.

One way to evaluate successfully is to ask yourself a series of questions that make you reflect critically on the work you have carried out. Try to work your way through the research process and evaluate every stage. This will ensure that you reflect thoroughly on the work you have done. Think about the following.

Planning

- Did you plan the project well?
- Did you produce an effective plan?
- Did you keep to the plan? How did this affect your work – positively or negatively?

Secondary research

- Did you review an effective range of secondary research in relation to the topic you chose to study?
- Were the sources up to date?
- Were the sources valid and reliable? How do you know and what difference did this make to the work?
- Did you carry out enough secondary research before you designed the primary research?
- How did the results for the secondary research help you with the primary research?

Primary research

You need to evaluate each primary research method you used. The following questions can be applied to most research methods as a way of starting the evaluative process:

- Was this an effective choice of research method for the chosen topic?

- Did you plan the method well?
- Was the sample used appropriate? How did this impact on the validity of the work?
- Did the method gain the information you hoped for? If not, why not?
- Were the results presented appropriately?
- Was there any 'misuse' of the research within the project? For example, on reflection, were any of the research methods 'designed' with a particular outcome in mind? As an example, questions may have been worded specifically to elicit particular responses.
- Were there any errors or bias evident that might have impacted on the results?
- Did you follow data protection and confidentiality conventions appropriately?
- On reflection, were there other research methods that you could have used that would have provided more effective results?
- If you were to continue with the research, what would you do next and why?

The report

Think about the following questions when writing your final report.

- How far did your findings reflect the original research question?
- Did your findings triangulate and how does this impact on the findings of the project?
- Is there anything you could have changed to improve the validity and reliability of the work?
- Did you carry out an effective discussion of your findings? Were comparisons drawn between the findings of different research methods?
- How did your findings compare to current research in the area? Did they support the current thinking? If not, why do you think that was?
- How might your research findings impact on your practice in the future?
- Are there potential areas for further development of your research?

Recommendations based on research findings

The results of research can impact on work with children in many different ways. Essentially, they enable us to have a better understanding of a child's world and help adults find ways to improve that world. They should provide an understanding of how children can be provided with the most effective care and education. They can be used to:

- extend knowledge of different aspects of children's development and care
- evaluate the services provided and identify how they might be improved to meet the users' needs
- monitor the development of children against norms and identify ways to support their development
- review services provided and identify any areas where there may be gaps
- develop new ways of working.

A significant amount of research is commissioned by the government, and this is used to inform both policy and practice. It is through research that the quality of a child's care and education can be improved. In this way, research can have an immense influence on the life chances of children both now and in the future.

Continued professional development

Once you have qualified and have secured a post working in early years education, it is important that you keep up to date with new thinking in the field. This is called continuous professional development or CPD. This could be in the form of a course which updates you or in the form of personal research. Professional development ensures your own skills are kept up to date but can also contribute to developing your own skills and practice.

Assessment practice 13.4 3D.P6 | 3D.M4 | 3D.M5 | 3D.D2

Once you have completed your research project, you need to show that you can reflect on your work, evaluate it and identify ways in which it might influence your practice in the workplace.

You need to:

- reflect on your research findings and describe how they relate to the original research question you set yourself
- analyse the effectiveness of each of the research methods you have used, discussing the strengths and weaknesses of each and remembering to comment on any sources of bias or error and how this might impact on the findings
- consider whether you can improve on your research in any way. If so, explain how you would do this and the implications it could have on the work
- discuss the extent to which your findings could be implemented in early years work.

Further reading and resources

Green, S. (2000) *Research Methods in Health, Social and Early Years Care*, Cheltenham: Nelson Thornes.

Hucker, K. (2001) *Research Methods in Health, Care and Early Years (Professional Development)*, Oxford: Heinemann.

Website

Science Museum: www.sciencemuseum.org.uk

Ready for work?

Ben Hunt Preschool manager

All professionals in early years settings use research skills as part of their everyday work. For example, you might need to find some information about a condition that one of your children has or you might be concerned that a child in your care is not developing at the pace you would expect. In both of these scenarios you could observe the children and compare your findings against theory.

In our preschool, members of staff use their research skills to collect information about the children they look after and make judgements about their development. They then use this information to provide activities and experiences that move children on to the next stage of their learning.

Skills for practice

- Visit an early years setting and try out a time sample. Choose a child to watch over a period of an hour. Record everything they do. What conclusions can you draw from your observations?

- Choose a topic of interest to you in the area of early years. Carry out literature research and summarise your findings into key points.

- Choose a stage of development, for example, 0 to 3 months, 9 to 12 months, 12 to 18 months or 2 to 3 years. Research the physical development you would expect to see at your chosen stage of development. Devise a checklist that you could carry out to assess the physical skills of children in your chosen age range against these expectations.

Introduction

All children have rights. It does not matter where they live or whether they are rich or poor. Their rights are enshrined in UK legislation. Knowing about children's rights will help you to understand the role of adults in protecting these rights and supporting children and their families to access health, education and social care services. You will also explore early years education, curriculum frameworks and how settings are inspected. As you gain experience in working with children you will develop an understanding of the importance of working closely with other professionals to improve outcomes for young children and their families.

Assessment: You will be assessed by a series of assignments set by your teacher/tutor.

Learning aims

In this unit you will:

A understand the provision of health, education and social services for children and their families

B understand the context in which early years education is provided

C understand the role of multi-agency work for children and their families.

Although I knew about some of the services that are available, until I started studying this unit I hadn't realised that children have a right to these in law. Young children can't stand up for their own rights so they rely on us as adults to make sure they receive the services they deserve.

Chloe, *a learner on an early years course*

Health, Education and Social Services for Children and Their Families

14

BTEC Assessment Zone

This table shows you what you must do in order to achieve a **Pass**, **Merit** or **Distinction** grade, and where you can find activities to help you.

Assessment criteria		
Pass	Merit	Distinction
Learning aim A: Understand the provision of health, education and social services for children and their families		
3A.P1 Explain the services and benefits children and families have a right to access, to include: • health • education • social services. **Assessment practice 14.1** **3A.P2** Explain why families may need to access named services. **Assessment practice 14.1**	**3A.M1** Assess how services and benefits support children and families, with examples. **Assessment practice 14.1**	**3A.D1** Evaluate the extent to which services and benefits could impact on outcomes for children. **Assessment practice 14.1**
Learning aim B: Understand the context in which early years education is provided		
3B.P3 Explain the differences between settings which provide for children's early years education. **Assessment practice 14.2** **3B.P4** English Explain how early years education is inspected in the home country. **Assessment practice 14.2**	**3B.M2** Compare the advantages and disadvantages to children and families of different types of early years education. **Assessment practice 14.2**	
Learning aim C: Understand the role of multi-agency work for children and their families		
3C.P5 Explain the role of a multi-agency approach in work with children and families. **Assessment practice 14.3**	**3C.M3** Discuss how multi-agency working contributes to meeting the needs of children and families, with examples. **Assessment practice 14.3**	**3C.D2** Evaluate the extent to which multi-agency working might impact on outcomes for children. **Assessment practice 14.3**

English   English Functional Skills signposting

How you will be assessed

This unit will be assessed by a series of internally assessed tasks set by your teacher/tutor. Throughout this unit you will find assessment practice activities that will help you work towards your assessment. Completing these activities will not mean that you have achieved a particular grade, but you will have carried out useful research or preparation that will be relevant when it comes to your final assignment.

In order for you to carry out the tasks in your assignment, it is important that you check you have met all of the Pass grading criteria. You can do this as you work your way through the assignment.

If you are hoping to gain a Merit or Distinction, you should also make sure that you present

the information in your assignment in the style that is required by the relevant assessment criterion. For example, Merit criteria require you to assess, compare and discuss, and Distinction criteria require you to evaluate.

The assignment set by your teacher/tutor will consist of a number of tasks designed to meet the criteria in the assessment criteria table. This is likely to consist of a written assignment but may also include activities such as:

- a leaflet
- a case study
- a presentation
- a guide to services.

Getting started

How many different services for children and families can you think of? Work in a small group and share your ideas. Write each idea on a separate sticky note. Then, sort the services under the following headings: health, education, social services.

Understand the provision of health, education and social services for children and their families

Statutory services are provided by central or local government. These services may be organised in different ways but are there to meet children's education, health and welfare needs. Many of these services are accessed by the vast majority of families, for instance, nurseries, schools and health services, but there are occasions when families need additional support to help them maintain the health and well-being of their children.

Legislation that supports the rights of children and families

Everyone has rights that are set out in law. Some legislation, such as human rights laws, protects the rights of all people. Other legislation, such as the Children Act 1989, protects the particular rights of children and their families.

The United Nations Convention on the Rights of the Child (UNCRC)

In 1989 the fundamental rights of children worldwide were agreed. They were set out in an international agreement known as the United Nations Convention on the Rights of the Child (UNCRC).

The UNCRC comprises 54 Articles, and of these, 40 Articles deal specifically with the rights of the child. For example, Article 24 states that 'every child has the right to the best possible health' and Article 28 that 'every child has the right to free primary education'.

Source: United Nations Convention on the Rights of the Child, UNICEF.

> **Research**
>
> You can find more information about the Articles that describe the rights of all children by visiting the UNICEF website. You can access this website by going to www.pearsonhotlinks.co.uk and searching for the ISBN of this title: 9781447970972.

In 1991 the UK ratified the rights set out in the UNCRC. This means that UK law must be compatible with each right.

Legislation and frameworks

Table 14.1 summarises the key legislation and frameworks that underpin children's rights to health, education and social services.

> **Key terms**
>
> **Child poverty** – according to the UK government, children and families are deemed to be living in poverty when their reported income is less than 60 per cent of the UK median income before housing costs have been paid.
>
> **Holistic** – all the child's needs, to include physical, emotional, social and cognitive.
>
> **In need** – this refers to children who are unlikely to maintain, or be given the opportunity to maintain, a reasonable standard of health or development, or whose health could be impaired without the support of local authority services. It also includes children who are disabled. (Source: Adapted from Section 17 of The Children Act 1989.)

Table 14.1 Legislation and frameworks

Legislation	Aims and objectives
National Health Service Act 2006	Everyone has the right to a free and comprehensive health service. This Act defines the duties of the Secretary of State to provide for: • the improvement of physical and mental health • the prevention of ill-health, diagnosis and treatment.
National Service Framework for children, young people and maternity services 2004	Confirms the right of children to a good start in life. It identifies problems relating to health inequalities and the need to deliver individualised health care, which provides for children's **holistic** needs. It establishes the rights of children and their families to high-quality integrated services.
Children Act 1989	Relevant to England and Wales. It is based on the principle that the child's needs are paramount. It defines the duty of the local authority to identify those children **in need** and to provide services to meet those needs. It also establishes the concept of parental responsibility.
Children Act 2004	Relevant to England and Wales. Extends the 1989 Act requiring local authorities to identify children's additional needs and to show how they plan to deliver coordinated responses. Every Child Matters outcomes were developed in response to this Act, now referred to as 'Help Children Achieve More'.
Childcare Act 2006	Sets out the rights to childcare for England and Wales, including free education for children aged 3 to 5 years. Aims to improve the outcomes and reduce inequalities between children by establishing a Sure Start children's centre in every community. Includes a requirement to provide information and support for parents. Brings together Help Children Achieve More and the EYFS curriculum to form an early years curriculum framework (EYFS) for children aged 0 to 5 years.
Education Act 2011	Confirms the rights of children to full-time education from 0–17 years (2014) and 0–18 years (2015) in England and Wales. Establishes the responsibility of parents or carers to ensure that their children receive education. Incorporates the Code of Practice for Special Educational Needs and Disability (see below). It gives children with special educational needs (SEN) the right to education in mainstream schools.
Code of Practice for Special Educational Needs and Disability 2014	Early education settings and schools must give regard to the Code when providing for children with special educational needs. Establishes children's right to have their needs assessed quickly and for appropriate support to be put into place. The Code also outlines the rights of parents or carers to advice and information. The 2001 Code was revised in 2014 so that it covers children and young people up to the age of 25.
Children and Young Persons Act 2008	Extends the statutory framework for children who are in care in England and Wales. It protects children's rights to high-quality care and services appropriate for and adapted to their individual needs. It places a duty on local authorities to appoint an independent person to look after the interests of children in care and to provide them with support and advice.
Child Poverty Act 2010	Aims to reduce inequalities, and the associated disadvantage, for children and families. Part 1 of the Act relates to the whole of the UK and requires strategies to be put into place. This Act sets targets for a minimum income for families by the year 2020 to reduce poverty. The **Child Poverty** Strategy of each home county provides the framework for the Act.

Services and benefits

Local authorities have a duty to improve the well-being of children and young people. They must put into place a Children and Young People Plan (CYPP) to show how they will do this. The CYPP shows the strategic goals set out by local authorities for children and young people in their area.

Health care services

Health care is provided by the National Health Service (NHS) and is the responsibility of the Department of Health. All families with young children need access to a wide range of health care services. Parents often feel that they are constantly at the doctors' surgery or baby clinic as children are prone to common infectious illnesses and minor accidents. The primary health care services available through GP surgeries, baby clinics, dental practices or optometrists are universal services and meet the majority of the health needs of children and families. Some children may face acute health problems that require access to secondary health services. These are provided by hospitals, A & E units or specialist health centres, through planned or unplanned admissions. Children with chronic conditions such as asthma or diabetes, or with a disability, will require long-term specialist health services.

Health surveillance

Health and development reviews are a free entitlement for all children and their families, starting with the baby in the womb and continuing at regular intervals throughout early childhood. Reviews are carried out by health visitors, GPs or practice nurses and include:

- identifying the strengths and needs of the child and family, including factors that may put children at risk of illness or abuse
- observing and taking measurements of growth and development – where children are not following expected patterns of development, support can be put in place to promote development and lessen long-term problems
- providing information, advice and responding to concerns – this **empowers** parents to make healthy choices for their children and family
- detecting abnormalities – identifying health or developmental problems so that support or medical or surgical interventions can be offered.

Key term

Empower – to enable individuals to make choices about their own lives.

Screening

Screening tests form part of the child health surveillance programme. Soon after birth babies are examined for abnormalities of the heart, hips and eyes, and testes (in males). Within a few days blood spot screening (heel prick) takes place, and this identifies children who may have or develop serious but rare diseases such as sickle cell disorders or cystic fibrosis. Within the first few weeks of life babies also undergo a hearing test. Before children start school they will have further hearing and vision screening tests.

that may cause serious complications or even fatality. Infectious diseases such as measles and mumps are becoming far less common, and polio has now been eradicated from the UK. When the majority of children are vaccinated, this also reduces the likelihood of the disease passing to those who are not immunised.

Immunisation

Health professionals have a responsibility to inform parents about the benefits of immunisation. Immunisation may be accessed in different settings such as baby clinics or GP surgeries, or given by the school nurse. Vaccines are available to all babies and young children to protect them against infections

Research

For more information on the immunisation programme for the UK, visit the NHS website. You can access this website by going to www.pearsonhotlinks.co.uk and searching for the ISBN of this title: 9781447970972.

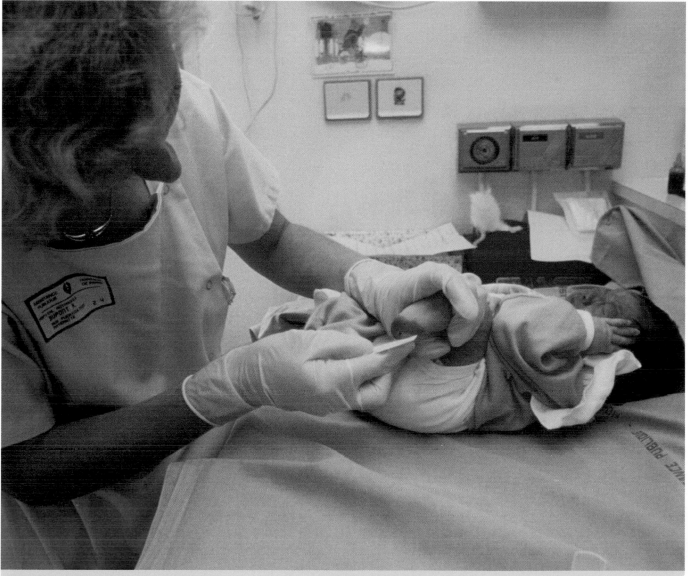

This baby is having a blood spot screening.

Children's social services

Children's social services are the responsibility of each local authority. From time to time children and their families may need additional support. This may be provided by family support workers, or by voluntary organisations such as Home Start. Children's social services provide support for the family when there are concerns about a child's welfare or when they are at increased risk of harm or abuse. Social services are also responsible for **looked-after children** or those in the process of being placed for adoption. Social workers aim to work in partnership with parents, empowering them to make the necessary changes to improve the well-being, and ensure the safety, of their children. However, the child's needs must come first, and in exceptional circumstances social workers have the powers to apply for a care order to remove children to a place of safety, such as foster care or a residential home.

Theory into practice

Find out more about the work of children's social workers on the government's education website by going to www.pearsonhotlinks.co.uk and searching for the ISBN of this title: 9781447970972.

Key term

Looked-after children – children who are in residential care, such as foster care or a residential home.

Early years education

The Department for Education has overall responsibility for children's services and education. Each local authority has a duty to ensure that there is sufficient good-quality early years provision in its area. Education does not start when a child enters school at the age of 5 years but at birth. Research shows that the learning and development that take place in these first five years are critical, as they provide a firm foundation for the child's development and attainment. This stage is referred to as the Early Years Foundation Stage (EYFS). From the age of 5, education becomes compulsory and children must attend school full time. From 5 to 7 years is referred to as Key Stage 1. Care and education are provided by a wide range of settings, and these are explored more fully in the next section. All home countries must provide for children's educational needs but the curriculum phases are different in Scotland and Northern Ireland.

Entitlement to education

Children are entitled to 15 hours free education and care per week (10 hours per week in Wales) for 38 weeks of the year. In England, children from disadvantaged families are entitled to this from the age of 2 to the age of 5. Other children qualify from the age of 5. The aim of this entitlement is to improve social mobility for disadvantaged children. In Northern Ireland, where children start compulsory education at 4, there are entitlements to free places in early years settings during the preschool year.

Link

Go to Section B in this unit to find more information about the types of education settings and services.

Benefits

Parents may be eligible for a range of benefits, designed to help alleviate the effects of child poverty. Poverty is more than just the lack of income. Poverty affects all aspects of life for the child and family by reducing access to suitable housing, leisure facilities, health care and educational opportunities. The government's Child Poverty Strategy aims to address the causes of poverty for children and families in an attempt to reduce inequalities and improve outcomes. Figure 14.1 shows the financial support that is available to families.

The way that tax credits are worked out is quite complicated and depends on income and the number of children in the family. Extra credit is also available for parents of disabled children who are claiming disability living allowance or whose child is registered blind. Some families are able to claim additional credits to pay for childcare.

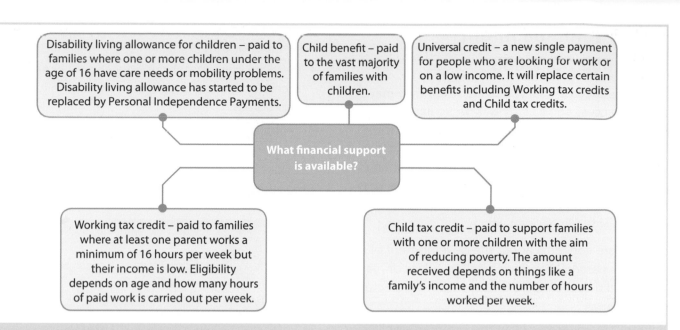

Figure 14.1 The financial support that is available to families

Information for families about education and services

There are many places where families can find information about education and services. Some of the sources of information are listed in Figure 14.2. Since 2013, in some areas of the UK, Universal Credit has replaced a number of benefits, including Child Tax Credits and Working Tax Credits. If you are already claiming benefits, you will be told when Universal Credit will affect you.

Research

You can find more information about the services that are available by visiting the websites for the National Association of Family Information Services and Directgov. You can access these websites by going to www.pearsonhotlinks.co.uk and searching for the ISBN of this title: 9781447970972.

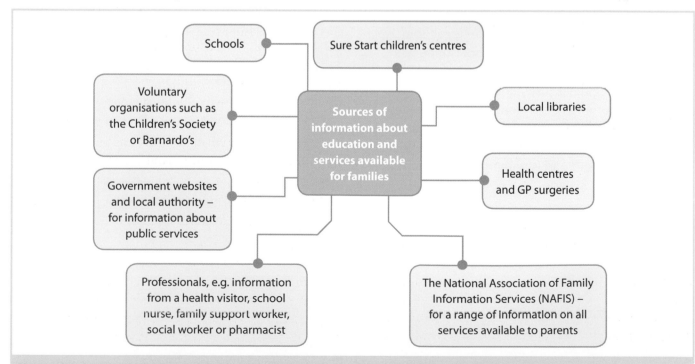

Figure 14.2 Sources of information about the education and services that are available

Why families might access services

There are times in everyone's life when they may need to access services. This is particularly true of families with young children. Sometimes families require advice so that they can resolve a problem themselves. However, there may be times when their needs are more acute or complex, and in this case support from one or more specialist services may be needed. This can happen when:

- there are concerns about the development of a child – parents may notice it themselves or may be told that their child is not reaching expected milestones
- there are concerns about the health of a child – this may be a minor or more serious illness
- a child has a special educational need or mobility problem
- a child requires emergency health care for serious illness or injury
- there is lack of knowledge – about immunisation or diet and nutrition, for instance
- a family is in debt and does not have enough money for basic needs such as food and clothing

- a child is at risk of harm or abuse – from a family member or others
- there are concerns about education – where to access education or concerns about a child's lack of progress
- a referral is made by a childcare professional
- a parent or carer is unable to provide care for a child because of their own physical or mental health problems or a disability.

Reflect

Some families are reluctant to access services. They are sometimes referred to as 'hard to reach families'.

- Discuss reasons why families may not access services with your supervisor or manager.
- Suggest three ways in which you could encourage families to access services.

Key term

Curriculum – all of the experiences and learning that are provided by a setting.

Assessment practice 14.1

3A.P1 | 3A.P2 | 3A.M1 | 3A.D1

There are three children in the Cooper family. Sam is 5 years old and attends the local primary school. Sam is doing well at school but he has cerebral palsy, which affects his mobility. Alice is 3 years old. She has just started nursery school for three mornings each week. During a recent review, concerns were raised about her speech and language development. The baby, Jack, is just 2 months old and is meeting the expected milestones for his age.

The family finds it quite a struggle to make ends meet. Mum, Claire, does not work at present but hopes to go back to working part-time when Jack is 6 months old. Dad, Jason, works long hours as a security guard but his income is quite low.

1 Explain the services and benefits that the Cooper family has a right to access.

2 Give reasons for why the family may need to access the services and benefits you identified.

3 Suggest ways in which the services and benefits are likely to support the family, giving examples.

4 Evaluate how each service and benefit that the family may access could contribute to the outcomes for Sam, Alice and Jack.

B Understand the context in which early years education is provided

Early years education takes place in a range of settings. It may be provided by the local authority, private or voluntary organisations, or in the child's own home. Until the term after the child's fifth birthday, when full-time education becomes compulsory, it is often sessional or part time. Although there is no requirement for parents to send their child to an educational setting until they reach 5 years, many parents choose to do so as it gives their children the opportunity to socialise with children of the same age. They can also take part in a wide range of play and hands-on activities that promote their all-round development.

Types of settings

Whatever the context of early education provision and type of setting, practitioners have a responsibility to provide a challenging environment and deliver a **curriculum** appropriate for the needs and age group of individual children. Some children attend more than one setting, for instance, a nursery class and childminder. The majority of primary schools offer extended services from 8.00 a.m. until 6.00 p.m., often referred to as 'wrap-around' care. Schools may also run holiday schemes.

Table 14.2 lists a variety of educational settings open to children.

Table 14.2 Types of educational settings

Setting	Description	Type
Nursery schools and classes	Provide early education for children from 3–4 years. They may be separate from or attached to a local mainstream school or managed separately. Usually part-time. Some preschool classes may form part of an independent school and be privately funded. Others may be run by third-sector organisations such as Barnardo's.	• Local authority • Private • Voluntary
Sure Start children's centres	Provide part- or full-day care and education for children aged 0–5 years. Centres also provide integrated health and care services for children and families. Their main purpose is to improve the outcomes for children and their families, focusing on those that are disadvantaged.	• Local authority
Day nurseries	Provide part- or full-day care and education for children aged 0–5 years. Sometimes based in the workplace.	• Local authority • Private • Voluntary
Playgroups	Offer part-time, sessional care and education for children aged 2–3 years. Playgroups are run by volunteers but must be registered and run by a qualified leader. They are often located in local community halls or schools.	• Voluntary

continued

Table 14.2 (continued)

Setting	Description	Type
Childminders	Childminders provide care and education for children in their own homes. Where this is provided for children under 8 years and over 2 hours per day, childminders must be registered and accredited.	• Private
Reception classes	Classes within a mainstream school (see below) providing full-time education for children from 4 years until they begin statutory education at the age of 5.	• Local authority
Primary schools (mainstream)	Provide full-time education for children from 4–11 years. From the reception class (4–5 years) children progress to Year 1 (5–6 years) and then to Year 2 (6–7 years).	• Community Schools are entirely run by the local authority (LA). • Some schools such as Foundation and Trust schools are run by a governing body in consultation with the LA. • Voluntary aided schools are usually faith schools and are partly funded by the LA. • Voluntary controlled schools are similar but are run by the LA.
Free Schools or Academies	The nature, organisation and curriculum of Free Schools and Academies are varied. They are accountable for the outcomes of children but are not required to follow the EYFS or the National Curriculum. Some offer nursery facilities.	• Independent from local and national government but publicly funded through the Education Funding Agency (EFA). • Set up and run by community groups including charities, parents, businesses, universities or other interested educational groups.
Special schools	Some children with a learning disability or physical disability may attend a special school if this is appropriate. Special schools may be community or foundation schools, or independent.	• Local authority • Private
Independent schools	Sometimes called private schools. They provide statutory education from 5 years. Usually they have preparatory classes for children from the age of 3 years. Some private schools follow particular teaching methods or a philosophy, such as Montessori schools or Steiner Waldorf schools. Private schools must provide an appropriate curriculum but do not have to follow the EYFS or National Curriculum.	• Privately funded

The structure of early years education

In England, early years education is divided into two distinct phases, the Foundation Stage and Key Stage 1.

Early Years Foundation Stage

This ranges from 0 to 5 years. At this stage education is not compulsory. The Early Years Foundation Stage (EYFS) provides the curriculum framework.

Primary education to Key Stage 1

From the term following a child's fifth birthday, full-time education becomes compulsory. At primary school the National Curriculum provides the curriculum framework.

The Early Years Framework

The EYFS was introduced in 2008 and revised in 2012 and 2014. It provides a mandatory curriculum framework for children from birth until the end of the reception year in registered early years settings. During their early years, children's learning will be supported through play and hands-on activity. Practitioners must provide a high-quality environment and design a curriculum that takes into account three characteristics of learning: **active learning**, **creating and thinking critically**, and playing and exploring.

Areas of learning

The EYFS identifies three prime areas of learning:

- personal, social and emotional development
- communication and language
- physical development.

There are also four specific subject areas: literacy, mathematics, expressive arts and design, and understanding the world.

> **Research**
>
> You can find out more about the revised EYFS and the characteristics of learning in Unit 12 on pages 25–57 or by visiting the Foundation Years website. You can access this website by going to www.pearsonhotlinks.co.uk and searching for the ISBN of this title: 9781447970972.

> **Link**
>
> Go to Unit 2 in Student Book 1 to find more information about the importance of play for children's learning and development.

Key Stage 1 curriculum

At Key Stage 1 the curriculum becomes a little more formal. The National Curriculum (NC) forms a major part of the whole curriculum for children attending state-maintained schools. It is divided into four key stages. Key Stage 1 is the curriculum framework for children aged from 5 to 7 years. There are two underlying principles or aims of the NC, which must be adhered to. These are as follows.

- Children must be prepared for the opportunities, responsibilities and experiences of later life.
- There must be opportunities for spiritual, moral, mental, physical and cultural development.

At Key Stage 1, the National Curriculum comprises the ten **statutory** subject areas shown in Figure 14.3. Religious Education is also a statutory subject but is not part of the National Curriculum. Guidelines for teaching Citizenship, and Personal, Social and Health Education (PSHE) are also included but these aspects of the curriculum are non-statutory.

> **Key terms**
>
> **Active learning** – the process by which children concentrate and keep on trying if they encounter difficulties, and enjoy their achievements.
>
> **Creating and thinking critically** – when children have and develop their own ideas, make links between ideas and develop strategies for doing things.
>
> **Statutory** – set down and regulated by law.

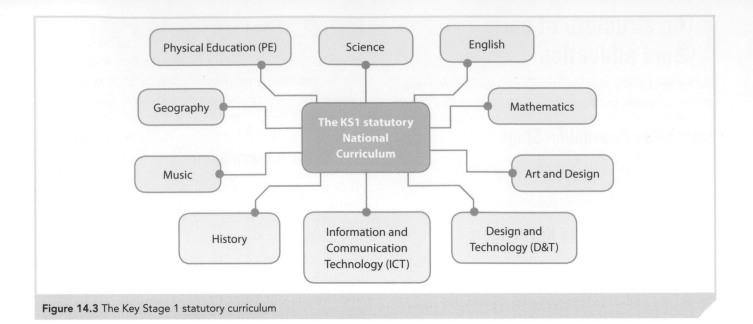

Figure 14.3 The Key Stage 1 statutory curriculum

Settings must provide indoor and outdoor learning opportunities for young children.

For each statutory and non-statutory subject area, there is a programme of study. Programmes of study provide the knowledge, understanding and skills that must be taught. However, they do not prescribe the ways in which subjects should be taught. Children continue to benefit from play and **experiential learning** methods that they enjoyed in the Foundation Stage.

Key term

Experiential learning – taking meaning from direct experience and hands-on activities.

In Wales, the statutory school age is 5 years, as in England, but the curriculum phases are a little different. The Flying Start programme provides guidance for the education and welfare for children aged 0 to 3 years. Children then progress to the Foundation Phase – the statutory curriculum for children aged 3 to 7 years. The Foundation Phase comprises seven areas of learning, including the requirement for Welsh language development. Children do not progress to the Welsh National Curriculum until Key Stage 2 at the age of 7 years.

In Northern Ireland, the statutory school age is 4 years. There is a preschool curriculum for settings for children aged 3 to 4 years. Children do not access the Foundation Stage curriculum until they start school at 4 years. The curriculum stages for Northern Ireland are as follows.

- Preschool:
  - 3 to 4 years
- Foundation Stage:
  - 4 to 5 years (Primary 1)
  - 5 to 6 years (Primary 2)
- Key Stage 1:
  - 6 to 7 years (Primary 3)
  - 7 to 8 years (Primary 4).

The Foundation Stage and Key Stage 1 curricula for Northern Ireland comprise areas of learning similar to England. You can find out more detail about the curriculum phases in Wales and Northern Ireland by going to the websites for the Welsh Government and Department for Education (Northern Ireland) respectively. You can access these websites by going to www.pearsonhotlinks.co.uk and searching for the ISBN of this title: 9781447970972.

Assessment

Children develop at different rates so will reach the expected goals or levels relating to each area of learning at their own pace. Individuals may even achieve at different levels across the areas of learning or subjects, for instance, achieving the goals expected for their age in literacy but not in mathematics. It is therefore important that curriculum planning takes account of the stage the child has reached and not their age.

Assessment is the method by which progress and achievement are measured. Ongoing assessment, described as **formative assessment**, is an essential part of the planning cycle. How would we know what to plan for the next stage of learning without knowing what a child already knows or can do? You will probably see practitioners making notes of their observations as they interact with children. You will also see that practitioners keep samples or photographs of children's work.

Summative assessment provides information on what children know and can do at a set point in time. It is a statutory requirement and the data is sent to the local authority. During the Foundation Stage, when a child is 2 years old, practitioners carry out a progress check against the three prime areas of learning. Then, at the end of the reception year, when a child is 5 years old, practitioners complete an EYFS Profile for the child. They make judgements about each child's knowledge, understanding and abilities relating to the EYFS areas of learning.

During Key Stage 1, at the end of Year 1, children must undergo a statutory phonics test. Then, at the end of Key Stage 1, at the age of 7 years, children are formally assessed by their teacher in reading, writing, speaking and listening, mathematics and science. Their progress is measured against the expected levels of attainment for each subject. The information provided by these assessments is important in helping teachers plan for the next stage of children's learning and development.

Key terms

Formative assessment – assessment that takes place during the learning process, or 'assessment for learning'.

Summative assessment – assessment of what a child knows and can do at the end of a period of learning, or 'assessment of learning'.

The role of inspectorates

The Education Act 2005 (Section 5) sets out the legal requirements for the inspection of schools. In England, childcare and education services including schools are regulated and inspected by the Office for

Standards in Education, Children's Services and Skills (Ofsted). The type of inspection will depend on the setting, the ages of the children and the type of care being provided. The Childcare Act 2006 provides a legal framework for registration and inspection of early years care and education, and care of children and young people under 18 years.

If you work in Wales or Northern Ireland, it is important that you find out about the inspectorate for your own home country. In Wales, Estyn is the inspectorate for schools and for nurseries that are maintained or receive funding from local authorities. A separate inspectorate, the Care and Social Services Inspectorate Wales, inspects childcare services. In Northern Ireland the Education and Training Inspectorate (ETI) inspects preschool settings and schools.

Registration

Those providing care and education for young children must register. To do this, providers must show that they meet minimum requirements, for instance, that staff are suitable and have appropriate qualifications and that the environment will meet the welfare requirements of children. There are two types of registration:

- the Early Years Register – for individuals and settings providing care for children up to 5 years, such as nurseries, preschools, childminders and playgroups
- the Child Care Register – for people providing care for children from 5 years to 8 years.

Inspection of early years education settings

Early years education settings are inspected on a regular basis. This is done with little notice or sometimes with no notice at all. Inspections are usually completed in half a day. During the inspection of early years settings an inspector will check that the requirements of the Early Years Foundation Stage framework are being met. They will look for evidence that:

- the children are being well looked after with regard to their health, social and emotional development, and well-being
- the environment is safe and stimulating
- the setting is being well managed
- the setting is providing opportunities for high-quality learning that lead towards the EYFS goals for children aged from 0 to 5 years
- the setting is supporting children's development.

Inspection of childcare providers

Inspection of childcare providers is done with a lighter touch, with the process taking less than 2 hours. Unlike early years settings, inspections are random unless Ofsted receives a complaint about a setting. The purpose of the inspection is to check provision against the requirements of registration, for instance, that the person providing care is suitable and that the environment is safe and meets welfare requirements.

Children should be stimulated and have opportunities for development. Playing board games stimulates children's social skills.

Inspection of schools

Ofsted is responsible for ensuring that schools meet the required standards set out in the Education Act 2005. School inspections will also include inspection of early years provision where this is managed by the school. Inspections usually take place every few years, but timing varies depending on how well the school has done in previous inspections. The key aims of inspection are to:

- evaluate the effectiveness of the provision to meet the care and educational needs of children
- identify areas of provision that need to improve.

Inspectors base their evaluations on information provided by the school, by talking to parents, staff and children, and by direct observation. You may have been aware of an inspection that took place at your own school. Can you remember being asked questions about your experiences?

As well as academic progress, inspectors look at how well the school provides for children's holistic needs, including:

- how well the children are doing with the curriculum, including the National Curriculum attainment targets
- the quality of teaching and learning happening both in and out of the classroom
- whether the school is providing equality of opportunity. The school must demonstrate that it meets the needs of all children regardless of race, culture, disability or individual need
- the processes in place to safeguard children from harm
- how well the school works with parents and outside agencies to improve the well-being and outcomes of the children.

How inspection reports are used

The purpose of inspection is two-fold. First, and most important, it works to raise the standards of early years provision. Reports indicate the extent to which standards have been met: that is, where settings are doing well in providing for children's needs, or in some instances not so well. These reports are then used as part of each setting's continuous review and development. Action plans must be put in place to develop areas of provision where improvement is needed. This could be one aspect of the setting, for instance, relating to health and safety, the quality of play provision or how well it provides for children's special educational needs. Improvements in standards will be measured at the next inspection.

Second, inspection reports can help indicate to parents which setting will best provide for their child's needs. Reports can be accessed from the setting or Ofsted by anyone with an interest in finding out how well a setting is doing. Although most parents will visit the setting or school where they intend to send their child, inspection reports provide them with additional information about the quality of care and education that their child will receive.

Produce an article for a local parenting magazine that:

- explains the difference between at least four different settings that provide early years education (to include private, voluntary and state provision)

- explains how each setting will be inspected
- identifies the main features for each of the four settings, comparing the advantages and disadvantages of each one for the child and their family.

C Understand the role of multi-agency work for children and their families

In your role as childcare practitioner you will be expected to work alongside professionals from other agencies, such as health, children's social care and education, and perhaps even the police or voluntary organisations. This is referred to as multi-agency working.

What is multi-agency working?

Multi-agency working is when professionals from different services work together in collaboration with parents to improve the outcomes for children. You may also hear the terms 'joint working' or 'partnership working' being used. Professionals who work together are not always based in the same organisation or setting but they will contribute to the assessment of children's needs, share information and work towards improving the outcomes for children. In this way, children and their families are placed firmly at the centre of any reviews, planning and delivery of services. Membership of the team will vary depending on a specific child's needs. Multi-agency working is essential when children and families need support from more than one agency, for instance, when a child in need has a disability, is at risk of harm or abuse or is looked after.

The following services may work together to support children and families:

- schools
- early years settings
- housing authorities
- benefit agencies
- health services
- advocacy services
- hearing units
- social services
- foster care
- child psychology services.

The role of multi-agency work

Multi-agency working is not a new way of working. There have been examples of agencies cooperating and working together for many years. However, until more recently this way of working has been ad hoc and service-led, rather than being led by the needs of children and their families. In 2003, following the death of Victoria Climbié, a report highlighted that failures of professionals to share information had contributed to her death. This resulted in the Children Act 2004 and the legal requirement for agencies to work more closely together in the interests of children and families.

The role of multi-agency working is to achieve a holistic approach to assessment and delivery of services, by providing:

- easier access to services for children and families
- early intervention
- better outcomes for children and families
- integrated support, enabling children to stay with their families or in their local school.

Research suggests that it is this holistic approach of multi-agency working that improves the outcomes for children. In Unit 1 you explored how each area of a child's development is interlinked, so you can understand that for support to be effective, all of the child's needs must be considered. Putting in place services to meet a child's health needs, for example, will not address their emotional and social needs.

Multi-agency working means that families only deal with one person. Families find this far less stressful than having to meet with lots of different professionals or having to travel to different settings. Children with complex needs may require as many as ten different services. Effective coordination of these services ensures that support can be put in place immediately. Delays or inappropriate or insufficient support may put children's health and well-being at risk. The delivery of the most appropriate service, delivered at the right time, improves outcomes for children and their families.

For children who are in need or at risk or have a special educational need, well-targeted support means that their needs can be provided for in their own home and/or their local school. For instance, a child with a disability may continue to attend their local mainstream school because their health care worker and physiotherapist work in partnership with the teacher and parents. Working as a team to support the needs of the whole family may reduce the risk of children being taken into care. For example, by giving parents advice and practical help, such as information on benefits or support for their own health needs, they will be more able to provide care for their own children.

Children in need

Under the Children Act 1989, Section 17, there is a duty on local authorities (LAs) to 'safeguard and promote the welfare of children within their area who are "in need"' (see the legal definition of 'in need' in the Glossary section). LAs must provide 'a level of services appropriate to those children's needs'. The most effective way that LAs can carry out their duty is for services to work together. When concerns are raised that a child is in need, it is important to carry out an initial assessment as soon as possible. The purpose of the assessment is to identify a child's holistic needs at an early stage so

that support can be put in place before the family reaches crisis point.

Children with special educational needs

The SEND Code of Practice 2014 requires that children's educational needs are assessed and that their needs should be met in a mainstream setting or school. When early years practitioners or teachers become concerned that a child is not achieving the level expected for their age, they will need to assess the child's needs. Once a child's needs have been established, an Individual Learning Plan (ILP) will be agreed by the setting and any other relevant agencies.

Support for children with SEN is a staged approach. Children are identified at the first stage when professionals working together in the child's own setting are able to provide for all their needs. This stage is called Early Years Action (for children under 5 years old) or School Action (from the age of 5 years). Children who do not make progress at this stage, or have been identified as having more complex needs, will require support from services outside the school. This stage is called Early Years Action Plus or School Action Plus. The school or early years setting will lead on the assessment but information may also need to be gathered about the child from other agencies and the parents. Agencies may include, for instance, an educational psychologist or hearing support worker. Children may require a Statement of Educational Needs when additional finance and resources are needed to support more complex needs.

> **Link**
>
> Go to Unit 19 to find more information about working with children with additional needs.

Children at risk

When concerns are raised about a child's safety and welfare, children's social services have a duty to investigate if there is 'reasonable cause to suspect that a child ... is suffering or is likely to suffer **significant harm**' under Section 47 of the Children Act 1989. A core assessment of the child's needs will then be carried out, drawing on information from their initial assessment and from relevant professionals.

If concerns are substantiated, a child protection conference will be held, led by a social worker and involving a number of agencies – for instance, a health worker, police officer and early years practitioner. A detailed Child Protection Plan will then be agreed, in partnership with the child's parents, that identifies the services required to ensure the safety of the child and supports them and their family.

How agencies work together

Multi-agency work can be organised in different ways. Agencies may be fully integrated or come together to work in partnership for a particular purpose. There are also times when professionals contact each other informally for advice and information. Some examples are given below, but as you explore multi-agency working in your own area you may find variations on the following models.

- Multi-agency panel

Professionals from a range of different services or agencies such as health, education and social services come together to form a 'panel' to discuss particular cases where there are problems faced by children and their families. Panel members may carry out casework and report back, or one professional may be appointed as the lead. In this model each panel member continues to be based within their own service or agency and is responsible to a manager there. Multi-agency panels may be formed

when staff from one setting, for instance, a nursery, identify that a child and their family require support from other services, such as behavioural support or a housing association.

- Multi-agency team

Although team members may continue to have links to their own 'home' agency to undertake training and access resources, they will work under the leadership of one manager. This is a more permanent arrangement than a panel, with professionals being appointed or sometimes seconded to the team. They will work towards the same goal – to improve the outcome for the child and their family. An example of this model is a special school that employs early years practitioners, teachers and a school nurse, but other professionals such as hearing support workers are seconded or appointed to meet the particular needs of individual children.

- Integrated services

These are similar to multi-agency teams, but are fully integrated. Professionals work together under the same manager to deliver services to children and their families. An advantage of this model is that right from the start there is a shared philosophy, shared methods of working and well-established communication channels. A good example of this model can be seen in a Sure Start children's centre where a range of services (for instance, health services, breastfeeding and weaning support groups, parenting classes, family support workers, nursery and playgroups) are available within one building.

Support centred on the child

Whichever model of multi-agency working is in place, in order to be effective the support must be centred on the child. This process is sometimes referred to as the Team Around the Child (TAC). Also key for successful team working are the following.

- Shared aims and purpose – it is important that, when working together, professionals have agreed ways of working, a clear purpose and mutual respect and trust.
- Effective channels of communication – communication will be far more effective where services are integrated, as there will be a shared language and methods of working.

The cycle of integrated assessment and support

Agencies must work together at each stage of the process from the initial assessment until the planned outcomes are met. This means that the review, which follows a period of support by agencies, may not be the final stage in the process but may lead to further assessment and planning. Support for children and their families must, therefore, be viewed as a continuous cycle.

Assessment

An assessment of a child's needs may be initiated and led by any agency, so all adults who work in children's services must be familiar with current assessment processes. The exception is when children are considered to be 'at risk', in which case a social worker from the local authority or the National Society for the Prevention of Cruelty to Children (NSPCC) will lead. Whichever agency leads, professionals from different services will work together to share information about the child and their family. When sharing information it is essential for professionals to observe confidentiality. This means that parents must always be consulted before sharing information, unless there is concern that this would put the child at risk of harm or abuse.

Information should include the strengths and interests as well as the needs of the child. The situation of the family must also be considered, as this will affect support planning and the role the parents will play. For instance, a health visitor may provide information about the child's health and their home environment, a social worker on the parents' ability to provide support, a hearing support worker on the extent of a child's hearing loss or a teacher about a child's behaviour and academic achievement. Parents know their child best, so wherever possible they, and if appropriate the child, should contribute to the assessment.

Planning

Following assessment, a plan will be agreed on how the five outcomes – be healthy, stay safe, enjoy and achieve, make a positive contribution and achieve economic well-being – can best be achieved. The format of the plan will depend on the child's needs. For instance, an Individual Learning Plan (ILP) is for children with SEN, while a Child Protection Plan is for children at risk of significant harm or abuse. Each agency will share its particular area of knowledge and expertise, aiding decision making about the best way to provide support and, where necessary, solving problems. By working together in this way professionals are able to coordinate support more effectively, ensuring that there is no duplication of services or, worse, that some of the child's needs go unnoticed.

Each plan will be agreed by the professionals involved, and should include:

- a lead professional to coordinate assessment, planning and reviews and to be the first point of contact for parents and other professionals
- the short- and long-term targets for the child and family
- detail about how these can be achieved
- the timescale for support and review
- the roles and responsibilities of each agency and the parents in providing support
- resource requirements.

Support

Once the plan is in place the lead professional must continue to coordinate the support, but each agency will be accountable for delivering their part of the plan. Support may be provided directly, for instance, a learning support assistant who works alongside a child in the classroom, or indirectly, such as advice given to a teacher by a child psychologist on ways to manage a child's behaviour.

Even though a date will have been agreed for review, it is important that progress is constantly monitored by each professional, to ensure that support plans are appropriate and that they can continue to be delivered. They must also inform the lead professional if the child or family's circumstances change at any time. When professionals work together in one setting they may find that there is a merging of roles, so it is important that they are clear about their individual responsibilities. Although this can be a barrier to effective working, the sharing of knowledge and expertise in delivering the plan can ultimately be of benefit to the child, family and the professionals involved.

Review

A review date must be agreed as part of the plan. The lead professional will then arrange the meeting and invite professionals from each agency and the parents. They will discuss what has gone well and what support has not been effective and the reasons for this. The result of the review may be that the child has met the identified targets and that their family no longer requires support from all or some of the agencies in the team. When some or all of the targets have not been met, the support may need to continue or be adapted. In some cases the child may need additional and/or specialist agencies to be involved. An amended support plan will then be put in place and the cycle will continue.

Further reading and resources

Barker, R. (2008) *Making Sense of Every Child Matters*, Bristol: Policy Press.

Walker, G. (2008) *Working Together for Children: A Critical Introduction to Multi-Agency Working*, London: Continuum.

Working Together to Safeguard Children: A guide to inter-agency working to safeguard and promote the welfare of children (Department for Education, 2013).

Websites

Department of Health: www.dh.gov.uk

Department for Education: www.gov.uk/dfe

Office for Standards in Education, Children's Services and Skills: www.ofsted.gov.uk

Public services: www.gov.uk

National Health Service: www.nhs.uk

Universal Credit: www.gov.uk/universal-credit

Ready for work?

Sonia Kaney
Family support worker based in a children's centre

How long have you been working as a family support worker?

I worked as a volunteer for the first six months alongside a colleague. When I completed my childcare course three years ago I was appointed full-time.

What does your work involve?

My work is really varied. I usually go into the homes of families with young children to provide support but I also lead groups at the children's centre. For instance, the last one was about how to prepare simple, nutritious meals. During my visits some families need more practical help and others more emotional support. A few months ago I visited a mum who found it really difficult to leave the house and was nervous of meeting others. This meant that she was not turning up for her toddler's health reviews and immunisations. I went with her to the children's centre and introduced her to the health visitor and two other mums. Now that she has got to know other mums I have noticed that she is visiting the centre regularly.

What knowledge and skills do you need to be a family support worker?

It is so important that you get on with people. You need to be a good listener and non-judgemental. Most important are good observational skills and knowledge of child development. Family support workers see families regularly and are often the first to notice that there may be a problem, that a child may not be developing as expected or may be at risk of abuse.

What do you enjoy about your job?

The work can be quite tough at times and writing reports is not my favourite task! Despite this I get on really well with other professionals at the centre and learn a great deal from them. When I work alongside a family and see them beginning to take more control of their own lives it gives me a great deal of satisfaction. I really feel that I'm making a difference.

Skills for practice

Professional relationships with adults

You should consider ways to build professional relationships with adults. Use the following tips to help you.

- Ask advice from colleagues at your placement and perhaps make suggestions.
- Use role play to practise using the telephone and speaking with a professional tone in a range of scenarios.
- Greet parents and other visitors with a smile and address them appropriately.

Introduction

The food children eat affects their health and development in many ways. The nutrients provided by food influence children's physical and intellectual development. Social skills are developed at mealtimes, and food can also have an impact on behaviour.

Most children enjoy cooking, as it provides a positive social activity. Cooking involves both mathematical and scientific skills. Preparing and eating food can also develop language skills. Growing the food that children then cook or eat adds another dimension.

Snack and meal provision are common in many day-care settings and you may be required to prepare food for children. It is important that you understand how to do this safely as well as how you can make the most of these learning opportunities.

Assessment: You will be assessed by a series of assignments set by your teacher/tutor.

Learning aims

In this unit you will:

A1   understand how to provide food for children to encourage health and development

A2   understand the role of the adult in encouraging children to develop healthy eating habits

B   understand the role of the adult in preparing and serving food safely.

> Whatever childcare setting you work in, you will need to know something about nutrition and food provision. Many settings involve the provision of food either as snacks or lunch and you need to be able to encourage children to eat healthily. Adults have a strong influence on what children eat, and food can also be used as a vehicle for learning.
>
> Abigail Fleming, *a nutritionist*

Food and Mealtimes in the Early Years

15

BTEC
Assessment Zone

This table shows you what you must do in order to achieve a **Pass**, **Merit** or **Distinction** grade, and where you can find activities to help you.

Assessment criteria		
Pass	**Merit**	**Distinction**
Learning aim A1: Understand how to provide food for children to encourage health and development **Learning aim A2:** Understand the role of the adult in encouraging children to develop healthy eating habits		
3A1.P1 Explain the impact of diet on children's health and development. **Assessment practice 15.1**	**3A1.M1** Analyse a child's diet in relation to current expert guidance. **Assessment practice 15.1**	**3A.D1** Evaluate the extent to which an early years setting contributes to children's health and development through the provision of food. **Assessment practice 15.3**
3A1.P2 Explain how to work with parents in early years settings to meet children's individual dietary needs. **Assessment practice 15.2**	**3A1.M2** Discuss the role of partnership working with parents in relation to children's attitudes to food. **Assessment practice 15.3**	**3A.D2** Recommend improvements to an early years setting's contribution to children's healthy eating habits. **Assessment practice 15.3**
3A2.P3 English Explain how children's attitudes to food are influenced. **Assessment practice 15.3**		
3A2.P4 Explain the role of adults in developing children's healthy eating habits. **Assessment practice 15.2**		
Learning aim B: Understand the role of the adult in preparing and serving food safely		
3B.P5 Explain responsibilities and practices for working safely in an early years setting when preparing and serving food to children. **Assessment practice 15.4**		

English / English Functional Skills signposting

How you will be assessed

This unit will be assessed by a series of internally assessed tasks set by your teacher/tutor. Throughout this unit you will find assessment practice activities that will help you work towards your assessment. Completing these activities will not mean that you have achieved a particular grade, but you will have carried out useful research or preparation that will be relevant when it comes to your final assignment.

In order for you to achieve the tasks in your assignment, it is important that you check you have met all of the Pass grading criteria. You can do this as you work your way through the assignment.

If you are hoping to gain a Merit or Distinction, you should also make sure that you present the information in your assignment in the style that is required by the relevant assessment criterion. For example, Merit criteria will require you to discuss and analyse, and Distinction criteria will require you to evaluate and make recommendations for improvements.

The assignment set by your teacher/tutor will consist of a number of tasks designed to meet the criteria in the assessment criteria table. This is likely to consist of a written assignment but may also include activities such as:

- case studies
- a leaflet
- observations.

Think about your own eating habits.

- How do you think these were formed?
- Who influences what you like and dislike?
- How have adults shaped your food choices throughout your life?

A1 Understand how to provide food for children to encourage health and development

A well-balanced diet is essential for all children for healthy growth and development. Providing food that is nutritious and also appeals to children can be challenging. This section will help you to understand the nutritional needs of children and the food that will provide the necessary nutrients to meet these needs.

Nutrients required for health and development and foods that contain them

An understanding of the nutrients required by children is essential if you are to provide them with a healthy diet. These nutrients need to be provided through food whatever the age of the child, but the amounts that are needed may vary.

There are five main dietary nutrients:

- proteins
- fats
- carbohydrates
- vitamins
- minerals.

Proteins

Proteins provide essential amino acids, which are needed for the growth and repair of our body's cells. They are particularly important for babies and young children. Proteins have to come from food and therefore are essential in the diet. Foods that contain all the essential amino acids are known as

high biological value (HBV) foods. Foods that are sources of protein but do not contain all the essential amino acids are known as low biological value (LBV) foods. If two LBV foods are eaten together, one may compensate for the deficiencies in the other – beans on toast is a good example. This is known as the complementary action of proteins.

Protein has another important function, which is to act as a secondary source of energy. The body's first sources of energy are fat and carbohydrate, but if energy is not available from these sources, it will use protein to keep going.

Figure 15.1 outlines the functions and sources of protein.

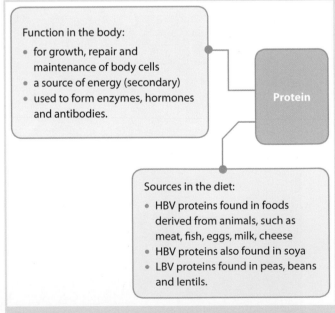

Function in the body:
- for growth, repair and maintenance of body cells
- a source of energy (secondary)
- used to form enzymes, hormones and antibodies.

Protein

Sources in the diet:
- HBV proteins found in foods derived from animals, such as meat, fish, eggs, milk, cheese
- HBV proteins also found in soya
- LBV proteins found in peas, beans and lentils.

Figure 15.1 The functions and sources of protein

Fats

Of all the nutrients, fats contain the highest amount of energy: 9 kilocalories per gram. Therefore, too much fat in the diet can contribute to obesity, in both adults and children. Fat can be saturated or unsaturated. Animal fats are generally saturated and should be eaten in moderation. Saturated fat comes from foods such as butter, lard, fatty meats, full-fat milk, chocolate and cheese. Eating a lot of saturated fats can increase the amount of cholesterol in your blood. High levels of cholesterol can increase your risk of heart disease. Vegetable and fish fats are usually unsaturated. Eating foods high in unsaturated fats can decrease the amount of cholesterol in your blood, and therefore contribute to a healthy lifestyle. Fat has the effect of making foods more palatable (pleasant to taste), and for this reason it is easy to eat too much of it.

Figure 15.2 outlines the functions and sources of fat.

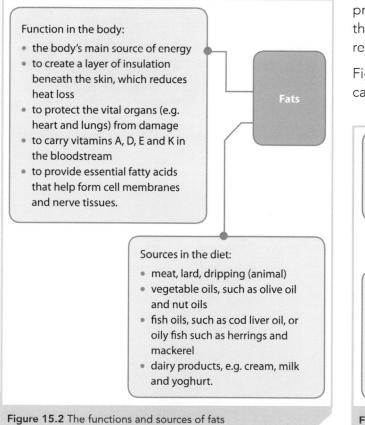

Function in the body:
- the body's main source of energy
- to create a layer of insulation beneath the skin, which reduces heat loss
- to protect the vital organs (e.g. heart and lungs) from damage
- to carry vitamins A, D, E and K in the bloodstream
- to provide essential fatty acids that help form cell membranes and nerve tissues.

Fats

Sources in the diet:
- meat, lard, dripping (animal)
- vegetable oils, such as olive oil and nut oils
- fish oils, such as cod liver oil, or oily fish such as herrings and mackerel
- dairy products, e.g. cream, milk and yoghurt.

Figure 15.2 The functions and sources of fats

Carbohydrates

As much as 50 or 60 per cent of the energy in our diet should come from foods containing carbohydrate. Carbohydrates have an energy value of 3.75 kilocalories per gram. They are divided into the following three sub-groups.

- Monosaccharides or simple sugars – these are the simplest kinds of carbohydrate molecule.
- Disaccharides, or sugars, such as sucrose (found in cane sugar) and lactose (found in milk).
- Polysaccharides, or complex carbohydrates, including starch (found in potatoes) and cellulose (found in lettuce).

Sugar is easily digested and therefore provides an 'instant' source of energy. Complex carbohydrates, such as starchy foods and cellulose, take longer to break down in the body and therefore provide a slow release of energy.

Some carbohydrates (in the polysaccharides group) provide what is known as dietary fibre. Fibre increases the water content in the body and helps the stools remain soft, thereby helping to prevent constipation.

Figure 15.3 outlines the functions and sources of carbohydrates.

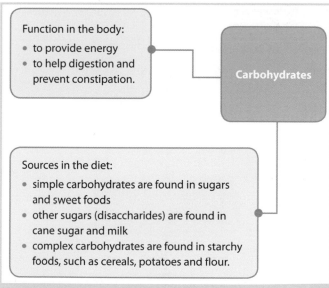

Function in the body:
- to provide energy
- to help digestion and prevent constipation.

Carbohydrates

Sources in the diet:
- simple carbohydrates are found in sugars and sweet foods
- other sugars (disaccharides) are found in cane sugar and milk
- complex carbohydrates are found in starchy foods, such as cereals, potatoes and flour.

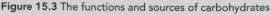

Figure 15.3 The functions and sources of carbohydrates

Vitamins and minerals

Vitamins and minerals are also known as **micronutrients** as they are needed in small quantities in the diet. Proteins, fats and carbohydrates, on the other hand, are known as **macronutrients** as they are needed in larger quantities.

Vitamins and minerals are **organic** compounds and are essential for life even though they are only needed in small quantities. Except for a few vitamins and minerals, the body cannot **synthesise** these and, therefore, they must be included in the diet regularly. Vitamins are divided into two groups according to how they are dissolved and carried in the body, as shown in Figures 15.4 and 15.5.

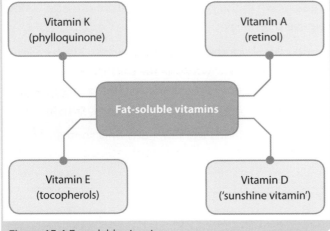
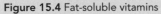

Figure 15.4 Fat-soluble vitamins

- Vitamin K (phylloquinone)
- Vitamin A (retinol)
- Fat-soluble vitamins
- Vitamin E (tocopherols)
- Vitamin D ('sunshine vitamin')

Green leafy vegetables, carrots and tomatoes are a good source of vitamins.

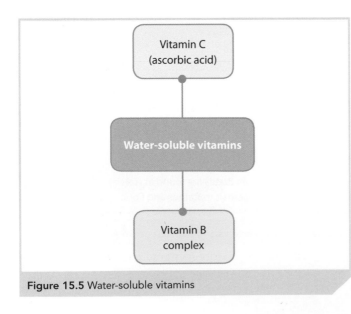

Figure 15.5 Water-soluble vitamins

- Vitamin C (ascorbic acid)
- Water-soluble vitamins
- Vitamin B complex

Dairy products are also a good source of vitamins.

Tables 15.1, 15.2 and 15.3 provide a description of the vitamins and minerals, together with their function in the body and main sources.

Table 15.1 Fat-soluble vitamins

Fat-soluble vitamin	Function	Sources
Vitamin A (retinol) Vitamin A comes from two sources. In animal products it is found in the form of retinol and this is the form the body uses. In vegetables, it is found in the form of beta-carotene.	• Vital for the formation of a pigment in the eye (rhodopsin, or visual purple) which helps the eye adjust to the dark • Contributes to maintenance of the skin • Used in the development of the skeleton including the skull and the vertebral column	• Rich sources: liver oils such as cod liver oil or halibut liver oil • Good sources: liver, carrots, spinach, butter, margarine • Useful sources: cheese, eggs, tomatoes, milk, salmon, herrings
Vitamin D Vitamin D is known as the 'sunshine vitamin' because the body can make vitamin D itself with the action of sunlight on the skin.	• Essential for the formation of bones and teeth • Promotes the absorption of calcium and phosphorus by the small intestine • Aids the withdrawal of calcium from the bones to maintain the correct amount of calcium in the blood	• Fatty fish such as salmon, herring and sardines • Dairy products such as butter, eggs, milk, cheese and margarine • Sunshine on the skin
Vitamin E (tocopherols) Studies have shown that a deficiency of Vitamin E in rats leads to degeneration of the muscles.	• Essential for normal **metabolism**	Most foods contain a trace of vitamin E. Good sources include: • seed oil, particularly wheatgerm • eggs • liver.
Vitamin K (phylloquinone) Vitamin K is needed in small amounts in the body. Although many diets are deficient in Vitamin K, it is produced by bacteria in the large intestine. Half the daily requirement can be met by this.	• Important component in blood clotting	Good sources include: • liver • green leafy vegetables • milk.

Table 15.2 Water-soluble vitamins

Water-soluble vitamin	Function	Sources
Vitamin C (ascorbic acid) Vitamin C is highly unstable and easily lost in cooking and food preparation through heat and oxidation. It can be lost from fruit and vegetables as they are cut, as well as being destroyed by heat. In cooking, it leaches into the cooking liquid. Therefore, to maximise vitamin C intake, you should cut up fruit and vegetables close to the cooking time, cook in a small amount of liquid for the least amount of time possible and use the cooking liquid in gravy and sauces.	• To make the connective tissue which binds body cells together • Essential in the manufacture of blood and the cell walls of blood vessels • Aids resistance to infection – it is believed it helps fight the common cold but there is no definite evidence to prove this • Deficiency may lead to slow repair of cells after injury	• Good sources include citrus fruits, blackcurrants and vegetables. • Potatoes are also a good source of vitamin C for the British. Although there is not a high amount in them, they are a staple of the British diet. As so many potatoes are eaten, they make up a significant source.
Vitamin B complex • Vitamin B1 (thiamin) • Vitamin B2 (riboflavin) • Niacin • Vitamin B6 (pyridoxine) • Vitamin B9 (folic acid) • Vitamin B12 (cobalamin)	• Essential for the release of energy from proteins, fats and carbohydrates • Needed for growth and normal functioning of the nervous system • Maintains muscle tone • Formation of red blood cells • Deficiency may lead to a feeling of being run-down, tiredness, loss of appetite or retarded growth in children • In severe cases, deficiency can cause nervous diseases such as beriberi, pellagra and anaemia	Good sources include: • brown rice • offal, such as liver or kidney • milk • eggs • fruit and vegetables • flour and most breakfast cereals – it is added by law.

Table 15.3 Minerals

Mineral	Function	Sources
Iron Iron is found in the body in the form of haemoglobin in the red blood cells. Red blood cells have a lifespan of about four months, after which they are replaced.	• Formation of haemoglobin in red blood cells, which enables cells to carry oxygen around the body to other cells and tissues • Important during growth spurts – particularly necessary during childhood • Important for brain development and immune function	• Animal sources include offal such as liver and black pudding, as well as eggs and fish. • Vegetable sources include green vegetables, cocoa, parsley and flour.
Calcium Calcium works hand in hand with phosphorus. If there is a lack of calcium in the diet, this can lead to stunted growth, badly formed teeth and rickets in children. Children require 600 mg/day.	• Necessary for the formation of the skeleton – strong bones and teeth • Necessary to help the blood to clot • Helps the normal functioning of the muscles	Good sources include: • milk and milk products such as yoghurt • tinned fish, particularly where the bones are eaten, including salmon • hard water • green vegetables • flour, as calcium is added during manufacture.
Phosphorus Phosphorus works in conjunction with calcium. It is the second most abundant mineral in the body and is found mainly in the bones.	• Contributes to the formation of strong bones and teeth • Essential component of the blood • Necessary for metabolism, to harvest energy from foods	• Present in most animal and vegetable foods and therefore a deficiency is unknown. • Phosphates are added to some foods during manufacture.
Iodine There is between 20 and 50 mg of iodine in the body; 8 mg is found in the thyroid gland. A deficiency of iodine can lead to lack of energy and obesity. It can also lead to goitre, which is a swelling thyroid gland in the neck.	• Essential component of hormones manufactured by the thyroid gland in the neck, including thyroxine, which control the body's metabolic rate • The recommended daily intake is very small – 0.05 to 0.30 mg/day	• Good sources include seafood and seaweed. • Iodine can be found in plant foods but the amount depends on the soil in which they are grown and therefore the amount is irregular.
Zinc Zinc is a trace element that is found in most foods, particularly in association with protein.	• Essential for tissue growth • Required for enzyme reactions in the body	Good sources include: • oysters • kidney • green vegetables • wholegrain cereals.

Guidelines for providing food and drink

When babies are born, they are able to suck but not bite or chew. Their digestive system is not able to digest solid food and they are born with the sucking reflex. This means that their diet has to be a liquid one: milk. Human babies are either breastfed or bottle fed with milk that has been modified to suit young babies. Whether to breast- or bottle feed can be a difficult decision for parents – there are advantages and disadvantages to both feeding methods.

Breastfeeding

Health experts recommend that breastfeeding is best for the human baby. It is believed that breastfeeding for the first six months gives babies a good start in life.

Breast milk is very complex and therefore no formula can match it exactly. It contains exactly the correct balance of proteins, fats, vitamins and minerals for a baby as well as delivering the correct amount of calories. This means that breastfed babies are less likely to become overweight than bottle-fed babies. They are also less likely to suffer from dehydration or from excess mineral intake. The protein in breast milk is easily digested and more of the essential components are absorbed into the baby's body.

Another advantage of breast milk is that it helps to protect the child from infections. First feeds, before the milk fully comes in, contain colostrum, which provides the baby with antibodies. These help babies fight infection and increase their resistance to a wide range of infections, including chest and urinary tract infections. It also contains a laxative, which allows the baby to cope with small amounts of milk while its kidneys adjust to life outside the womb. Formula milk does not contain these antibodies.

Some researchers believe that breastfeeding can help bonding between the mother and baby as it creates a special kind of closeness.

Bottle feeding

Not all women are able or want to breastfeed. Some women choose to breastfeed for the first few months and then move to bottle feeding as the child grows. Every mother is different and will do what they feel is best for their baby. If a mother does not want to breastfeed or wants to stop, bottle feeding is the alternative.

If bottle feeding is chosen, formula milk must be used. A baby cannot be given cow's milk as a drink, as it has too much protein and lacks important nutrients. Cow's milk should not be given to a baby as a drink until they are 12 months old.

Modern formula milks have been developed to replicate breast milk as closely as possible. They are made from dried cow's milk that has been modified to make it more digestible for a young baby. Most formulas are based on whey or casein, and these are the main source of protein. Whey-based formulas are usually given to young babies as they replicate breast milk more closely and are easier for a young baby to digest. Casein-based formulas often contain more minerals and protein and are therefore suited to hungrier babies.

Formula milks are produced with clear instructions on how to make the feeds up to the correct proportions and consistency. It is important that these instructions are followed exactly. The formula should not be made stronger by adding more powder, as this makes the mixture too concentrated and can cause dehydration.

With bottle feeding, a mother can see exactly how much milk a baby has taken. However, it is important that a baby is not forced to finish a feed, as they may not need it all and excess calories will be converted to fat. This can lead to an increase in weight that can be difficult to shift later in childhood. However, if a baby is still hungry after a feed, an additional feed can be easily made up to satisfy that hunger. If breastfeeding, the mother's body quickly responds to the different demands of the baby and a suitable amount of milk is made for subsequent feeds.

Some women find breastfeeding in public embarrassing, despite it being seen as more acceptable than it used to be and supported by legislation. Despite this, both bottle and breastfeeding can be managed while mother and baby are out and about.

Weaning

Weaning – sometimes referred to as complementary feeding – is the process of expanding a baby's diet to include food and drink other than breast milk or infant formula.

Weaning should start from about 6 months. Although all babies develop at different paces, it is recommended that weaning should not be started with babies younger than 6 months for the following reasons.

- **Neuromuscular coordination** needs to be adequately developed and an infant of less than 6 months is unlikely to be able to maintain a suitable posture for swallowing. They are also unlikely to be able to move food from the front to the back of the mouth for swallowing.

- They are not usually willing to experiment with different flavours, textures and consistencies.

- The kidney function may not be mature enough to deal with the greater concentration of **solutes** and reduced fluid volume that is associated with weaning.

- Secretion of digestive juices in the gut is not adequately developed to cope with digestion.

- Absorption capacities of the small and large intestine are not adequately developed.

- The gastrointestinal system is more prone to food-related allergies such as **coeliac disease**.

- Children should not have too much energy-dense food too early as it may lead to obesity.

From about the end of the sixth month, babies can cope with soft foods of a slightly thicker consistency than milk, such as baby rice or baby rusks softened with milk. They can suck and swallow these feeds. Babies cannot bite and chew lumps of food until they are 5 or 6 months old.

Solid foods are introduced when milk alone is unable to meet a baby's nutritional needs. Signs that suggest a baby needs to start solids include:

- the baby still seems hungry after a good milk feed
- the baby starts to demand to be fed more often, suggesting that the milk feed is not satisfying them
- the baby starts to wake in the night for a feed after previously sleeping through.

The move from a wholly liquid diet to a solid one is a gradual process. Each stage builds on the previous one, ensuring that the baby's digestive system can cope with the changes in textures and types of food. Weaning has a number of stages.

> ### Key terms
>
> **Coeliac disease** – a digestive condition caused by gluten intolerance.
>
> **Neuromuscular coordination** – the joint operation of different muscles to produce a movement, e.g. raising your arm.
>
> **Solutes** – a substance that is dissolved in another substance.

6 to 9 months (Stage 1)

Weaning usually begins with offering some solid food after one milk feed during the day. First foods are simple unprocessed foods such as puréed vegetables or fruit, or non-wheat-based cereal such as baby rice mixed with milk. These foods are bland and are unlikely to upset the baby's digestive system. It is important not to give a wheat-based product at this stage, as wheat can upset the digestive system.

Recent guidance from health visitors on weaning includes an approach known as 'baby-led weaning'. This can be used alongside giving puréed foods or on its own. The idea is that you allow babies to choose what they eat from the outset. You offer them different foods cut to suitable sizes, and if they like a food, they choose to eat it. If they do not like a food, they will not eat it. This allows babies to enjoy the same foods as the rest of the family and develop their own tastes.

If the food is to be offered heated, make sure it is not too hot. Microwaves should not be used to heat baby food due to the hot spots that can occur. There are many ready-prepared first foods such as baby rice available. Remember to follow the instructions on the packet or jar if using commercially produced foods.

If, when starting to wean, the baby seems not to want the food, it is important not to force them to eat. Put the process on hold for a week and then try again.

Food is given in small amounts on a clean spoon or fingertip. Babies will take time to learn how to take food from a spoon and there will be spitting and mess as they learn. Often babies get frustrated when they first start solid food as they are used to the milk coming in a continuous flow, and eating is a slower process, with pauses.

Solid food should never be added to bottles as this can cause choking.

Table 15.4 summarises the foods to try and foods to avoid at Stage 1.

Table 15.4 Stage 1 of weaning: foods to try and foods to avoid	
Foods to try	**Foods to avoid**
• Vegetable or fruit purées (potato, yam, spinach, apple, banana) • Thin porridge made from rice, cornmeal, sago or millet • Rusks mixed with breast or formula milk	• Wheat-based foods such as bread or biscuits • Milk other than breast or formula • Eggs • Citrus fruits • Nuts • Fatty foods

Simple unprocessed foods such as puréed vegetables are unlikely to upset the baby's digestive system.

9 to 12 months (Stage 2)

Feeds still start with the breast or bottle milk but the amount of solid food is gradually increased. The amount given will vary according to the baby's appetite.

At this point, the number of feeds at which solids are given is gradually increased to two and then three.

Cereals should be given at one feed only, and other tastes introduced. It is probably wise not to introduce more than two or three new foods each week as this will enable you to identify whether any food seems to upset the baby.

There are lots of commercially prepared baby foods available for this stage but many parents choose to offer foods they are eating themselves. These foods need to be mashed, sieved or puréed. As the baby gets used to eating solids and chewing, the food can be prepared a little lumpier. Using foods that the rest of the family are eating is cheaper and babies also get used to eating like the rest of the family. Also, parents know what is in the food and can ensure it meets any special requirements, such as being halal or kosher.

Table 15.5 summarises the foods to try and the foods to avoid at Stage 2.

Table 15.5 Stage 2 of weaning: foods to try and foods to avoid	
Foods to try	**Foods to avoid**
• Purées that include meat, poultry or fish • Pulses, including lentils • Wider range of vegetables • Well-cooked eggs • Wheat-based foods	• Cow's milk as a drink • Goat's milk • Nuts • Spicy foods

This will mean that the baby takes less and less milk from the breast or bottle. The milk feed might now be limited to just the first and last feeds of the day. Diluted fruit juices and water should also be offered as drinks with meals.

Table 15.6 goes into more detail about what foods must not be given to children under 12 months. Note that nutritional advice can change and it is essential to check current guidelines regularly.

Table 15.6 Foods to avoid giving to children under 12 months

Food	Reason
Salt	Salt can cause problems for the kidneys and later health problems. Do not buy foods that have salt in them or add salt when cooking.
Honey	Sometimes honey can contain a bacteria that is dangerous to babies and can cause an illness called infant botulism. Honey can also cause tooth decay.
Sugar	Sugar can cause tooth decay, but also give babies a liking for sugary foods later on.
Whole or chopped nuts	These can be a choking hazard.
Raw or partially cooked eggs	Eggs are a good source of protein, but must be thoroughly cooked, as they can contain bacteria that can cause food poisoning.
Shark, marlin, swordfish	Fish is good for babies, but these fish can contain mercury and so should be avoided.
Low-fat, low-calorie foods	'Diet' low-calorie foods are not good for babies because they need foods that contain plenty of nutrients. Low-fat dairy products such as low-fat yoghurt should also be avoided.
High-fibre foods	Bran, wholemeal pasta and brown rice are good for adults but are very high in fibre and stop babies digesting other nutrients. Brown bread is fine.
Cow's milk	Cow's milk is not suitable as a main drink for babies under 12 months. Full-fat milk can be introduced after this time.

12 months plus (Stages 3 and 4)

Foods can get lumpier and may be mashed rather than puréed. Once babies can hold foods they can be given finger foods such as carrot sticks, pieces of apple or bread. Sweet biscuits should be avoided as this encourages babies to expect sweet snacks. Finger foods allow babies to practise chewing and will help them learn to feed themselves. Babies should not be left alone to chew – an adult needs to be near in case of choking.

Once the baby masters chewing, food only needs to be chopped, not puréed.

Table 15.7 outlines the foods to try at Stage 3 and Stage 4.

Case study

Moving on to solids

Jane is a new mother. She has a 3-month-old baby whom she has breastfed. She now wants to prepare for introducing solids and comes to you for some advice.

- What recommendations would you make in terms of introducing first solids?
- Devise a first weeks plan for 6 to 9 months and 9 to 12 months to help Jane with her menus.

Table 15.7 Stages 3 and 4 of weaning: foods to try

Stage		Foods to offer
Stage 3	• Introduction of lumpier foods and finger foods • Vitamin drops containing A, C and D for breastfed babies • Quantity of milk feed remains the same	• Two servings per day of foods high in carbohydrates, e.g. potatoes, yams • Two servings per day of foods high in protein, e.g. eggs, meat, fish, tofu, beans • Fruit and vegetables to be part of two or more meals per day
Stage 4	• Introduction of minced or chopped foods • Increasing quantities of food so that the baby has three main meals a day • Milk remains important (500–600 ml per day)	• Three to four servings per day of foods high in carbohydrate • Three to four servings of fruit and vegetables • Two servings of foods high in protein • Fruit and healthy snacks if baby is hungry between meals

Note: Salt, honey or sugar must not be added to, or already in, any of the foods.

Research

More information about weaning can be found on the NHS website, under the 'Healthy Eating' tab. You can access the relevant part of the website by going to www.pearsonhotlinks. co.uk and searching for the ISBN of this title: 9781447970972.

Children aged 1–5 years

By the age of 1 year, most infants are able to feed themselves. They will also have enough teeth to be able to bite and tear food. In the second year, molar teeth also develop and the ability to grind and chew food increases.

Portion size

Portion size is important, as large plates of food can be off-putting for children. Small children have high energy requirements in relation to their size but they are not able to eat large amounts of food at any one time. Therefore, they need to eat small portions frequently, and the foods need to be full of energy or 'energy rich'. This means their diet will contain foods that are proportionally higher in fat and lower in fibre compared to the ideal diet of an adult.

Use small plates to encourage children to eat what is in front of them – large plates of food can be off-putting.

This is also why children under 5 years should not be given skimmed milk as a main drink, as they need the calories provided by whole milk. Children at the age of 2 can, however, gradually move to semi-skimmed milk as a main drink if they are growing well.

Children also need more nutrients relative to their size than adults. Children often eat a smaller range of foods than adults, but the selection offered should be varied enough to provide a good mixture of nutrients in different amounts. All children should be encouraged to follow healthy eating guidelines, such as eating five portions of fruit and vegetables a day.

The amount children want to eat is often affected by their physical activity and physiological growth. This means children's appetites may fluctuate as their growth does. Parents sometimes worry if their child is small or appears to be eating very little. It is important that they do not force children to eat more or make a fuss of the amount they eat as this could have a negative effect. Remember that growth often happens in spurts, and as long as the child is healthy and is growing well overall, it is likely that all is well.

Prevention of dental decay

Tooth decay is common in children. There are a number of small changes that you can easily make to a child's diet to reduce the risk of dental decay. Figure 15.6 shows ways to reduce the risk of tooth decay.

Good dental hygiene routines are very important. Children should be encouraged to clean their teeth thoroughly at least twice a day using a toothpaste that contains fluoride. They should also go to the dentist every six months – starting this from an early age can help to prevent fear developing. Fluoride is routinely added to tap water and this can help reduce tooth decay.

This practitioner is helping children to brush their teeth.

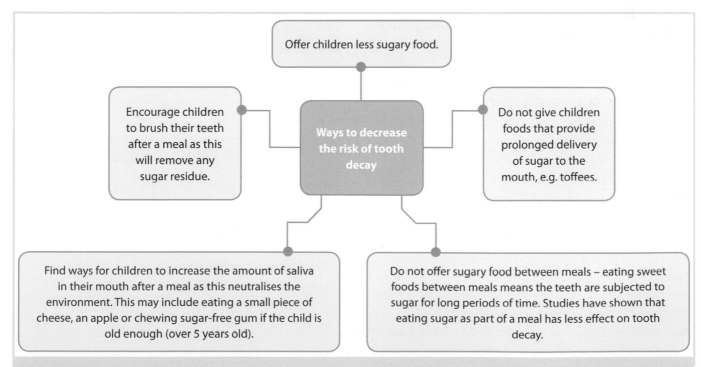

Offer children less sugary food.

Encourage children to brush their teeth after a meal as this will remove any sugar residue.

Ways to decrease the risk of tooth decay

Do not give children foods that provide prolonged delivery of sugar to the mouth, e.g. toffees.

Find ways for children to increase the amount of saliva in their mouth after a meal as this neutralises the environment. This may include eating a small piece of cheese, an apple or chewing sugar-free gum if the child is old enough (over 5 years old).

Do not offer sugary food between meals – eating sweet foods between meals means the teeth are subjected to sugar for long periods of time. Studies have shown that eating sugar as part of a meal has less effect on tooth decay.

Figure 15.6 Ways to decrease the risk of tooth decay

Working with parents and/or carers to meet individual children's food needs

Meeting children's individual food needs can sometimes be challenging for parents and carers. Parents and carers want their children to have a healthy diet but there may be factors that influence their diet such as allergies, food intolerance or restrictions due to social, cultural or religious reasons. This may mean that parents and carers need to adapt the way that food is prepared for the family to accommodate special diets. It is important that you understand the related issues so you can provide appropriate advice and support to parents and record dietary information for all staff in the setting.

Providing a healthy diet

There are some foods that you need to bear in mind when preparing foods for children.

Salt

It is important that salt is not added to a baby's food. A baby's digestive system cannot cope with more salt than that which is naturally found in food. Therefore, if you are cooking food for adults or older children that will also be puréed or mashed for a baby, salt should be left out of the cooking process. Babies and young children should also not be given salty snacks such as crisps.

Sugar

Extra sugar should not be added to food or drinks, as this can lead to tooth decay. Sugar is often listed on packets as glucose, sucrose, fructose, maltose, syrup honey or concentrated fruit juice, so you will have to read labels carefully to avoid it. Try to ensure that children are given as much savoury food as possible.

Allergies and intolerances

Parents and carers may decide to exclude certain foods from their children's diet, as they believe they are linked to **food allergies** or **intolerances**. A food allergy occurs when there is a reaction to certain food, and this happens every time that food is eaten. The body is actually producing antibodies to 'fight' the food and these can be detected in a blood test.

Physical signs of an allergic reaction might include a rash, breathing difficulties, swelling of the lips or throat, or hyperactivity.

A food intolerance also produces a reaction every time a food is eaten, but antibodies are not produced. However, a food intolerance can still provoke similar reactions to a food allergy.

In children, the incidence of food-related allergies and intolerances is very low, and therefore self-diagnosis is not recommended. Removing certain foods from a child's diet without proper medical advice could lead to under-nutrition. Any parent or carer who suggests that their child has an intolerance or allergy should be advised to seek confirmation from their doctor.

Medical advice will also determine whether a reaction to a food is the result of an allergy or an intolerance.

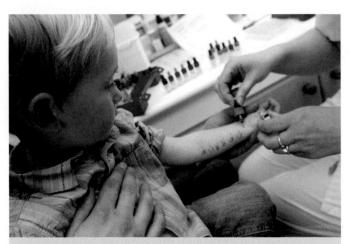

This nurse is administering an allergy test. Parents and carers should seek medical advice if they suspect their child has a food allergy or intolerance.

Key terms

Food allergy – when the body has an abnormal reaction to a food or a component of a food.

Food intolerance – when the body is hypersensitive to a food or a component of food; there is a reaction but the reason for this reaction is not always clear.

Foods that might cause reactions

Cow's milk, wheat and eggs are linked with allergies, and therefore babies should not be given them until they are at least 6 months (except cow's milk, which should not be given as a main drink until 1 year). They should then be introduced in small quantities and one at a time so any reactions can be seen. If there is a history of allergies in the family it is possible that they may be allergic as well. Egg yolk is more digestible than egg white, so this is often given first.

Cow's milk should not be used as the main drink until 1 year because of its low iron content, but it can be used in food preparation after 6 months. Once a baby starts having cow's milk, they should be given whole milk, not semi-skimmed or skimmed. Babies need a lot of energy for their size and so energy-rich foods are important.

Goat's milk and sheep's milk can also cause allergic reactions. Goat's milk is low in folic acid, one of the most important vitamins. These milks need to be boiled and cooled before use if they are not pasteurised.

Nuts should not be given to babies or children under 5 because they could choke on them. Finely ground nuts may be given after 6 months.

Food additives are used in ready-made foods, which we tend to eat a lot of these days due to our busy lifestyles. Manufacturers use additives to make foods last longer as well as to improve the appearance and flavour of foods. Food additives can have a negative effect on young children by contributing to allergies and hyperactivity. Therefore, it is wise to try to reduce the amount of foods that contain artificial additives in a young child's diet.

Restrictions due to social, cultural or religious reasons

Many communities are made up of people from different cultures and religions, each with their own customs. Many of these customs relate to food. Most have particular foods linked to festivals or dates of religious significance. Sometimes this means that a food is forbidden, for different reasons.

Table 15.8 outlines some food restrictions linked to different cultures.

If you are working with children from cultures that have rules relating to food, it is important that you fully understand their dietary limitations and that you respect and follow them.

Table 15.8 Food restrictions relating to different cultures and religions

Religion and restrictions	Special food practices	Food preparation
Judaism • Do not eat pork. • Only eat fish with fins and scales. • Do not eat shellfish. • Do not eat foods containing meat and milk at the same meal.	• Do not prepare food on the Sabbath (Saturday). • There should be six hours between eating meat and dairy foods.	• Meat and poultry must be kosher – animals are killed in a particular way to drain the maximum amount of blood. • Separate cooking equipment must be used for meat and dairy products.

continued

Table 15.8 (continued)

Religion and restrictions	Special food practices	Food preparation
Islam • Do not eat blood. • Do not eat pork or pork-related products. • Do not consume alcohol. • Only eat with the right hand – the left is considered unclean.	• Ramadan is a period of fasting during which Muslims do not eat between sunrise and sunset – they eat light meals during the hours of darkness. • Ramadan lasts for one month and the timing varies from year to year.	• Animals must be ritually slaughtered with a blow to the head, and certain words must be spoken while this happens. • Meat slaughtered in this way is called halal.
Hinduism • Do not kill or eat any animals. • Do not eat cheese prepared in Western cultures. • Hindus are usually lacto-vegetarians. • Strict Hindus are vegan.	• Society is based on **castes**. • Hindus from upper castes cannot eat with those from lower castes.	• Ritual bathing is carried out and clean clothes are put on before food is prepared.

Key term

Caste – a system of dividing society into classes or different social groups.

Assessment practice 15.1   3A1.P1 | 3A1.M1

Produce a booklet for new parents that explains the importance of nutrition for children's health and development.

In the booklet, discuss the extent to which children's health and development can be affected by their diet. Make sure you give examples and refer to expert guidance on nutrients, portion size and the prevention of dental decay.

A2 Understand the role of the adult in encouraging children to develop healthy eating habits

Healthy eating habits are formed from the moment a child starts to eat solid food and can impact on an individual's health throughout their life. Therefore, it is important that children form healthy eating habits early on. There are many ways you can help and support children to do this as you will read about in this section. It is important that you work closely with parents and/or carers.

Helping children develop healthy eating habits

Children's food preferences begin to develop between the ages of 1 and 5. Therefore, it is important at this time to encourage children to try as many different foods as possible. This will allow them to experience different tastes and textures.

Parents and carers may not eat a variety of foods for different reasons. Some families are on low incomes and may have access to a smaller range of foods, therefore children may not have a suitably balanced diet. Others may follow particular diets from personal choice, for example, being a vegan, or for health reasons, such as having coeliac disease. In these cases, it is important that parents give children foods that they may not eat themselves to make sure they have a balanced diet.

Regular meal patterns are established in the early years and, as part of this, children's eating patterns should fit in with those of the family as this helps them develop social skills. Structured eating patterns will help children become used to eating regular meals with nutritious snacks in between. Children do need to snack in between their main meals to meet their nutritional and energy requirements. These snacks should be savoury, such as raw vegetables or cheese, rather than sweet – although fresh fruit is acceptable. Drinks should not contain sugar.

Children's diets need to be balanced. This means that they must contain all the necessary nutrients in the correct proportions. The Food Standards Agency has provided the information in Figure 15.7 as a set of guidelines for what constitutes a healthy and balanced diet.

Healthy eating guidelines should be applied with caution. A low-fat or high-fibre diet would prevent a child from obtaining the energy and nutrients they need. However, a diet that is low in salt and sugar is advisable as it develops good eating habits and prevents a child getting used to sugary foods which can lead to tooth decay.

Attitudes towards food

There are many factors that can affect children's attitudes to food.

Rewards and treats

When food is offered as a reward for something, such as 'being good' or going through an experience that may cause anxiety, such as going to the dentist, it is often sweet food such as cakes, chocolate or sweets. Using food as a reward is tempting and may work in the short term but it may also lead to weight problems later in life. It can make a child think of sweets as 'nice' foods and other foods such as vegetables as 'not-so-nice' foods.

If you want to use food as a reward, try making fruit a reward from an early age or, better still, use outings such as trips to the park or to the beach as rewards instead.

Use the eatwell plate to help you get the balance right. It shows how much of what you eat should come from each food group.

Fruit and vegetables

Bread, rice, potatoes, pasta and other starchy foods

Meat, fish, eggs, beans and other non-dairy sources of protein

Foods and drinks high in fat and/or sugar

Milk and diary foods

Department of Health in association with the Welsh Government, the Scottish Government and the Food Standards Agency in Northern Ireland.

Figure 15.7 The eatwell plate (© Crown copyright 2011)

Association with love and nurturing

Food is often associated with love and nurturing. Many family occasions are celebrated with food, and this food is not always healthy – for example, cakes for occasions such as birthdays and Christmas, or chocolate eggs at Easter. Many parents feel that being able to provide these types of foods for their family is a sign of being a good parent.

However, it is important to separate food as an essential care-giving task from a means of showing love. Love should be demonstrated in other ways, such as hugging and through words.

Insistence on finishing food

Parents sometimes believe it is important that children finish everything on their plate. Some parents insist on children doing this before they can have a dessert or before they are allowed to get down from the table. This may be as a result of their own childhood, if their own parents insisted on the same. They see food that is left as a waste.

Generally, children will eat what they need. Insisting that they finish what is on their plate means that they learn to monitor how much they eat by external factors rather than by internal cues such as how hungry they feel and what they actually need for good health. It can lead to eating more calories than they need, and therefore to obesity. It can also make mealtimes quite stressful for children, when they should be enjoyable.

A better way may be to involve children in serving themselves and making it clear that they should only take what they can eat.

It is also important to remember that in some cultures it is seen as a custom to leave a little bit of food on your plate.

Working with parents and carers to develop healthy eating habits

There are many reasons why children choose the foods they eat, but for many children, the main influence on their diet and eating habits will be their parents and/or carers and their family (see Figure 15.8).

It can be difficult to advise parents and carers on how to eat healthily without causing offence. You need to have a good understanding of the family situation in order to do this effectively.

For example, a family living on a low income may have a limited choice of food because of their budget. A low income not only affects what you can buy but also other issues such as what transport is available. Food is cheaper and there is a wider selection in large supermarkets, which tend to be out of town and so may be inaccessible to some families. Families on low incomes may have to shop in local shops where prices are higher and there is less choice. This will impact on a child's diet.

If the parents or carers suffer from disabilities or medical conditions such as arthritis, the child's diet may be affected. Arthritis, for example, makes it difficult to carry out tasks that require fine motor skills such as preparing and cooking food. This may lead to the family relying on convenience foods, which often lack nutrients, for a large part of their diet.

Healthy food choices will also be affected by parents' and carers' own knowledge of food and cooking as well as their willingness to prepare a healthy diet. Their own diets may be influenced by the jobs they have. If they work long hours, they may not want to spend a lot of time preparing fresh foods when they get home and may opt for a convenience meal instead.

The foods available locally will also impact on food choice. Regional variations mean different areas have different fresh produce. For example, in areas of the country where fruit is grown, this will be readily available during the summer season. If you live near the coast, fresh fish is usually obtainable but in other areas it may not be.

If parents and carers are able to find fresh foods that are in season, these are generally cheaper. However, preservation techniques and the improved transport system mean that many foods are available all year round.

When advising parents and carers, it is important to do so with sensitivity. You may decide to make healthy eating information readily available for them through leaflets or websites. You may also consider holding a healthy eating information session to encourage parents and carers to share tips on helping their children to eat healthily with each other. It is quite common for nurseries and schools to send home information on healthy lunchboxes and to have a healthy eating policy, so this would provide an avenue for offering guidance and advice to all parents and carers.

Assessment practice 15.2   3A1.P2 | 3A2.P4

Many early years settings provide advice to parents and carers on ensuring their children have a healthy diet.

1 Devise a leaflet that a nursery could give to parents and carers to highlight how they can work with practitioners to meet their child's nutritional needs.

2 Explain how adults can encourage children to develop healthy eating habits.

Reflect

Make a list of all the food you ate yesterday. Write down why you ate the foods you did. How do they fit with Figure 15.8?

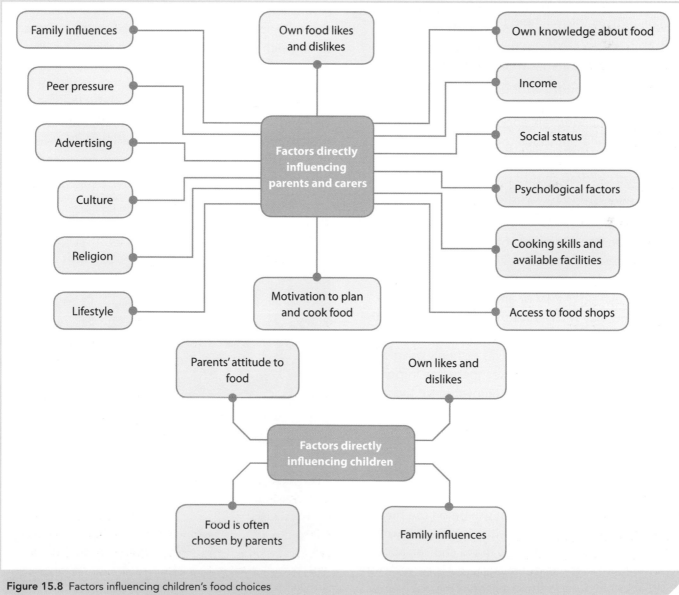

Figure 15.8 Factors influencing children's food choices

Case study

Feeding a family

Nadia is a single parent with two children aged 5 and 7. She is on a limited income and is concerned that their diets are not as healthy as they could be. Both children attend school and have school dinners.

1 What factors might affect what the children eat?

2 Nadia's 7-year-old daughter wants to take a packed lunch to school. How could Nadia ensure that she has a healthy lunch?

3 What advice would you give Nadia to help her provide a balanced diet for her children on a budget?

■ Encouraging enjoyment of food

Preparing meals can be stressful, as it takes skill and organisation to bring a meal together at the right time. However, starting children off with good eating habits will lead to a lifetime of healthy eating. This is why it is important that mealtimes are enjoyable for children, as this will help them develop a good relationship with food.

You can make mealtimes more enjoyable by making sure you have enough time to enjoy the experience. This means being able to sit down with children, eat in a relaxed manner, talk about different things and experience different foods together. A rushed meal will be a stressful one and certainly not a fun one. Adults and children should eat the same foods, and this will also ensure that you are not spending lots of time preparing different food for the children.

Talking is an important part of the mealtime experience and distractions will affect that. It is difficult to hold a conversation with others if they have one eye on the TV or are texting on their phone. You may wish to set the rule of 'no TV' at the table. Eating together gives you an opportunity to communicate with children. This not only develops their social skills but also makes them feel important, making the experience more enjoyable for them.

Encouraging independence through self-serving

Getting children involved in the meal will help them become more interested in their food. While you may not want them to decide what will be on the menu all the time (you might end up with chips at every meal), you could encourage them to make choices about how the food that has been prepared is served. You could also encourage them to serve themselves, as

this promotes independence and also helps ensure that they take the amount of food they feel they can eat.

Adults eating with children

At mealtimes adults act as role models for children. Adults and children should eat the same foods, and this will encourage children to expand their tastes. Eating with children helps to teach them social skills and good manners – these habits are likely to stay with them for the rest of their lives. Therefore, it is important that adults fully participate in the meal as well and are not distracted by texting or reading at the table, for instance. They should be fully involved in discussions as this is an opportunity to spend 'quality time' with children.

This family look like they are enjoying their meal – sit down with children and create a relaxed atmosphere.

Involving children in food preparation

Being involved with food provides children with many learning opportunities. Activities that involve food can develop physical, social, emotional, numeracy and language skills. Children can be encouraged to be part of the meal planning and then the shopping for food. The discussion and counting involved develops language and maths skills almost without children realising. It also gets them interested in food so they are more likely to want to eat it.

Cooking

Cooking is fun and you can get them involved in cooking at an early age. Children find cooking exciting, as it gives them quick results. The fact that they can eat the results of their efforts – usually very quickly after finishing the task – adds to this enjoyment. Encouraging children to cook gives them lots of opportunities to discover things for themselves. Children can gain a great sense of achievement from cooking because it is so immediate.

Activity

Increase the fun aspect of cooking by encouraging children to look for 'faces' in the fruit and vegetables they are using. Raisins have faces, as do potatoes and carrots, as a result of the indentations that occur naturally on their surfaces.

1 Encourage children to look for faces as they shop for and prepare food.
2 Talk about the 'strange' names some foods have, such as 'spring onions', which could lead to bouncing around the kitchen.
3 Look for opportunities to explore unusual foods, such as purple carrots and Jerusalem artichokes.
4 What other ways can you think of to make cooking fun?

Cooking can offer many opportunities for learning. It encourages creativity, and develops self-confidence as well as self-esteem. You can talk about where our food comes from and what is healthy food and why, and what is not.

When planning to cook with children, you will need to think about safety issues, particularly when cooking with very young children. This may mean that you need to do more of the preparation if the child is too young to use a knife, for example, or to stir hot foods. Nevertheless, you can still make sure they are fully involved in the process of stirring and mixing or putting the mixture into tins.

Be ready for a mess – children are likely to be messy when preparing food but this is part of the fun. They can also be involved in the clearing up. It is important that they do this, as it is one of the least enjoyable parts of the cooking process.

If you are making something that cooks in the oven, you can use the opportunity to discuss how they think the mixture will change in terms of appearance, texture and taste as it goes through the cooking process. You will need to adjust your language to suit the age of the child but this is a good opportunity for learning. It also starts them off developing a skill they will use for the rest of their lives.

Activity

1 Find a simple recipe that you could make with children.
2 Go through each of the stages of the recipe and explain what learning opportunities there might be for children.

Growing food

Children like to be involved in growing food that they can then prepare, cook and eat. Again, growing food provides lots of opportunities for learning as it gives them the opportunity to experience the natural world and learn where food comes from.

Many nurseries and primary schools have a growing area. You do not need a traditional garden or vegetable patch to grow food. You can grow small amounts of food in tubs or window boxes, or even on a window sill.

Growing food from seed can take time and therefore it will be important to hold children's interest by looking at the progress regularly.

It may be an idea to start with a food that grows quickly, and cress is a good example. You can grow cress inside on the window sill, where children can see it change.

You might also consider buying plants from a garden centre to reduce the waiting time. Also, some plants are easier to grow if you start with a plant, rather than a seed, and success is important in maintaining children's interest in the first instance.

These children are enjoying being in their setting's growing area.

If you do want to grow plants from seed, consider the following points when deciding what seeds to grow with children:

- Choose plants that are easy to sow with large seeds, such as courgettes, as this will make it easier for children to handle them.
- Choose seeds that germinate quickly to keep children's attention.

- Choose plants you can grow in the same place as you sow the seeds so you do not have to transplant seedlings.
- Choose plants that will crop quickly.
- Choose plants that require minimal care other than watering and feeding.
- Choose plants that will continue to crop over a period of time.

Plants you may want to consider include courgettes, tomatoes, salad leaves and strawberries.

Assessment practice 15.3   3A2.P3 | 3A1.M2 | 3A.D1 | 3A.D2

Write an article for a magazine for early years professionals explaining how children's attitudes to food are influenced both at home and in the early years setting. In it:

- analyse how working in partnership with parents in early years settings can contribute to the provision of food that encourages children's health and development
- evaluate the extent to which adults in early years settings could contribute to children's health and development through the provision of food
- recommend how a setting could improve their contribution to children's healthy eating habits.

B Understand the role of the adult in preparing and serving food safely

When preparing food for children, it is important that this is carried out in a hygienic way. Unhygienic food preparation methods can lead to food poisoning. This can be severe if it happens to vulnerable groups, such as children, who may not be strong enough to cope with the illness. Therefore, it is essential that you follow good hygiene practices, whether you are preparing food in a setting or in the home.

Responsibility to comply with food safety legislation

Anyone who prepares food for others has a responsibility to ensure that food is safe to eat and

will not cause food poisoning. This means that anyone preparing food must meet current food hygiene regulations. Food poisoning can make children extremely ill and, in some cases, it can be fatal. Therefore, it is essential that you are fully up to date with hygiene practices and follow them effectively. Food hygiene regulations may differ in other countries so it is important that you follow those relevant to the situation you are in.

Food Safety Act 1990

The Food Safety Act 1990 aims to protect consumers by:

- preventing illness from the consumption of food

- preventing consumers from being misled as to the nature of the food they are purchasing
- ensuring that all food produced for sale is safe to eat, of high quality and not misleadingly presented.

This Act made it illegal to sell food that has been contaminated or adulterated or is unfit for human consumption. This is why sell-by and use-by dates are used on pre-prepared or packaged food. It is also an offence to label or advertise food in a way that misleads the customer. The Act made it possible to prosecute companies and individuals who do not follow it.

Food Safety (General Food Hygiene) Regulations

These are regulations made under the Food Safety Act 1990. They apply to all types of food and food businesses but do not cover domestic preparation in the home. They do cover non-commercial activities such as charity events.

These regulations detail standards that must be followed in premises where food is being prepared. These standards state that food premises must be kept clean and in good repair. There are also regulations about design and layout, hand-washing facilities and toilets, hot and cold running water, ventilation, lighting and changing facilities.

Activity

The Food Safety Regulations state that there must be changing facilities away from the food preparation areas where staff preparing food can change from their outdoor clothes. In addition, the toilet facilities must not open on to the food preparation area. There should also be a separate hand-washing basin from the basins used for food preparation.

Why do you think these regulations exist?

The Regulations also explain the requirements for food preparation areas. There are specific requirements for rooms in which food is being prepared that include how the ceilings, floors and windows are built and what facilities are needed for cleaning utensils and equipment as well as food.

There are specific guidelines on waste disposal, as poor disposal of waste can lead to food contamination.

They also outline how different types of food should be stored to reduce the risk of contamination.

In addition, the regulations give guidelines for staff preparing and serving food. This includes ensuring that staff follow good personal hygiene rules and are trained in these. They also make clear that staff should not work if they are ill.

Safe working practices when preparing food

Children are particularly vulnerable if they suffer from food poisoning, because they are less able to cope with the symptoms than healthy adults. Preventing food poisoning is easy if you understand how bacteria multiply. If you understand this, then you can easily take steps to reduce the risk of poisoning.

How do food poisoning bacteria multiply?

To prevent the growth of harmful bacteria, you need to understand the conditions in which they grow and multiply. To grow and reproduce, bacteria require a number of conditions occurring at the same time. Figure 15.9 outlines these conditions.

Bacteria also need time to multiply; however, once the conditions in Figure 15.9 are met they multiply very fast. Bacteria multiply by a process called binary fission every 20 minutes. This means that every 20 minutes the number of bacteria doubles. Therefore, the longer the bacteria are in positive conditions for growth, the more they will reproduce.

It is therefore essential to wash your hands thoroughly before handling food and after handling raw meat. You should also ensure any cuts you may have are covered.

Reflect

Most of the food we buy in supermarkets is preserved in some way so that it lasts longer and does not suffer from decay. Food might be frozen, canned, pickled or dehydrated. How do these methods prevent food-poisoning bacteria from growing?

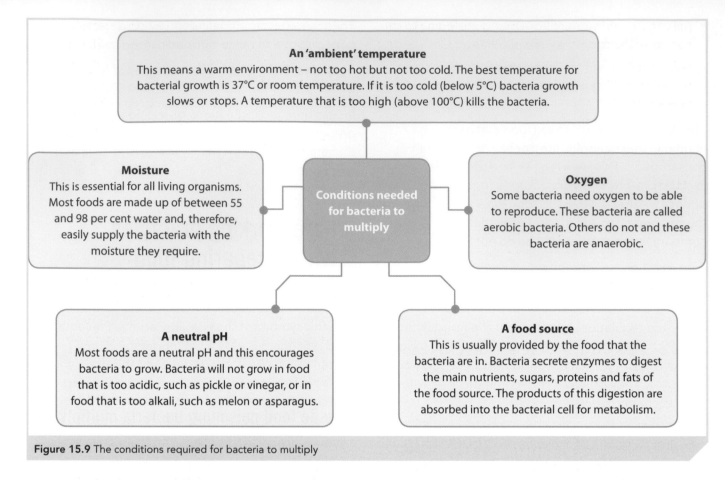

An 'ambient' temperature
This means a warm environment – not too hot but not too cold. The best temperature for bacterial growth is 37°C or room temperature. If it is too cold (below 5°C) bacteria growth slows or stops. A temperature that is too high (above 100°C) kills the bacteria.

Moisture
This is essential for all living organisms. Most foods are made up of between 55 and 98 per cent water and, therefore, easily supply the bacteria with the moisture they require.

Conditions needed for bacteria to multiply

Oxygen
Some bacteria need oxygen to be able to reproduce. These bacteria are called aerobic bacteria. Others do not and these bacteria are anaerobic.

A neutral pH
Most foods are a neutral pH and this encourages bacteria to grow. Bacteria will not grow in food that is too acidic, such as pickle or vinegar, or in food that is too alkali, such as melon or asparagus.

A food source
This is usually provided by the food that the bacteria are in. Bacteria secrete enzymes to digest the main nutrients, sugars, proteins and fats of the food source. The products of this digestion are absorbed into the bacterial cell for metabolism.

Figure 15.9 The conditions required for bacteria to multiply

Preparing food for children with allergies or intolerances

When preparing food for children who suffer from food allergies or intolerances, you have to consider other factors in addition to preventing food poisoning. Incorrect food choice or preparation can lead to illness.

- Nut allergies – children with nut allergies are very sensitive to any trace of nuts. Therefore, it is important that you do not prepare or serve any food with nuts in, even if it is not being served to the person with the nut allergy, as they may suffer a reaction just by being close to nuts.

- Coeliac disease – if a child suffers from coeliac disease they cannot eat foods containing wheat. Wheat causes damage to their small intestine, so food is not digested properly. This will result in diarrhoea and malnutrition, as nutrients from food are not absorbed. People with coeliac disease cannot eat many common foods that are typically made from wheat, such as bread, biscuits and cakes. Wheat is also found in many processed foods as a thickening agent as well as being used

to coat foods such as fishfingers. When preparing food for a coeliac, most basic foods, such as meat, fruit, vegetables, cheese, potatoes and rice are suitable but other baked products need to be made with suitable flour, such as rice flour.

Research

To find out more about coeliac disease, visit the Coeliac UK website. You can access this website by going to www.pearsonhotlinks.co.uk and searching for the ISBN of this title: 9781447970972.

- Lactose intolerance – some children suffer from lactose intolerance. Lactose is the sugar found in milk. The body does not produce enough of the enzyme lactase which is needed to digest milk. As the milk sugar cannot be digested as it should be, it passes into the large intestine, where it causes irritation, pain and diarrhoea. Children with lactose intolerance need to avoid cow's milk. However, they can usually drink goat's or ewe's milk as these are low in lactose. Children with lactose intolerance will not necessarily have to avoid all milk and dairy products, as usually small amounts can be consumed without side effects. Cheese and yoghurt can usually be eaten as well, as they only contain a small amount of lactose and so do not cause any symptoms.

Procedures for safe food practice

The main reasons for food poisoning are bad temperature control or food being stored incorrectly. Food poisoning often happens because food is prepared too far in advance, cooled too slowly, stored incorrectly – for example, at room temperature – not reheated sufficiently or incorrectly thawed.

Food can also be contaminated with pathogenic micro-organisms or the toxic chemicals produced by micro-organisms. This is usually caused by poor food hygiene practices.

Did you know?

Some foods are naturally poisonous because they contain toxins, for example, some mushrooms, and red kidney beans (if not cooked correctly). Food can also be contaminated with toxic chemicals such as lead, copper or agricultural pesticides and herbicides. Also, chemicals such as disinfectants may contaminate food during growth, storage, preparation and/or cooking.

When food is fresh and being stored, or when it is being prepared for cooking and eating, it can be contaminated with bacteria. There are a number of simple actions that you can take to reduce the risk of food poisoning.

Personal hygiene

Personal hygiene is very simple but can also be easily forgotten when you are busy. Remember the following things.

- Wash hands thoroughly before preparing food and between handling different foods.

- All humans carry the staphylococcus bacteria on their skin and in their nose and throat. This is why you should not touch your face, hair or nose when preparing food.
- Always cover your hair or tie long hair back to keep it from falling in food – this is a physical contaminant.
- Do not cough or sneeze over food, as the droplets in the air from the sneeze or cough can transfer food-poisoning bacteria directly on to food.
- Always wash hands after using the lavatory. Salmonella is found in the human gut and therefore, bodily fluids can be a direct and indirect source of food poisoning. Salmonella can live for up to three hours on unwashed hands.
- Do not smoke when preparing food. As well as the potential for ash to drop in the food, you will constantly touch your face as you smoke the cigarette.
- If you are ill, you should not prepare food for others, as you may inadvertently contaminate food.

Food storage

Storing food correctly is important to ensure that bacteria are not given a chance to start to multiply. To prevent this happening, you should ensure that you remove the conditions in which bacteria multiply easily, as described previously. In addition:
- always choose foods that look fresh
- choose foods within their use-by dates
- use a cool bag to transport cold and frozen foods from the supermarket to home to prevent its temperature rising to one at which bacteria might start to multiply
- put frozen and chilled foods away immediately after purchase to keep them at their correct temperatures
- make sure the fridge is between 0 and 5°C and the freezer below −18°C
- store cooked and raw food separately in the fridge as raw food can contaminate cooked food
- store cooked meat above raw meat to avoid blood dripping on to cooked meat or other food that will contaminate them.

Food preparation

Good food preparation is essential to ensure that any bacteria are killed or that the conditions in which bacteria thrive are removed. Make sure you follow the personal hygiene guidelines. Pets should not be allowed in the kitchen, as they can carry bacteria.

When preparing food, remember the following things.

- Eat foods by their use-by dates – these are there as a guide to freshness.
- Always work in a clean area and clean the work surfaces and utensils as you go – this will reduce the risk of cross-contamination.
- Always prepare different foods in different areas – for example, fresh vegetables may have soil on them so they should be prepared away from other foods to ensure that the soil does not contaminate them.
- Use separate utensils to prepare raw and cooked foods.
- Thoroughly defrost frozen food before cooking it.
- Make sure cooked foods reach a temperature of over 63°C – they should be piping hot.
- Check meat and poultry with a food thermometer to make sure the right temperature has been reached. Juices should run clear.
- Keep hot foods hot and cold foods cold.
- Do not keep food warm for long periods of time, and particularly not between 5 and 63°C, as bacteria multiplies rapidly at this temperature range.
- Cool foods as quickly as possible and within 1.5 hours – cover and store in the fridge or freezer.

Heating and reheating food

Heating or reheating food has the potential to cause food poisoning if not carried out thoroughly. It is essential to remember that the food should be piping hot before it is served – over 63°C. Lukewarm food is an excellent breeding ground for bacteria.

If using pre-prepared food, follow the instructions carefully.

Cleaning routines

Effective cleaning is important to reduce the risk of food poisoning. Cleaning removes dirt, food residues

and grease, all of which could attract bacteria. Cleaning may use:

- detergent – a mix of chemicals which will remove the grease, dirt and food particles but not kill germs or food poisoning bacteria
- disinfectant – this will reduce any micro-organisms to a safe level. This is either done with hot water or chemicals or a combination of both.

Cleaning should be carried out in a systematic way, working from clean to dirty surfaces. It is important that you use the correct equipment and chemicals to ensure effective cleaning. You should wear different clothes for cleaning the kitchen and toilet areas. Water should be changed frequently, as soon as it looks dirty, to ensure effective cleaning. Cloths should be disinfected after use.

Assessment practice 15.4　　　3B.P5

Following food hygiene guidelines is essential if you want to prepare food that is fit to eat and will not cause ill health. However, in a busy work environment, it is easy to forget these practices.

1 Prepare a poster outlining food hygiene and safety tips, which could be displayed in a food preparation area in an early years setting.

2 Produce a section for an employees' handbook that gives further information to supplement the poster.

Further reading and resources

Barasi, M. (2007) *Nutrition at a Glance*, London: Wiley-Blackwell.

Lean, M. (2006) *Fox and Cameron's Food Science, Nutrition and Health* (7th edition), London: CRC Press.

Websites
Baby Centre: www.babycentre.co.uk

Baby Weaning: www.babyweaning.com

Food Standards Agency: www.food.gov.uk

Healthy Food Healthy Planet: www.healthyfoodhealthyplanet.org

KidsHealth®: www.kidshealth.org

Ready for work?

Seb Bevan Deputy manager of a day nursery

The daily routine of the nursery includes snacks and lunch to ensure the children keep their energy levels up. We believe that it is important to provide healthy food at different times of the day. We always provide a cooked meal at lunchtime made from fresh ingredients. Many of our children eat their main meal with us in the middle of the day and therefore it is important that it is nutritious and healthy.

Knowledge of nutrition is essential to ensure that we plan healthy meals. It means we can be sure that the meals the children eat are contributing to a balanced diet.

Mealtimes are also important social occasions for the nursery. We always sit down together to eat. The nursery staff join the children as they can model good manners. Lunchtimes are another opportunity to develop language and social skills.

The meal offers the opportunity for children to develop confidence serving each other – they really enjoy getting involved. Eating with other children also encourages them to try new flavours or foods.

Sometimes we involve the children in preparing a part of the meal or one of the snacks we have mid-morning or mid-afternoon. We may use some of the vegetables we have grown with the children in our garden and this adds extra interest to the activity.

Anyone who works with children should take advantage of the opportunities that using food as a learning tool can bring.

Skills for practice

Caring skills

Practise doing these things to improve your skills with food.

- Develop a list of quick, healthy, nutritious snacks and main meals that you could prepare for a preschool child.

- Plan a food-based activity that will not involve cooking, which you could carry out with a 4-year-old child. Try making sandwiches that you then cut into different shapes or, as a treat, cornflake cakes (children just need to stir the mixture). Watch how the children respond to the activity and listen to the language they use. Think about how you could develop their learning.

- Sit with a child during lunch. Help them to develop their fine motor skills with the cutlery.

Tips for weaning

- Go at the baby's pace – starting solid food is a change for them as they are used to a totally liquid diet. It will take time.

- Try not to rush a baby when they are eating or force them to eat more than they want. It is important to make eating a time to chat and enjoy each other's company. If food is refused, call an end to the meal.

- Try to use foods that the family is eating as soon as possible. This will help the baby learn to like a range of ordinary foods and will help avoid a fussy eater in the future.

- Fresh foods, puréed or mashed, should form the basis of a baby's diet. Use commercially prepared baby foods when in a hurry or as a convenience but not as the main component.

Introduction

In this unit you will look at how to meet the varying needs of children under 3 years, including their nutritional requirements. You will also look at the skills and qualities you need to work with children in this age range. It often takes a particular type of person to work enthusiastically and sensitively with children under 3 years. It is essential to understand child development and the specific needs of this age group. A good starting point is to revise your child development knowledge for children aged 0 to 3 that you covered in Unit 1.

Assessment: You will be assessed by a series of assignments set by your teacher/tutor.

Learning aims

In this unit you will:

A   understand how to meet the nutritional needs of children under 3 years

B1 understand how to meet the specific developmental needs of babies under 1 year

B2 understand how to meet the specific developmental needs of children from 1 to 2 years

B3 understand how to meet the specific developmental needs of children from 2 to 3 years

C   understand the skills and qualities needed to work with children under 3 years.

> Working with children under 3 years is hard work but immensely interesting and satisfying. Their rate of development in all areas is considerable as they move from being quite vulnerable to gaining independence and confidence. The speed of their growth and development can be quite breathtaking and one of the many joys of working with this age group is to share with them the many changes that take place.
>
> Penny Tassoni

Working With Children Under 3 Years

16

BTEC
Assessment Zone

This table shows you what you must do in order to achieve a **Pass**, **Merit** or **Distinction** grade, and where you can find activities to help you.

Assessment criteria

Pass	Merit	Distinction
Learning aim A: Understand how to meet the nutritional needs of children under 3 years		
3A.P1 I&CT Explain the nutritional needs of children from birth to 3 years of age. **Assessment practice 16.1**	**3A.M1** Discuss the importance of ensuring the nutritional needs of children from birth to 3 years are met. **Assessment practice 16.1**	**3A.D1** Evaluate how an early years setting provides for the nutritional needs of children under 3 years, making recommendations for improvements. **Assessment practice 16.1**
3A.P2 Describe the role of adults in early years settings in the preparation and feeding of children from birth up to 2 years. **Assessment practice 16.1**		
3A.P3 English I&CT Plan a menu for one day in an early years setting to meet the nutritional and energy needs of children aged 2 to 3 years. **Assessment practice 16.1**		
Learning aim B1: Understand how to meet the specific developmental needs of babies under 1 year **Learning aim B2: Understand how to meet the specific developmental needs of children from 1 to 2 years** **Learning aim B3: Understand how to meet the specific developmental needs of children from 2 to 3 years**		
3B1.P4 Describe how adults in early years settings respond to the individual needs of babies in care routines while meeting the needs of others in the group. **Assessment practice 16.2**	**3B1.M2** Analyse the ways in which adults in early years settings can meet the specific developmental needs of babies under 1 year old. **Assessment practice 16.2**	**3B.D2** Evaluate the effectiveness of creating an environment for children from birth to 3 years that supports and promotes different areas of development and learning. **Assessment practice 16.5**
3B1.P5 Explain the features of a sensory environment in an early years setting for babies under 1 year. **Assessment practice 16.2**		
3B2.P6 Describe how to create an environment in an early years setting for children aged from 1 to 2 years where they feel secure and supported in active exploration. **Assessment practice 16.3**	**3B2.M3** Analyse how the environment and communication aid the development and learning of children aged from 1 to 2 years using examples. **Assessment practice 16.3**	
3B2.P7 Explain the role of adults in supporting the development of communication of children from 1 to 2 years. **Assessment practice 16.3**		

continued

Assessment criteria (continued)

Pass	Merit	Distinction
3B3.P8 Describe accessible activities and routines which involve children aged 2 to 3 years to help promote their social, emotional and developmental needs. **Assessment practice 16.4**	**3B3.M4** Analyse how adults and accessible activities and routines contribute to the social and emotional development and positive behaviour of children from 2 to 3 years. **Assessment practice 16.4**	
3B3.P9 Explain the role of adults in promoting positive behaviour with children from 2 to 3 years. **Assessment practice 16.4**		
Learning aim C: Understand the skills and qualities needed to work with children under 3 years		
3C.P10 Explain the skills and qualities needed for work in early years settings with children under 3 years. **Assessment practice 16.5**	**3C.M5** Analyse the importance of the adult in presenting a professional and positive role model to children under 3 years in an early years setting. **Assessment practice 16.5**	

English English Functional Skills signposting   **I&CT** Information and Communication Technology Functional Skills signposting

How you will be assessed

This unit will be assessed by a series of internally assessed tasks set by your teacher/tutor. Throughout this unit you will find assessment practice activities that will help you work towards your assessment. Completing these activities will not mean that you have achieved a particular grade, but you will have carried out useful research or preparation that will be relevant when it comes to your final assignment.

In order for you to carry out the tasks in your assignment, it is important that you check you have met all the Pass grading criteria. You can do this as you work your way through the assignment.

If you are hoping to gain a Merit or Distinction, you should also make sure that you present the information in your assignment in the style that is required by the relevant assessment criteria. For example, Merit criteria will require you to discuss and analyse, and Distinction criteria will require you to evaluate.

The assignment set by your teacher/tutor will consist of a number of tasks designed to meet the criteria in the assessment criteria table. This is likely to consist of a written assignment but may also include activities such as:

- a good practice guide
- a presentation to your peers and teacher/tutor
- observations and case studies.

Getting started

Make a list of ways in which adults can support 2-year-olds. When you have finished this unit, see if you can add to this list.

A Understand how to meet the nutritional needs of children under 3 years

The first three years of life are characterised by significant physical growth and development. This is made possible partly by the nutrition that babies receive. In this section, you will look at the nutritional requirements of children in the first three years and how to meet them.

Nutritional requirements in the first six months

In the first six months of life, babies' nutrition is gained from milk. This will be either human breast milk or formula milk.

> ### Link
>
> Go to Unit 15, Section A1 to find more information about why bottle feeding or breastfeeding may be chosen.

Formula milk

There are different types of formula milk, and in order to meet babies' nutritional needs it is important that they are given the correct type and quantities.

Types of formula milk

The majority of formula milks are made from modified cow's milk, to which vitamins and minerals are added. The composition of a formula milk – the amounts of proteins, fats, minerals and vitamins it contains – will depend on the age of the child.

A good starting point is to understand that formula milk is available in two forms:

- ready-to-feed – a sterilised, made-up formula sold in cartons. This can be given straight to the baby at room temperature or warmed up
- powdered – this has to be made up by adding water.

Preterm babies

Wherever possible, human breast milk is given to preterm babies. Where this is not available, a formula specially made for preterm babies is available. This contains more protein and fat than formula milk for full-term babies.

Newborn babies up to 6 months

Until they are 6 months old, babies should be given 'first' infant formula when they cannot be breastfed. First formula is whey-based and it is not recommended that other types of formula milk are used, unless under the guidance of a health professional. This formula is also thought to be sufficient for the first 12 months, after which babies can be given ordinary cow's milk as a drink.

Whey-based versus casein-based formula

While whey-based formula milk is recommended by health professionals, some parents choose to give their babies casein-based formula milks.

These milks are often aimed at hungrier babies and many parents believe that by giving them this type of formula milk, their baby will sleep for longer. This is disputed by health professionals.

Follow-on milks

These are formula milks that contain additional fat and protein. They are casein-based, but are not suited to the nutritional needs of babies under 6 months. Though they are suitable for babies over 6 months old, they are not considered necessary by health professionals.

Soya milk

Soya milk is made from soya beans. This type of formula milk is not recommended for babies unless advised by a doctor or health visitor. The usual reason for a baby to be given soya milk is because of an allergy. If you are working with a baby with a milk (lactose) allergy, you should never feed them any form of cow's milk, including formula.

How much formula milk should a baby have?

The amount of formula milk a baby should have depends on their weight. As a guide, use 150–200 ml per kg in 24 hours – so a newborn baby weighing 4 kg would need 600–800 ml in total per day. As young babies have small stomachs, this amount would be divided into several feeds. Most newborns feed every three hours at first, but after around six weeks they often settle into a four-hourly feeding pattern. However, it is best to feed on demand.

Research

Work out what type and how much formula milk a baby of 5 months weighing 7 kg would need in a day.

The advantages of breastfeeding

Health professionals, including health visitors, paediatricians and dieticians, recommend breastfeeding for babies in their first months of life. Reasons for this include:

- promoting attachment between baby and mother
- providing easily digestible milk, the composition of which adjusts according to the baby's needs and demands
- passing on antibodies from mother to baby, which strengthen the baby's immune system
- the provision of milk 'on tap' at just the right temperature.

Link

Go to Unit 15, Section A1 to find more information about the advantages of breastfeeding.

How to support breastfeeding mothers

It is known that breastfeeding is good for babies and so it is important that you find ways of supporting breastfeeding mothers. Some mothers will want to breastfeed their children when they are with you and others might want to express milk for a bottle that can be given later. There are several ways in which you can support breastfeeding mothers, as Figure 16.1 shows.

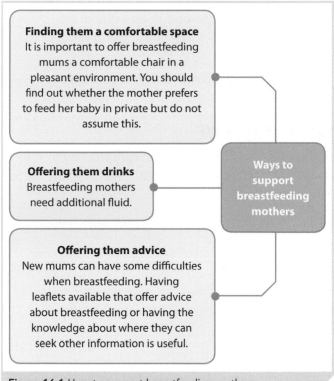

Finding them a comfortable space
It is important to offer breastfeeding mums a comfortable chair in a pleasant environment. You should find out whether the mother prefers to feed her baby in private but do not assume this.

Offering them drinks
Breastfeeding mothers need additional fluid.

Offering them advice
New mums can have some difficulties when breastfeeding. Having leaflets available that offer advice about breastfeeding or having the knowledge about where they can seek other information is useful.

Ways to support breastfeeding mothers

Figure 16.1 How to support breastfeeding mothers

Preparing and storing feeds

It is important that you know how to prepare and store feeds hygienically. This reduces the risk of a baby contracting food poisoning. The information that follows is based on guidelines that were current at the time of writing.

You should regularly check information and best practice relating to all aspects of infant feeding.

Sterilisation of equipment

When babies are bottle fed with infant formula or breast milk, it is important that the bottles and equipment used are sterilised first. This includes the bottles, teats and anything else that will be in direct contact with the milk. Before sterilising, you should:

- wash hands thoroughly using soap and hot water
- wash feeding and preparation equipment thoroughly in hot soapy water, using brushes for teats and bottles
- after washing feeding equipment, rinse it thoroughly under the tap.

Commercial sterilisers

Many settings will have commercial sterilisers. You should find out how to use these in accordance with the manufacturer's instructions.

Boiling method

Another method of sterilisation is by boiling. You can sterilise feeding equipment in boiling water but you must check first that the equipment is suitable for sterilising in this way. If it is, use the following method.

1 Fill a large pan with water.
2 Place the feeding equipment in the pan, making sure there are no air bubbles inside it.
3 Cover the pan with a lid and bring to the boil.
4 Boil the water for at least 10 minutes, making sure the pan does not boil dry.
5 Keep the pan covered until the equipment is needed.
6 Wash your hands thoroughly and clean the surface you will be using, before removing the equipment.

7 If the bottles are not being used immediately, assemble them with the teat and lid in place to prevent the inside of the sterilised bottle and the inside and outside of the teat from being contaminated.

Remember never to leave hot pans and liquid unattended. Make sure the area is safe to prevent burns and scalds.

Any unfinished milk needs to be thrown away at the end of the feed.

Preparation of powdered formula feed

After all of the equipment used to feed the baby has been sterilised, use the following steps to prepare a powdered formula feed.

1 Put on a clean apron. Wash your hands thoroughly with soap and water and then dry them.
2 Boil fresh tap water in a kettle.
3 Allow the boiled water to cool to no less than 70°C. This is important because temperatures below 70°C will not kill any bacteria present in the powdered milk and so there is a danger of food poisoning.
4 Check that you are preparing the correct formula for the baby.
5 Follow the manufacturer's instructions and pour the correct amount of boiled water into the sterilised bottle. The water should always be poured into the bottle first.
6 Follow the manufacturer's instructions and add the exact amount of formula. This will be in proportion to the weight of the baby. Adding more or less powder than instructed could make the baby ill.

7 Reassemble the bottle following the manufacturer's instructions.

8 Shake the bottle well to mix the contents.

9 Cool the bottle quickly to feeding temperature by holding the bottom of the bottle under a running cold tap, or placing it in a container of cold water.

10 Check the temperature by shaking a few drops of the formula onto the inside of your wrist – it should feel lukewarm, not hot.

11 Throw away any feed that has not been used within two hours.

More information about how to sterilise feeding equipment and prepare powdered formula feed can be found on the NHS website. You can access this website by going to www.pearsonhotlinks.co.uk and searching for the ISBN of this title: 9781447970972.

Storage of powdered infant formula

Tins of infant formula should be kept in a dry cupboard. Each tin should be labelled with the name of the child it belongs to.

Did you know?

The practice of making up babies' feeds in advance and storing them is no longer recommended.

Storage of ready-to-feed infant formula

Ready-to-feed formula should be kept in a dry cupboard until it is ready to be used.

Storage of human breast milk

Breast milk that has been expressed can be frozen or kept in the fridge for three days, assuming the fridge temperature is between 5°C and 10°C. It can be kept for five days if the fridge temperature is 4°C or less. It is important that breast milk is labelled with the following information:

- who the milk is for
- when the milk was expressed
- when the milk should be used by.

How to bottle feed a baby

Feeding should be a relaxing and pleasurable time for a baby. It also needs to be safe. Ideally, bottle feeds should be given by the child's **key person**, as this supports the attachment process. Interaction is a key part of feeding babies, so you should talk to them, sing and make eye contact. You must also avoid rushing. Find out from parents about whether their baby needs **winding** and if so, how they normally do this.

Key terms

Key person – a practitioner designated to take responsibility for a child's emotional well-being by having a strong attachment with them and a good relationship with their parents.

Winding – a process to help babies expel any air trapped in their digestive system during feeding.

Use the following steps for bottle feeding a baby. Warning: Do not ever leave a baby alone with a bottle.

1 Check that the feed in the bottle is the correct one for the baby you are giving it to.

2 Find somewhere comfortable where you can sit with the baby.

3 Show the baby the bottle, and gently incline the baby.

4 Put the teat on the baby's lips and wait for the baby to accept it – do not force the teat into the baby's mouth.

5 Slightly angle the bottle so that the baby is only sucking milk, not air.

6 Look at the baby all the time you are feeding them, and talk or sing.

7 Be sensitive to the baby by noticing if they turn away their head or push the bottle away when they need a rest or have had sufficient milk. Do not force the baby to keep feeding.

8 If necessary, wind the baby in the way that the parents have indicated.

9 Unused milk should be discarded.

How to bottle feed a baby.

Weaning

Weaning or complementary feeding is the process by which babies move from a liquid-only diet to a mixed diet of solids and liquids.

Why weaning is important

Weaning is important for many reasons. First, weaning provides babies with additional energy and iron from the added food that is introduced into their diet. These support growth and also maintain health. Babies who are not weaned at 6 months are likely to become anaemic, as the natural reserves of iron that they received in the womb from their mother will run out. Babies will also lack the energy needed to promote their physical development.

The chewing of foods also develops the muscles in the mouth that will help babies produce speech sounds. This is why it is important that once babies have begun the process of weaning, they are given foods that require them to do some chewing.

When to start weaning

The current guideline is that babies should begin this process at 6 months and that they should have a milk-only diet until this point. This is because early weaning is linked to obesity, **food allergies** and digestion difficulties. It is thought that babies' digestive and immune systems are not ready for solid food until 6 months. Having said this, in some cases health professionals will suggest earlier weaning if a baby is showing signs of needing additional nutrients.

Key term

Food allergy – when the body has an abnormal reaction to a food or a component of a food.

Research

Many baby foods are labelled as being suitable for babies from 4 months, despite clear advice from the World Health Organization that early weaning is not desirable. Many health professionals are unhappy about this as they claim that this is misleading for parents.

- Find out about how baby foods are labelled.
- Look at the websites of baby food manufacturers. What advice do they give parents?

Foods to offer

The Food Standards Agency suggests that weaning is a four-part process.

Link

Go to Unit 15, Section A1 to find out about the stages of weaning and what foods to offer at each stage.

Baby-led weaning

Baby-led weaning is an approach that has become popular with some parents. The idea is that babies learn to feed themselves and choose what and how to eat. Instead of the traditional staged approach, babies are encouraged to help themselves to a range of foods, usually as part of a family meal. Babies can pick up the foods that they like the look of and then explore them using their mouths.

Advocates of baby-led weaning suggest that this approach prevents babies from becoming fussy eaters and also encourages them to chew early on. They also say that by missing out the spoon-feeding stage, babies have more control and independence, which is good for their emotional development.

Criticisms

However, baby-led weaning is still controversial. Critics point to an increased risk of undernourishment, as babies only take in small amounts of food at first and often spend longer playing with their food than actually eating – as baby-led weaning is not meant to include any spoon-feeding. Another criticism is that babies are more in danger of choking with this method, although advocates suggest that this is not such a problem and that usually the baby is only gagging. A final point everyone agrees on, including those in support of baby-led weaning, is that it can be very messy.

Middle ground

While some parents will choose baby-led weaning and stick to its philosophy rigidly, many parents use a combination of the traditional staged technique along with some baby-led weaning. In practice this means that the baby will be given opportunities to play with food items, but parents will also do some spoon-feeding as well.

Research

Find out more about the baby-led weaning approach.

- Ask parents about what they have chosen and what they do at home.
- Find out how your placement setting approaches weaning.

Find out more about baby-led weaning by going to www.pearsonhotlinks.co.uk and searching for the ISBN of this title: 9781447970972.

Meals, snacks and drinks

In Unit 15, you looked at the range of nutrients that children need. Young children cannot manage with just three large meals a day – their stomachs are small

and they will need snacks in between. This means that meals and snacks should be carefully planned. Below are some points to read alongside Unit 15.

Energy requirements

The amount of energy a child needs depends on many factors, but particularly their amount of physical activity. It is useful when planning meals, snacks and drinks to have some idea of how many calories a child should have over a day. This information is in Table 16.1.

Table 16.1 Average daily energy requirements for under-3s

Age	Energy requirements (calories)	
	Boys	Girls
1 year	765	717
2 years	1004	932
3 years	1171	1076

Source: Dietary Reference Values for Energy (2011), Scientific Advisory Committee on Nutrition.

Research

Nutritional guidelines are often being updated. This means that you should always check you are aware of the latest recommendations. A good source of information about young children's nutrition is the Caroline Walker Trust. Look out for their detailed guide to planning meals for under-3s in their booklet 'Eating well for under-5s in child care'. You can access this website by going to www.pearsonhotlinks.co.uk and searching for the ISBN of this title: 9781447970972.

Fruit and vegetables

It is recommended that the under-3s should taste five different fruits or vegetables every day. You do not need to provide adult-sized portions. Fruit and vegetables can make excellent snacks, for example, carrot sticks, apple slices and orange segments.

Drinks

Water can be offered for children to quench their thirst, but whole milk is also a good drink as part of a meal or snack. Semi-skimmed milk can be offered after the age of 2 years, but only if the child is otherwise eating well. Sugary or fizzy drinks are not appropriate and may give children a taste for sweet things, even if they are sugar-free. Eating sweet things can cause dental decay.

As soon as children are able, you should help them to use an open cup rather than a beaker. This is important for their sense of independence and also for developing their physical skills.

This child will soon be ready to try an open cup.

Snacks

It is worth thinking of snacks as mini meals and being aware that they should be part of the overall calorie and nutritional intake of the child rather than being considered separately. It is also useful to get children into good habits with eating snacks, such as sitting down to eat rather than wandering around. Snacks should not be so filling that children will not be hungry for their meals.

Meals

From around 2 years, many children start to have clear preferences for and dislikes of certain foods. It is important that we make sure that mealtimes remain relaxed – we might want to encourage children to try new foods or to finish a particular food, but should avoid confrontations. Most toddlers can be tempted to try things if they are arranged into faces or pictures on the plate. Some foods can also be 'disguised' by cooking them with others or by chopping them up small.

Vitamin D

For the first time in many years, some children in the UK are now deficient in vitamin D. This deficiency can cause a bone disease known as rickets. Sunshine is the best source of vitamin D, but it is now also being suggested that more vitamin D should be included in young children's diets. Good sources of vitamin D are tuna, sardines and eggs as well as fortified breakfast cereals.

Assessment practice 16.1

3A.P1 | 3A.P2 | 3A.P3 | 3A.M1 | 3A.D1

You have been asked to write a feature by an early years magazine about how your early years setting meets the nutritional needs of children under 3 years. The editor has asked that the article covers the following.

1 The importance of meeting the nutritional needs of children and an explanation of what these are.

2 The role of adults in early years settings in the preparation and feeding of children aged 0 to 2 years.

3 Examples of daily menus that meet the nutritional guidelines for children aged 2 to 3 years.

4 An honest account of how your early years setting provides for the nutritional needs of children under 3 years, including its strengths and weaknesses as well as how the early years setting might improve its practice further.

B1 Understand how to meet the specific developmental needs of babies under 1 year

Working with babies under 1 year is very rewarding. They develop quickly, but they also have specific needs. In this section, we look at how to work sensitively with babies in this age group.

Tuning in to babies

As you saw in Student Book 1, babies need to develop attachments to the people who look after them. These will include their parents and other family members, and also their key person. If you care for a baby, it will be important to 'tune in' to that baby. This means learning to recognise how they express their feelings and needs.

A good starting point when tuning in to a baby is to begin by talking to the baby's parents. They can tell you about their baby's reactions, preferences and little ways. Parents can also teach you to interpret their babies' cries. This is important, as although there are some similarities between babies' cries, they do differ.

As well as finding things out from parents, you also need to observe babies as you work with them, as this will soon help you to work out how they like to be held, how long they take to respond and what they like looking at or doing.

'Tuning in' to a baby is likely to occur more quickly when you are involved in their personal care and when you look for opportunities to hold and make eye contact with them.

Responding to distressed babies

When babies are distressed, it is very important that you find ways to comfort and reassure them.

How would you tune in to this baby?

To do this you must stay calm yourself. This is essential, as babies can tell by your tone of voice, facial expression and the way you are handling them if you are anxious or stressed.

Babies cry for a reason, and it is important once you have picked a baby up to work out why they are crying. While you are doing this, keep talking to the baby in a soothing voice and try gently rocking them or stroking their back.

Pain caused by injury or illness

Babies who are screaming may be in pain. Have a quick look to see if there are any visible signs of illness, injury or other things that might cause them discomfort.

Look at where the baby touches themself, as this may indicate the source of the pain. For instance, babies often tug at their ears when they have an ear infection.

Did you know?

Look for a rash, especially if the baby has a fever and an unusual screaming cry, as this can be a sign of meningitis.

Research

Find out more about the signs of meningitis in young babies by visiting the Meningitis Trust's website. You can access this website by going to www.pearsonhotlinks.co.uk and searching for the ISBN of this title: 9781447970972.

Wind

Some babies can become very distressed shortly after a feed, as trapped wind in their stomachs causes pain. You can wind a baby by putting them over your shoulder and gently but firmly rubbing their back. Alternatively, you can sit them upright on your lap and rub their back. Apart from dissipating the pain, these actions may simply help to soothe the baby.

Tiredness

Some babies cry when they are tired. This tends to be an intermittent cry and so you may need to put the baby down to sleep, but then stay with them. Many babies respond to being rocked or stroked if they are finding it hard to fall asleep. Always check on a sleeping baby according to the procedure of the setting.

Separation anxiety

From around 7 months, babies will start to resist being separated from their parents. At first, resistance might be quite slight, but as babies develop, they will cry and become very distressed. Recognising separation anxiety is important, as it means that you will need to work on developing a stronger bond with the child. If a baby remains distressed, it is important to contact the parent.

Unexplained crying

You have looked at some of the usual reasons why babies may cry. It is also important to take unexplained crying seriously. If you cannot soothe a baby, you should always report your concerns quickly to your line manager and, if you have the authority, to the child's parents. You should also let parents know if a baby is crying more than usual even after they have calmed down.

Unexplained crying could be a sign that the child is unwell, even if no temperature is recorded. The child could be lonely and need companionship, or the crying could be an attempt to communicate. Speaking and reassuring the child can help them to understand that they do not need to worry.

Things can change rapidly with a newborn child, so any crying should never be overlooked.

Responding to individual needs in care routines

The way that you care for each baby will depend on their individual needs and also parental preferences. It is important to follow these carefully for a number of reasons.

Routines should be similar to those at home

Wherever possible, you should stick to the same sleep, feeding and nappy changing routines as those that parents use. This makes it easier for the baby to settle and feel secure. If you work closely with parents this information will be shared and when there are changes at home, these can also be implemented in the setting.

Routines must meet babies' individual needs

Care routines also need to be individualised to ensure that each baby's needs are met. It may be that one baby has a particular formula milk or another needs different skincare products. Respecting these preferences ensures that individual babies' needs are met, and also that no allergic reactions are triggered.

Avoidance of institutionalisation

Where there are a number of babies in a group who may spend long periods away from their parents, there is a danger of institutionalisation if care routines are not individualised. Institutionalisation is considered problematic as it reduces the amount of stimulation and personal attention that babies receive.

Balancing individual babies' needs with others' needs

In an ideal world, every baby would have their own key person while in group care. The reality is that babies may be cared for alongside other babies or, in the case of home-based care, with older children. Balancing the needs of the group with individual needs can be tricky.

Being organised

The key to successful group-care work is good organisation and planning. You should think ahead about what each child is likely to need in terms of feeding, play and care routines. Then you should try to prepare as much as you can, for example, getting the nappies ready for changing routines, or putting out activities and toys for older children.

Universal appeal

Where you have more than one child in your care, it is worth looking out for activities that will appeal to children of varying ages, such as blowing bubbles or moving to music. Such activities can be enjoyed by more than one child at once and older children can be watched by younger ones, who learn from them.

Quality time

It is important to prioritise certain times with babies, particularly those linked to care routines such as feeding and nappy changing. Again, organisation is important. If you have an older child with you, you may need to make sure that this child has something to do while you are feeding the baby or, when you are looking after babies together, you could put out a treasure basket activity for the baby who is not being fed.

How to prepare a sensory environment

Babies need plenty of stimulation. They gain this primarily from being with an adult and being held, talked to and read to. However, babies also need opportunities to use their five senses in ways that stimulate them. This means that we need to create a sensory environment for babies, both indoors and out.

Sound

There should be objects that make sounds available for babies to use, such as rattles and squeaky toys. In addition, many settings have outdoor wind chimes. It is also important to sing to babies. You can use a soundtrack for support if you are not confident at singing.

Vision

Babies are keen to look around. It is therefore helpful if there is a range of different colours, including pastels and patterns, in their environment. Babies are also fascinated by faces, so photographs are very appealing, as are mirrors for them to look into. Many settings put mirrors and different brightly coloured objects outdoors as well as inside.

Taste

A sensory environment should include the food that is offered to babies as they are being weaned and afterwards. Babies react to the taste of things and will have clear preferences. Trying out plenty of new foods can help babies become adaptable rather than fussy eaters. In addition, babies also explore using their mouths.

Babies can be stimulated by providing objects that make a sound.

Link

Go to Unit 2 in Student Book 1 to find more information about how babies explore using their mouths.

Smell

Many settings make use of sensory bags that have different smells, such as lavender bags. In some settings, the staff plant sensory gardens that contain plants such as herbs, which provide different smells.

Did you know?

When you introduce an aroma for the first time, monitor babies carefully. Some smells can trigger asthma attacks.

Texture

Babies' skin is very sensitive. They can feel texture with their feet as well as their hands. When creating a sensory environment, it is worth thinking about putting different textures on the floor as well as what things feel like when they are held.

Objects and toys to support oral exploration

All babies take items into their mouths. This is the key way in which they explore and gain sensory stimulation.

In addition to presenting natural objects for babies to choose from, we should also make sure to provide other objects and toys to allow sensory exploration. These might include household objects such as wooden spoons, hard fruit such as oranges, or different fabrics. You can give these to babies when they are sitting up or you are holding them on your lap.

Link

Go to Unit 2 in Student Book 1 to find more information about treasure basket play, in which groups of natural objects are presented for the baby to explore.

Texture, smell and shape

- Does the object have an interesting texture?
- Does the object have an attractive smell?
- Can the baby lift the object unaided?

There are no right or wrong objects or toys to use for this activity, but do consider the following questions.

Safety

- Is there a risk of choking?
- Are there sharp edges?
- Are there moving parts that might trap the baby's finger?
- Could any part of the object break off if the object was sucked?

Hygiene

- Is the object clean?
- Can it be easily cleaned after the baby has finished with it?

Assessment practice 16.2 | 3B1.P4 | 3B1.P5 | 3B1.M2

1 You have been asked to talk to prospective early years learners about working with babies. In your talk, you should cover:
   - why it is important for adults to respond to babies' individual needs in care routines and how this might be done at the same time as meeting other babies' needs in the group.
   - the importance of sensory environments for babies under 1 year and the features of such an environment.

2 You have also been asked to produce a handout for the learners that looks at the ways in which adults can meet the specific developmental needs of babies under 1 year old.

B2 Understand how to meet the specific developmental needs of children from 1 to 2 years

Children develop rapidly in this year and start turning from babies into toddlers. They begin to express themselves using words and also through movements. In this section, we look at how best to support children during this year.

Environments that support curiosity and exploration

Though a few babies stand and walk before their first birthday, most will start to do so during this year. This gives them great freedom, though even when they are still crawling they are keen to explore. It is therefore important to create environments that encourage curiosity and exploration while keeping children safe. Figure 16.2 shows the types of resources and activities that are usually provided, both indoors and out.

Providing musical instruments is a good way to stimulate children.

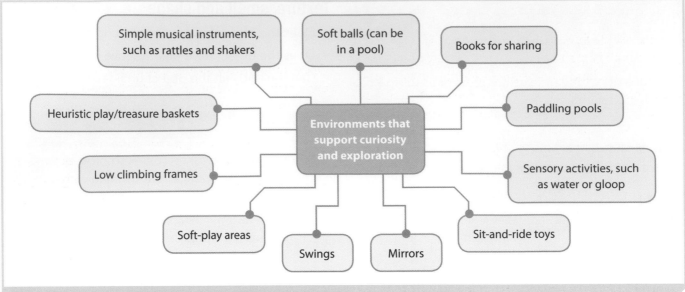

Figure 16.2 Environments supporting curiosity and exploration

Within the figure:
- Simple musical instruments, such as rattles and shakers
- Soft balls (can be in a pool)
- Books for sharing
- Heuristic play/treasure baskets
- Environments that support curiosity and exploration
- Paddling pools
- Low climbing frames
- Sensory activities, such as water or gloop
- Soft-play areas
- Swings
- Mirrors
- Sit-and-ride toys

Theory into practice

Make a list of ways in which your setting creates a stimulating environment for toddlers that allows them to explore.

Routines that value and respect children

Between their first and second birthdays, children will start to show signs of becoming independent. It is important, therefore, that you understand and respect their wishes wherever possible. A good starting point for this is through routine activities such as washing, feeding, nappy changing and dressing. Respecting children means being sensitive to signs that they want to do something for themselves, and to their preferences. You may, for example, ask a child whether they would like more to eat – if the child shakes their head, do not force them to eat more. Similarly, if a child is happily eating, but is doing so slowly, it is important not to rush them. Interestingly, rushing children often results in more problems and things actually taking even longer! Respecting children also means looking for ways of involving them in their care routines and, where appropriate, providing choices. You may, for example, ask children who should do the nappy change or, at mealtimes, which highchair they would like to sit in. It is important that choices are appropriate, as at this age children

are not able to take long-term decisions that will impact on their health and overall well-being.

Predictability and familiarity

Routines for this age group need to feel predictable. Children like to know what is likely to happen at nappy changing time, when dressing or during meals. Predictability is often linked to adults' behaviour rather than to keeping things exactly the same each time. Children need to know that the way that the adult responds to them and acts in a situation is unchanging. This is one reason why it is good practice for just a few core people to be involved with nappy changing and washing, as after all, this is intimate care. In many settings, there are also set places where meals, naps and nappy changes take place. Along with a predictable adult, this helps the child to feel more secure.

Transitional objects

Between the ages of 1 and 2 years, children tend to have some sort of comforter, which helps them feel secure, especially in new situations or when they are not with their parents. These are known as 'transitional objects'. Children use a surprising range of objects for this purpose, although cuddly toys, blankets and scraps of fabric are especially popular. As these are important objects for children it is usual for them to be readily available and to be offered if a child becomes distressed, or at nap time.

Defiance and resistance

From around 15 months until children are around 3 years old, they start to show signs of determination and independence. This often translates into moments of defiance. This can come as quite a shock for adults, especially parents. It is important to accept that this is part of the 15-month to 3-year profile, and that things will change once children have more language and cognitive development.

Remember that toddlers are not thinking about others' feelings when they are busy pulling all the books off a shelf – they are probably just enjoying the sensation. The term 'egocentric' is often used to describe young children. This is sometimes wrongly translated as 'selfishness' when it is really only about the child's stage of development. At this stage, children are only able to focus on what they are doing and how they feel.

Supporting emotions that change quickly

One of the many interesting things about working with children between 1 to 2 years is the way their emotions can change quickly. A 15-month-old child might cry because they cannot reach their beaker, but a moment later, the same child is likely to be laughing and smiling. This is normal for this age range but can take a little bit of getting used to. Emotions are liable to **fluctuate** and so tears and misery then laughter and smiles within a space of 10 minutes is pretty usual. It is important not to overreact and to stay calm when this happens and, above all, not to assume that children are being manipulative. They are simply showing typical development.

Key term

Fluctuate – to change quickly.

Using distraction to manage unwanted behaviour

Once babies are walking, a whole new world of exploration opens up to them. It is an exciting place filled with interesting objects and other children. Now that they can take things without the help of adults, they will often want to play with things that are either unsafe or not theirs. It is therefore normal for a toddler to wander over to another toddler and attempt to take whatever is in the other child's hand.

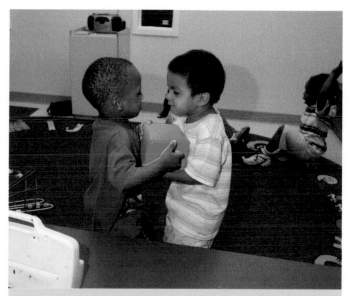

It is not uncommon for toddlers to show unwanted behaviour when they are able to walk. What would you do in this situation?

The usual strategy used to counter unwanted behaviour with this age group is distraction. Instead of focusing on what the child is attempting to do, you show the child something else that may be of interest to them. For instance, you could start singing or show them an alternative toy. Distraction has many advantages, but mainly it avoids unnecessary conflict and tears. It is also age appropriate. Trying to reprimand a child of this age or explain the error of their ways is pointless, as they do not have the language or cognitive skills to understand.

Using distraction

Cassie is a learner on placement in the toddler room. She is surprised to find how calm and happy the children are. At lunchtime, she spots that one toddler is helping himself to food from another toddler's plate. She tells the toddler to stop doing this in a firm voice. The toddler ignores her and carries on taking food. (The other toddler looks bemused but is not upset by this.) The room leader comes over and calls out the first toddler's name and smiles at him. She begins to clap her hands. All the toddlers start to join in. She starts singing a song and as she does so, she takes the toddler by his hand and steers him and his plate over to another part of the table.

1 Why did the toddler not stop when Cassie reprimanded him?

2 How was distraction used by the supervisor?

3 What were the benefits of using distraction?

Supporting communication development of children from 1 to 2 years

We know that adults need to communicate with young children in order to support their language development. As a key person you may do this in a variety of ways such as sharing books, playing simple games or just chatting and making eye contact as you are changing nappies or supporting mealtimes. Interestingly, when adults engage with children in this way, not only are they supporting their language development, but also their social and emotional development. The eye contact and interest as well as the sensitive interaction help children to gain reassurance, learn social skills and feel secure.

The years from birth to 3 are crucial in terms of children's communication and language development. From the ages of 1 to 2, children's **receptive language** will be expanding and from around 15 months, we should expect to be hearing some first words. The number of words that children produce will depend on many things, but crucially on how much adult interaction they have. The more time children spend with their key person engaging in activities, such as sharing books and playing simple games and during mealtimes, the better. When children of this age have opportunities for sustained interaction, they are more likely to understand what is happening. Increased interaction also means that these very young toddlers are more likely to feel emotionally secure.

Key term

Receptive language – language that a child can understand.

B3 Understand how to meet the specific developmental needs of children from 2 to 3 years

From 2 to 3 years, toddlers really develop. They gain in independence, confidence and also physical skills. While their language skills are developing, they are not yet able to totally express themselves, and this can lead to frustration. Working with this age group is fascinating, but also requires organisation to be able to meet their specific needs.

Assessment practice 16.3

You have been asked by your local early years network to report on how best to create stimulating and sensory environments that encourage communication for toddlers aged 1 to 2 years and help them feel secure and supported in active exploration.

They are particularly interested in the features and concepts that are important in environments for children aged from 1 to 2 years and how to create an environment in which children feel secure and supported.

They would also like you to cover the role of adults in supporting the development of communication of children from 1 to 2 years.

Your report should conclude with an analysis of how the environment and communication can aid learning development. This analysis should include examples.

Creating an environment that supports self-reliance

Toddlers enjoy being busy and independent. It is vital that you do not underestimate how much they are increasingly able to do for themselves. This should be reflected in the environment that you provide for them. Wherever possible, some resources should be easily accessible for them to help themselves. You also need to make sure that you give them plenty of opportunities to develop self-care skills such as dressing and feeding. When toddlers learn to do these things themselves, they will have a sense of achievement, although they will need to be allowed additional time. It is also important to judge sensitively whether a child needs help – ideally, you should ask the toddler if they need a hand.

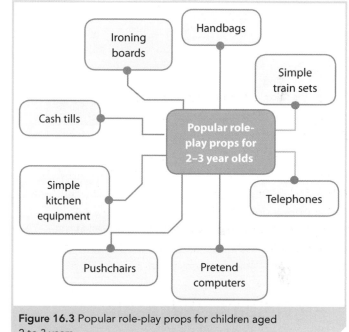

Figure 16.3 Popular role-play props for children aged 2 to 3 years

Creating experiences for role play

From around 2 years, most toddlers start to enjoy using props that they have seen adults using. This is their first step towards role play. They often enjoy the movements and actions, but how much they are actually 'pretending' varies. Providing props that toddlers can use is important, as these often help toddlers to feel 'grown up' and also encourage vocalisation. You may find that children who are closer to 3 years old and talking well sustain role play for longer periods and may start to play with other children. Figure 16.3 shows some popular role-play props that children enjoy using.

Involving children in routine activities

It is a common mistake to think that toddlers want to play all the time. While play should be a part of their daily activities, they also like helping adults – this provides additional stimulation and a change of pace. Tasks might be anything from helping to sweep the floor to putting laundry in the washing machine. This is easy to do in home-based care, but such opportunities may need to be created in group-care settings. By being involved in routine activities and tasks, toddlers gain a feeling of importance, and they also practise valuable physical skills, often involving fine motor movements. They will learn everyday vocabulary and enjoy chatting to you during the activity. When carrying out routine tasks with toddlers, it is important to be patient and expect that things will take longer than usual. Figure 16.4 shows some of the ways in which you can involve children.

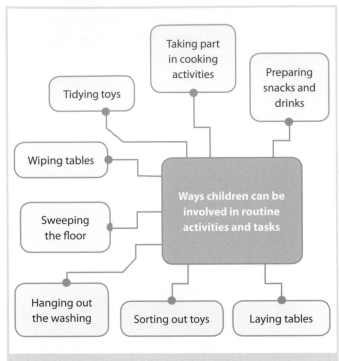

Figure 16.4 Ways to involve children in activities and tasks – can you think of other activities that 2-year-old children can be involved in?

The diagram shows "Ways children can be involved in routine activities and tasks" connected to:
- Tidying toys
- Taking part in cooking activities
- Preparing snacks and drinks
- Wiping tables
- Sweeping the floor
- Hanging out the washing
- Sorting out toys
- Laying tables

Providing manageable challenges

Two-year-olds do like to have some challenges, particularly mental and physical ones. It is therefore important to look for activities that will provide these. In addition to involving children in routine activities and tasks, you can also look at the types of toys, activities and resources that you provide. Heuristic play is a good example of this. With heuristic play, a range of objects – not toys – are put out for a toddler to explore. Toddlers can then make their own connections and challenges.

You also need to observe toddlers closely as they play and consider whether they are fully engaged – and if they are not, to think about whether the materials, activity or resources are sufficiently engaging.

Why is this a manageable challenge for this child?

Link

Go to Unit 2 in Student Book 1 to find more information about heuristic play.

Understanding impulsive behaviour

A major feature of 2-year-old children is their impulsive behaviour. This often takes people by surprise if they have not worked with this age range before. Most 2-year-olds are governed by what they see and what they feel like doing. 'I see, I want' is a good maxim to remember when working with this age group. Added to this, children of this age have developed quite fast reactions and can move quickly. This has many implications, particularly when it comes to safety. This is one reason why safety equipment must be used consistently with this age group.

The level of impulsiveness shown by this age group comes out in many ways: they may push another child down the slide if they are in the way or they may start banging a cupboard door because they like the feel of the action and the sound that it makes.

Factoring in impulsive behaviour

If you understand that children in this age group are likely to be impulsive, you can factor this in when working with them. It means that you might have equipment and toys ready for them so that they immediately have things to focus on. It also means that you might hide objects or items that you do not want them to have. You might also take certain safety measures, such as putting reins on children before you step outside for an outing.

Interestingly, as children's speech develops, they become less impulsive. This is because speech is linked to the ability to organise, plan and recognise consequences.

Research

1 Observe 2-year-old children in your setting. Can you see ways in which they are quite impulsive?

2 How does your setting manage this?

3 Now observe children aged 3 to 4 years. Can you see that most of them are less impulsive in their actions?

Guidelines for acceptable behaviour

It is important to have very realistic goals for toddler behaviour. These goals should be based on the usual patterns of child development for their age. Expecting children to behave in ways that are not linked to the usual patterns of behaviour is likely to cause conflict and frustration.

Link

Unit 7 in Student Book 1 looked at goals and expectations of behaviour. You should revisit these if you are working with this age group.

Remember that toddlers' willingness to comply will be variable, and that this is usual for the age group. This might mean that a child is fairly cooperative one moment, but then shows defiance or an impulsive behaviour later on.

It can be helpful to bear in mind the typical behaviours of this age group. Typically, children of this age:

- have no concept of sharing
- have no understanding that possessions belong to others
- are restless and active

- dislike sharing adult attention
- will snatch items from other children.

Temper tantrums

Many children under 3 will have temper tantrums. These vary in frequency and intensity from child to child. Temper tantrums are most likely to occur when a child is hungry, tired or feeling frustrated. A temper tantrum is a frenzy of uncontrolled emotion that can be triggered by a child seeing something they cannot have or being stopped from doing something. Children do not plan tantrums – they occur spontaneously.

Avoiding tantrums

Tantrums are negative experiences for everyone. Other children become anxious, adults are distracted from positive activities and the child having the tantrum also becomes very distracted. The best solution is to try to be organised so that, as far as possible, tantrums are avoided.

Tiredness

Tantrums are more likely to occur in children who are tired. A combination of tiredness and hunger increases the risk of a tantrum considerably. Making sure that children are getting around 12 hours of sleep in a 24-hour period is therefore a good starting point. This may mean moving nap times forward if a child seems particularly tired. For children who have many tantrums, it is worth finding out from parents how much sleep the child has and whether the parents need support with this.

Research

Read a booklet created for parents by the National Children's Bureau to inform them about children's sleep. You can access this booklet by going to www.pearsonhotlinks.co.uk and searching for the ISBN of this title: 9781447970972 .

Hunger

Children's brains need food. Impulsive behaviours that often cause tantrums are more likely to be exacerbated when children are hungry.

This means making sure that you have regular meal and snack times and that you are ready to be flexible with these if a child seems hungry.

Emotional security

Children are more likely to have tantrums when they feel insecure. A strong and effective key person system is therefore vital, and children in this age group need to spend plenty of time with their key person. Changes in the child's home life can also be a cause of tantrums. This may include the arrival of a sibling, the parents' separation or moving house. If this is the case, you will need to spend extra time with the child and you may also need to increase their nap times. This is because when children are going through changes in their lives, they are less likely to be sleeping well.

Good organisation and pace

Two-year-olds are busy people. Good organisation can prevent them becoming bored – plenty of resources and toys are needed. As toddlers will often want what another child has, a key strategy is to ensure that there are duplicates of favourite toys such as pushchairs. Playing with children gives you the opportunity to divert their attention and prevent problems from arising.

What to do if a tantrum occurs

There is a moment, just before a tantrum gets underway, when it might be possible to distract the child. Sometimes this works, other times not. If a tantrum does get underway, the best thing you can do is to reassure the other children that 'Dee is feeling a little angry now, but she will be all right' so they do not become distressed. You should then keep very calm and stay near the child. You may try to touch and comfort the child, but this is often unsuccessful and can provoke the child even more.

In some ways, it is good to see the tantrum like a storm and allow it to pass in its own time. Do not do or say anything to fuel it. Once the child has calmed down, act as if nothing particular has happened. Do not reprimand the child or talk about the tantrum. Some children may want a cuddle afterwards, while others may want to join in an activity. It can take time for some children to recover from a tantrum, so be ready to go at their

pace for a while. A few minutes after the tantrum, make sure the child is given plenty of praise and attention. This helps the child to learn that positive behaviours are valued and given attention. This is particularly important if the tantrum was triggered by attention seeking.

Assessment practice 16.4   3B3.P8 | 3B3.P9 | 3B3.M4

You have been asked to mentor a learner on placement who has not worked with children aged 2 to 3 years before. To help her, you have decided to write a guide to working effectively with children aged 2 to 3 years. Your guide should include:

- the type of accessible activities and routines that support the social and emotional needs of this age range
- the role of adults in promoting positive behaviour with children in this age range
- the effects on children's social and emotional development of having accessible activities and routines, as well as skilled adults working alongside children.

Assessment practice 16.5   3B.D2 | 3C.P10 | 3C.M5

You have been asked to give a presentation to a group of first-year learners about the role of adults and effective environments in relation to promoting the development of children under 3 years.

Your presentation should include examples and must cover:

- the extent to which the environment created by early years settings can support and promote each of the areas of development and learning
- the skills and qualities that adults need to demonstrate in order to work with children under 3 years
- the importance of positive role modelling by adults when working with children under 3 years.

C Understand the skills and qualities needed to work with children under 3 years

There are certain skills and qualities that you need if you wish to pursue a career working with under-3s. In this section, we look at what makes a successful under-3s practitioner.

Qualities you will need

There are particular qualities that practitioners who work effectively with children under 3 seem to have. Figure 16.5 shows these qualities. If you intend to work with this age range, you might like to reflect on whether you are able to demonstrate these skills, or are willing to work on developing them.

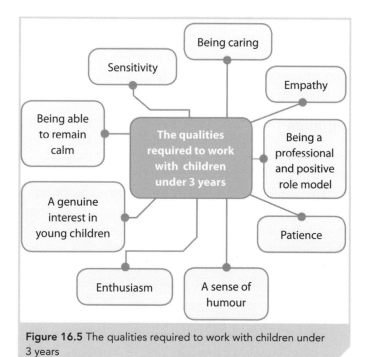

Figure 16.5 The qualities required to work with children under 3 years

Patience

While all people working with young children need to have patience, this is particularly important with this age range for a number of reasons.

First, babies and toddlers cannot be rushed. They do things in their own time and simple tasks such as dressing and getting ready to go out can be very protracted.

This age group is also fascinated by and keen to repeat certain play and activities. Toddlers will often want the same book read to them a number of times

or will be keen to repeat the same movement over and over again. While this is part of their learning, it does require that adults are patient and are able to maintain their own enthusiasm.

Finally, babies and toddlers can also have rapid changes in their responses. One moment a baby may be calm and settled but five minutes later might be quite irritable.

Sense of humour, enthusiasm and being a role model

Babies and toddlers can sense when adults are happy and fun to be with. Practitioners who work with babies and toddlers should show they enjoy being with them and should be playful. Babies and toddlers also like to be with people who have a sense of humour and who show this appropriately. It is important to be a positive role model.

Sensitivity, caring approach and empathy

There is a debate as to whether care, sensitivity and empathy can be taught or whether they come naturally. Regardless of this, these are qualities that you will need to have. Babies and toddlers need people to be very sensitive to their needs and who can respond with care and empathy. An irritable baby will need soothing and being talked to in ways that calm. Babies and toddlers are very attuned to tone of voice and facial expressions. Someone who is genuinely expressing empathy and care is likely to reassure and calm a baby or toddler. Children's speech and emotional development is linked to whether they are with people who can show sensitivity, care and empathy.

Calmness

Babies and toddlers need to feel safe with those who care for them. They can tell if a person is stressed, anxious or frustrated. This means you have to display calmness at all times, even if you are feeding a baby and at the same time a toddler wants the potty.

Genuine interest in young children

All of the qualities mentioned are easy to demonstrate if you have a genuine interest in young children.

If you are interested in toddlers' development, you are likely to find their need to repeat play activities over and over again fascinating. If you do not have this genuine interest, you are likely to find it boring.

Children are quick to sense whether or not you have this interest, and if you do not, they are likely to demonstrate this in their responses. Parents will also pick up on this.

Skills for work with children under 3 years

As well as specific qualities, there are some skills that are essential for work with under-3s. Figure 16.6 shows some key skills that are essential for working with this age group.

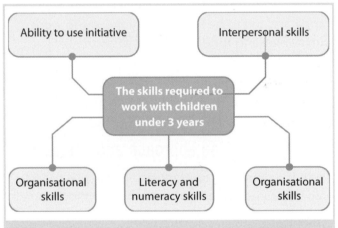

Figure 16.6 The skills required to work with children under 3 years

Literacy and numeracy skills

Childcare practitioners need to have good levels of literacy and numeracy as these are skills you will use all of the time. From September 2014, staff holding an Early Years Educator qualification must have achieved English and maths at grade C or above in their GCSEs if they are to count in staff:child ratios.

Interpersonal skills

It is essential that you are able to communicate with and respond to children, and also their parents or carers. Many parents will be leaving their children in someone else's care for the first time and will naturally be anxious about this. Good interpersonal skills can give parents confidence and allow you to communicate effectively with them. You also need to

demonstrate good interpersonal skills with children. They will learn a lot about how to relate to other people from watching you in action.

Observational skills

Throughout this unit you have seen the importance of observational skills. Good practitioners will be closely monitoring the children they are with and, while they may not write up every observation, they will be using what they have noted to do spontaneous planning. This will be in addition to the more formal observation and planning process described in Unit 9 in Student Book 1.

Organisational skills

If you work with the under-3s, you will need excellent organisational skills. This is because they cannot wait around for food, nappy changes or play activities. Babies need to be fed on time and nappies have to be changed promptly and correctly. Toddlers who are bored and are waiting around are likely to find their own amusements, and this might not be what you had expected.

Initiative

The ability to take the initiative often comes gradually and will be linked to your knowledge and growing confidence. It is important, though, to be 'quick on your feet' when working with this age group, as what may be required at any point in time may change. This means that if you are someone who likes to take their time or prefers to be told what to do, you may struggle to work with this age group.

Further reading and resources

Lindon, J. (2006) *Helping Babies and Toddlers Learn: A Guide to Good Practice with Under-threes*, London: National Children's Bureau.

MacIntyre, C. (2011) *Understanding Babies and Young Children from Conception to Three: A Guide for Students, Practitioners and Parents*, London: Routledge.

Robinson, M. (2003) *From Birth to One: The Year of Opportunity*, Oxford: Oxford University Press.

Ready for work?

Caroline Jenkins   Nursery worker

I have spent most of my career so far working in the baby and toddler room. I love it here and think that anyone working with babies and toddlers is very lucky. We see the babies when they first come and get to know the parents well. As most of our babies are with us for four years, it means that whenever we go outdoors or to another room, there are always 'our' children waving and talking to us. It does take a lot of patience working in the baby and toddler room, but it is also a lot of fun. I love the way that babies and toddlers become fascinated by things that when they are older will just be taken for granted. It is also amazing to see the way that they develop and their personalities start to shine through. Some babies are clearly bold, while others seem to be great thinkers.

Some people say that working in the baby and toddler room is boring. They have never been here! We take our children outdoors several times a day and always, unless it is really pouring down, for a long walk. Babies and toddlers always find things to notice and there is always plenty to talk about as we see cats, cars going by and the odd shopper. Back indoors, it's non-stop with nappy changes, mealtimes and activities. From early on we encourage the children to do as much as they are able and visitors are often surprised when they see the babies crawling with a nappy in one hand ready to bring it to the changing room!

Skills for practice

A dummy as a transitional object

Many toddlers become attached to a dummy. This is because the current advice for preventing cot death includes the use of a dummy when a baby is put to sleep up to the age of 12 months. The dummy is meant to keep the airways open.

As a result there has been an increase in the number of dummies being brought into settings by toddlers. This can create tension because if a toddler uses a dummy, they are less likely to interact with adults and also to show the full range of facial expressions. It is therefore recommended that the use of dummies should be restricted to nap times only.

Most settings have a policy about this and will explain the reasons for this policy to parents. Ideally, an alternative transitional object such as a cuddly toy should be encouraged. This can be introduced by the parents when the child is having a good time or a cuddle so that the child associates the object with being happy and feeling secure. It will take some time for this object to be accepted and then used by the child, but it is worth persevering with it.

Introduction

Working in a home-based setting can be a rewarding experience for early years practitioners. It provides opportunities for practitioners to develop close relationships with the children in their care, through supporting their development during the pre-school years.

This chapter will focus on key areas of the role, such as working with parents and networking with other agencies, as well as looking at ways of developing play and other learning opportunities for children in home-based settings.

Assessment: You will be assessed by a series of assignments set by your teacher/tutor.

Learning aims

In this unit you will:

A   understand the value of home-based care for children and families

B   understand how to establish a safe and healthy home-based environment

C   understand how to provide play for differing ages of children in a home-based environment

D   understand how to meet the personal, social and emotional needs of children in a home-based environment

E   understand the role of parents and other agencies as partners in home-based childcare.

By doing this unit I have increased my confidence and furthered my knowledge and understanding of how home-based practitioners work professionally to meet the needs of children and families. I hope that one day I'll be able to work with children in my own home and maybe even set up my own childminding business. Working as a childminder would enable me to carry on working even after I've started my own family.

Sarah, *a learner on an early years course*

Working With Children in Home-based Care

17

BTEC

Assessment Zone

This table shows you what you must do in order to achieve a **Pass**, **Merit** or **Distinction** grade, and where you can find activities to help you.

Assessment criteria		
Pass	**Merit**	**Distinction**
Learning aim A: Understand the value of home-based care for children and families		
3A.P1 Explain the benefits of home-based care for children and families. **Assessment practice 17.1**	**3A.M1** Discuss the extent to which home-based care benefits children and families. **Assessment practice 17.1**	
Learning aim B: Understand how to establish a safe and healthy home-based environment		
3B.P2 Describe the role of the home-based practitioner in keeping children safe, using examples. **Assessment practice 17.2**	**3B.M2** Analyse how children can be kept healthy and safe in a home-based environment, using examples. **Assessment practice 17.2**	**3B.D1** Evaluate how a home-based practitioner could contribute to children's health and safety more effectively. **Assessment practice 17.2**
3B.P3 Explain how to promote healthy lifestyles in a home-based environment. **Assessment practice 17.2**		
Learning aim C: Understand how to provide play for differing ages of children in a home-based environment		
3C.P4 Explain the role of observation in the provision of play in a home-based environment. **Assessment practice 17.3**	**3C.M3** Analyse the role of the adult in providing appropriate play experiences for children of mixed age ranges in a home-based environment. **Assessment practice 17.3**	
3C.P5 Explain, with selected examples, how to provide opportunities for play for children of mixed ages in a home-based environment. **Assessment practice 17.3**		
Learning aim D: Understand how to meet the personal, social and emotional needs of children in a home-based environment		
3D.P6 Explain how to meet the emotional health needs of children in home-based childcare. **Assessment practice 17.4**	**3D.M4** Analyse how home-based practitioners contribute to meeting the personal, social and emotional needs of children of mixed ages. **Assessment practice 17.4**	**3D.D2** Evaluate approaches and techniques home-based practitioners use to support children's personal, social and emotional needs in home-based childcare. **Assessment practice 17.4**
3D.P7 Explain how to support the positive behaviour of children of mixed ages in home-based childcare. **Assessment practice 17.4**		

continued

Assessment criteria (*continued*)

Pass	Merit	Distinction
Learning aim E: Understand the role of parents and other agencies as partners in home-based childcare		
3E.P8 English I&CT Explain, using examples, how home-based practitioners work with other agencies to support children and families. **Assessment practice 17.5**	**3E.M5** Analyse how the relationship between home-based carers, parents and other agencies can support children. **Assessment practice 17.5**	
3E.P9 I&CT Explain how home-based carers work in partnership with parents to support children and families. **Assessment practice 17.5**		

English English Functional Skills signposting   I&CT Information and Communication Technology Functional Skills signposting

How you will be assessed

This unit will be assessed by a series of internally assessed tasks set by your teacher/tutor. Throughout this unit you will find assessment practice activities that will help you work towards your assessment. Completing these activities will not mean that you have achieved a particular grade, but you will have carried out useful research or preparation that will be relevant when it comes to your final assignment.

In order for you to achieve the tasks in your assignment, it is important that you check you have met all of the Pass grading criteria. You can do this as you work your way through the assignment.

If you are hoping to gain a Merit or Distinction, you should also make sure that you present the information in your assignment in the style that is required by the relevant assessment criterion. For example, Merit criteria will require you to discuss and analyse, and Distinction criteria will require you to evaluate.

The assignment set by your teacher/tutor will consist of a number of tasks designed to meet the criteria in the assessment criteria table. This is likely to consist of a written assignment but may also include activities such as:

- a guidance document
- case studies.

Getting started

Remember a time when you were cared for by a relative or other adult, for example, before school.

With a partner, discuss how this felt. Were there things that you liked or disliked?

A Understand the value of home-based care for children and families

This section explores the value of home-based care in providing flexible and consistent care that is able to meet the individual needs of children. The home setting promotes real-life experiences for children and supports engagement with their local community.

Consistency of care and positive relationships

Home-based childcare is unique. It provides a relaxed family environment, a home-from-home experience, and studies show that this gives children the best start. It allows parents to choose a setting that may provide similar parenting styles, beliefs and cultures to their own.

Children are able to form secure attachments to one carer. This supports their emotional development by giving them the confidence and the opportunity to try out new things.

Home-based practitioners are able to form lasting positive relationships with families, and share their children's progress with them. These effective partnerships allow you, as a carer, to share observations of the children you look after and plan for their next steps. The continuity of care you provide will support both the child and their parents.

Individual children's needs can be met, and routines and activities can be flexible and spontaneous.

Imagine that you had planned to spend the day baking with the children, then wake up to find that there has been a heavy snowfall. Home-based childcare means you can quickly adapt your plans to make full use of the learning opportunities as a result of the weather. You can use this opportunity to play outside, make footprints, show the children what happens when you bring the snow inside, make winter pictures and so on.

Being responsive to children's individual needs

Home-based practitioners are well placed to support the needs of all children. As the **key person** they will form caring relationships with, and gather a huge amount of knowledge about, the children in their care. They will be able to provide support as children enter different stages of development and provide guidance for parents, for example, with potty training.

The home-based setting is often the most suitable one in which to provide care for vulnerable children. This could be because the numbers of children are fewer and the environment, equipment and resources can be easily adapted to meet the individual needs of the child. Many home-based practitioners provide childcare and/or **respite care** for disabled children.

Key terms

Key person – a practitioner designated to take responsibility for a child's emotional well-being by having a strong attachment with them and a good relationship with their parents.

Respite care – short-term care with the assistance of professional carers.

Flexibility to meet the needs of parents and children

Another benefit of home-based care is that children are often able to access services within their local community, such as baby clinics, local stay-and-play sessions, preschools, schools and after-school activities. This allows children to build on and maintain existing relationships while feeling part of their community.

Parents require a flexible service that meets their needs as working families. Whether they are working part- or full-time, home-based childcare can provide valuable before- and after-school care, part-of-the-day care, as well as overnight care to cover working shift patterns.

Home-based practitioners often have a good network of support and are able to provide holiday and sickness cover for each other in agreement with parents.

Caring for siblings together

In home-based childcare, siblings can be cared for together. This can support children and provide reassurance when settling in. Siblings can learn from each other and share experiences. This all helps support the children's emotional and social development and promotes their well being. In addition, parents have the convenience of only having to drop off and collect from one place.

Continuity of care through to teenage years

Many home-based practitioners recount their experiences of caring for children from when they were babies right up to secondary school age. They become part of the family, and children will often go back to visit their former childminder when they return from university.

Siblings are often cared for together in home-based childcare.

This strong attachment, together with the reassurance and continuity it provides, supports the child's development – particularly their emotional development and well-being. Home-based practitioners are well placed to support the many **transitions** that children go through, providing a smooth passage from one environment to another. They can work with parents to prepare children for change, and recognise the impact change may have on their emotional development.

Case study

Supporting transitions

When it was time for Paul to attend nursery, his home-based practitioner spent time talking to him about the things he would do there. With permission she took photographs of the nursery and they role-played the routines that he would have to follow. She visited the nursery with Paul and his mum, and shared with the nursery Paul's learning journal, so they could see all that Paul had achieved.

On the day that Paul started he had a book of photographs to take with him that showed where he would hang his coat, the teacher he would see and where he would have his lunch. This provided him with a visual story that enabled him to feel in control of his day.

In what way do you think the actions of the home-based practitioner helped:

1 Paul?

2 his mum?

3 the nursery?

Real-life learning experiences

Children are able to gain real-life learning experiences in a home-based setting. These are invaluable in making sure they are equipped and resilient to cope with their life ahead. Home-based practitioners are able to support the earliest speech and language development of children, and their high-quality interactions mean children are valued and able to develop self-esteem. The routines that take place, such as dressing, putting on shoes and feeding, allow children many opportunities to practise skills.

They are surrounded by everyday experiences that not only promote the child's learning but provide real enjoyment for both the child and the carer.

Caring for children in a smaller group

Home-based childcare provides children with the opportunity of being cared for in a smaller group. Their individual needs can be clearly identified and met, and children are able to form secure attachments not only with the key person but also with the other children. This is particularly beneficial for children with emotional development and confidence needs.

Assessment practice 17.1   3A.P1 | 3A.M1

Create a poster aimed at parents to be displayed in your local children's centre.

It should explain the benefits to children and their families of home-based childcare.

Include an evaluation of how home-based childcare contributes to meeting children's individual needs and also the needs of the child's family.

B Understand how to establish a safe and healthy home-based environment

Supporting children to keep safe and healthy is an important part of home-based childcare. This section looks at how you can promote children's independence while ensuring their safety and well-being.

Importance of identifying and managing risk

Like all practitioners, home-based child carers have a responsibility to keep children safe and healthy. Children are naturally curious and can have a limited awareness of how to stay safe. It is a legal duty for home-based practitioners to follow the regulatory requirements of their home country in relation to health and safety.

Link

Go to Unit 4 in Student Book 1 to find more information about health and safety requirements.

Research

Certain accidents and incidents must be reported by law. Research the Reporting of Injuries, Diseases and Dangerous Occurrences Regulations (RIDDOR) 1995 to find out what responsibilities you have under this Act.

They are also required to have a valid paediatric first-aid qualification, which is approved by the local authority and involves a minimum of 12 hours' training. Home-based practitioners must have a first-aid box available both within the setting and when out and about. It is also essential to seek appropriate parental permission relating to administering medicines or other treatment.

Home-based practitioners are required to follow specific policies and procedures for health and safety. These will depend on your home nation's regulatory

requirements. In England, these are the requirements of the Early Years Foundation Stage (EYFS) and in Wales, the National Minimum Standards for Regulated Childcare.

Did you know?

In order to comply with **regulations** and **legislation** relating to health and safety, home-based practitioners need to seek parental permission for a range of activities, including:

- administering medicines
- seeking emergency medical treatment
- taking children on outings
- taking photographs/videos of children
- applying sun cream.

This list is not comprehensive, and home-based practitioners have a responsibility to make sure that they refer to the regulatory requirements for their own home nation.

Key terms

Legislation – the act of making laws.

Regulations – legal requirements that have to be followed.

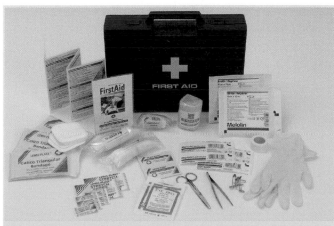

First-aid boxes should be up to date and complete.

Risk assessments

Risk assessments inside and outside the home-based setting will need to be carried out on a regular basis. This should also include regular outings such as the school run or one-off organised trips. A risk assessment must identify potential hazards and risks. When thinking about risk assessments, remember:

- a hazard is anything that may cause harm, such as chemicals, electricity or an open drawer
- a risk is the probability, high or low, that somebody could be harmed by these and other hazards.

For example, bleach left by the toilet is a hazard and there is a risk a child could be seriously harmed by this.

Activity

- Consider each room in your own house and the potential risks and hazards there.
- For each room, identify the particular hazard, then state what the risk to children may be. Finally, list the actions you could take to prevent harm to children. An example is below:
  - Identified hazard: Front door opens on to busy road.
  - Risk: Children may be able to leave premises.
  - Control measure: Supervision of children at all times and door locked with key accessible for emergencies.

Case study

Preventing harm

Mary is a registered childminder. She has two teenage sons who have left their razors and shaving foam out in the bathroom over the weekend. On Monday morning Mary is welcoming three children into her setting.

4 What steps should Mary take to prevent any harm to the children?

5 What might happen if she did not take these steps?

Involving children in managing risk

When children play it is important they are allowed the opportunity to take measured risks, as this will support their learning and development. By taking these risks children will learn a range of skills, including the ability to calculate the level of risk involved in an activity and to avoid and understand the consequences of dangerous situations.

Independence and resilience

Allowing children to make decisions during their play encourages them to become independent and builds their self-esteem. This resilience supports their ability to cope with life as they reach adulthood.

Reflect

James is a nanny caring for 2-year-old twins and he has decided that they are going to make a fruit salad. How can James take a measured risk that will allow the twins to take part safely and benefit from the experience? Think about the tools he might use and the levels of supervision he needs to ensure.

Research

Visit the Health and Safety Executive website for further information on managing risk. You can access this website by going to www.pearsonhotlinks.co.uk and searching for the ISBN of this title: 9781447970972.

Management of outings

It is important to risk assess both regular outings (for example, school runs) and one-off outings (such as a trip to the seaside) and seek parental permission in line with your home nation's regulatory requirements.

Inspection requirements

Remember to refer to your home nation's requirements in relation to managing risks for inspection.

The value of secure indoor and outdoor environments

Children's learning will flourish in a secure environment that allows them to experience situations in which they are able to learn to evaluate risk for themselves. Outdoor opportunities give children access to a variety of resources and a chance to improve their movement, coordination, control and use of their senses to learn about the world around them.

Home-based practitioners may care for their own children alongside the children they are minding. It is therefore important that they think carefully about how to balance the risk-taking of their own children with the need to ensure the safety of those in their care and the wishes of their parents.

■ The principles of safeguarding

Home-based carers have a responsibility to follow the regulatory requirements of their home nation. This would include the requirement to have a **safeguarding policy** and to follow the Local Safeguarding Children Board's **procedure**.

Link

Go to Unit 8 in Student Book 1 to find more information about safeguarding children.

Key terms

Policy – a written statement about what you will do.

Procedure – an explanation of how you will do something.

Safeguarding – the act of keeping children safe from harm.

Safe recruitment

Some home-based practitioners choose to work alongside others. They may work together as separate registered providers, or one practitioner may employ assistants or take on volunteers. In this situation the practitioner is required to seek permission from the regulatory body, who will check the proposed assistant's suitability. This will involve carrying out a Disclosure and Barring Service (DBS) check. The employer must ensure that the proposed assistant is suitably qualified and understands all the relevant policies and procedures, as well as provide and carry out inductions, supervision and appraisals.

Lone workers

Working alone or in isolation is a feature of being a home-based practitioner. This can make them more vulnerable to allegations of abuse. However, there are steps that practitioners can take to protect themselves.

- Behave professionally at all times.
- Ensure all accidents and incidents are recorded accurately and factually.
- Record all injuries children arrive with at the setting.
- Ensure parents sign records, or make a note if a parent refuses to sign.
- Ensure the rest of the family are also aware of their vulnerability to allegations.
- Encourage children to be independent.

Any concerns about a child need to be recorded and stored securely. This information is confidential and should only be shared with the appropriate professionals, in line with the setting's safeguarding procedure. As lone workers, home-based practitioners do not have a manager or designated officer within the setting. Instead, there is support and guidance available through organisations such as the Professional Association for Childcare and Early Years (PACEY) or the NSPCC.

Case study

Responding to allegations

John and Alice are registered childminders. Their daughter Sophie has just returned from university for the Christmas holidays. One evening, a parent of a child John and Alice care for, 3-year-old Frankie, telephones to say that Frankie is very upset. He has just told her that Sophie shut his finger in a door earlier that day.

1 How should the childminders respond to this allegation?

2 What steps could John, Alice and Sophie take to prevent this happening in the future?

Impact on own family

It can be very distressing if a home-based practitioner either is accused of abuse or has to manage a child protection case within the setting. If this does happen it is important to document all conversations and records.

The family may experience a range of emotions, including anger, shock and helplessness. These emotions are normal and support is available. It may be that legal advice is required, and this can be provided by the PACEY to its members or by the Citizens Advice Bureau.

Support of families

It is important to remain professional at all times. Families may be experiencing a wide range of emotions and may need to seek support from other agencies.

Promoting healthy lifestyles in a home-based setting

Practitioners working in the home are able to influence children and families to make healthy lifestyle choices. The flexibility of home-based care means that children can be actively involved in the planning and preparation of meals and hygiene practices. Home-based practitioners can also plan activities that support healthy lifestyles, such as setting up an assault course in the garden and asking the children to think about the impact of this on their body by taking their pulse at the end.

Food hygiene

Children can be seriously affected by food poisoning, so it is good practice for home-based practitioners to access guidance from the Food Standards Agency (FSA) and undertake basic food handling training. Children may have allergies, which the home-based practitioner may need to discuss with parents. Registered childminders are required to register as a food business operator with their local authority if they regularly provide snacks or meals to the children in their care.

Did you know?

The Food Standards Agency provides a free resource called 'Safer Food, Better Business' to support home-based practitioners when preparing, storing and cooking food. Download this resource from their website, which you can access by going to www.pearsonhotlinks. co.uk and searching for the ISBN of this title: 9781447970972.

Home-based practitioners need to consider a range of issues relating to food and nutrition, including:

- correct fridge/freezer temperatures
- correct methods of storage; e.g. of lunches
- correct thawing, heating and cooking of food
- sterilisation of bottles and/or storage of milk
- hygiene practices
- consideration of food allergies
- support and advice on good nutrition.

In England, the School Food Trust has produced voluntary nutritional guidance for early years practitioners. Support tools include menus and recipes, self-evaluation checklists and an early years code of practice for food and drink.

The Department of Health has also issued physical activity guidelines that explain the physical activity children require from birth to adulthood. Alongside good nutrition, physical activity ensures children have the best start in life and reduces the risk of ill-health.

You can access these guidelines by going to www.pearsonhotlinks.co.uk and searching for the ISBN of this title: 9781447970972.

Link

Go to Unit 15, Section B to find more information about food hygiene.

Assessment practice 17.2

3B.P2 | 3B.P3
3B.M2 | 3B.D1

Home-based practitioners often provide parents with a welcome pack explaining the service they offer, and giving them something to read before making their decision about whom to choose to care for their child.

Create two sections for the welcome pack.

1 A description for parents about how the home-based practitioner ensures children will be kept healthy and active.
2 An explanation of how the children will be kept safe while also being given the opportunity to take risks.
3 An evaluation of how home-based practitioners can contribute to children's health and safety more effectively.

C Understand how to provide play for differing ages of children in a home-based environment

Home-based childcare provides an environment in which children of differing ages can actively explore and learn through play. Ongoing observation and assessment ensure a range of play opportunities can be planned and children's progress can be recorded.

Recognising the play needs of children of differing ages

Children learn through play, so careful planning to ensure they have a range of opportunities is vital. Through observing the children in their care, childminders can recognise their likes and dislikes, strengths and areas for development. There are also many scenarios in which children can be observed naturally. These may include:

- playing in the park
- preparing snacks and eating meals
- at parent and toddler/childminding groups.

Link

Go to Unit 2 in Student Book 1 to find more information about recognising play needs at different ages.

Recording children's progress

Recording observations does not have to be time consuming. They can be recorded by taking photos, writing on sticky notes and using video.

Using their knowledge of child development, childminders can establish the current stages of development that children in their care have reached. This knowledge then allows them to plan effectively.

The Early Years Foundation Stage requires that childminders complete a progress check when a child is between the ages of 2 and 3. This is an assessment that identifies children's progress in the prime areas of learning and development. Through both the childminder's observations and parents' feedback, the progress check is intended to highlight areas where progress is being made and agree next steps, as well as identify where progress is less than expected.

Link

Go to Unit 9 in Student Book 1 to find more information about observations.

Case study

Recognising play needs

When Anna joined Ameera's setting at 3 years, Ameera decided that she needed to get to know Anna before she started planning experiences and opportunities for her. Ameera spent time discussing Anna's development with her parents, learning more about her background and early learning experiences. She spent time observing Anna in order to understand her current stage of development and what her interests were. She noticed that Anna really enjoyed listening to a nursery rhyme CD and began to sing along. This enabled Ameera to plan for Anna's next steps in her learning and development journey. Ameera had a nursery rhyme book that she shared with Anna, and used puppets and other soft toys to sing along with them.

1 What other activities/resources could Ameera provide to support Anna's interest in rhymes?

2 How might Ameera record these observations?

Planning for children's play

In order to meet the needs of individual children it is important to provide them with a range of activities. This helps them progress while allowing opportunities for the childminder to undertake further observation and reflection. By planning experiences and activities that are challenging but achievable, you will be able to support and extend every child's learning and development.

In a home-based setting, routines are a big part of a carer's day-to-day work and, with a bit of thought, they can be incorporated into activity plans. It is important to recognise the value of learning opportunities that can be gained from everyday routines.

Table 17.1 shows some examples of routines that provide potential learning opportunities.

Children's interests change over time, so you must be flexible in your approach. You need to ensure that you make the best of any opportunities that arise during the day. For example, if on the school run a child in your care spots a ladybird, this opens up opportunities for further discussion and exploration, which could also inform future planning.

Table 17.1 Routines with potential learning opportunities

Activity	Potential learning
Putting away shopping	• Counting • Colour matching • Sizes • Recognition • **Positional language**
Preparing food	• Weights and measures • Understanding the world
Laying the table	• Sorting • Matching • Language and communication

Involving children in the preparation of food is a good way to help them develop.

Home-based practitioners in England are required to follow the Early Years Foundation Stage framework for activity planning and observation. In Wales, the early years framework is called the Foundation Phase.

Different types of play for children of different ages

Home-based practitioners usually care for children of varying ages, so there will be times when they need to be encouraged to participate in different types of play. This can be achieved by good planning but also by having an adaptable and flexible approach. For example, if out on a walk, a 2-year-old child might learn about their shadows on the grass, whereas a baby might enjoy waving their hands in the sun. Both children could take part in tree rubbings so this might be a good activity to engage children in.

It is important to listen to children's views and opinions and to take these into account. There may be occasions when a child does not want to participate in an activity and, in this case, alternatives need to be provided.

Balancing child-initiated and adult-led play with children of different ages

As a home-based practitioner it is important to provide a balance of child-initiated and adult-led play. Adult-led activities could include things like cooking and story-telling. They can be used to develop language and introduce concepts. The learning process is more important than the end result. For example, when baking cakes it is the learning that takes place while working through the stages that is important rather than the appearance of the finished cake.

Home-based practitioners are able to support children of different ages in smaller groups by providing resources that support the varying ages and stages of development. If we take the example of baking cakes, younger children are able to feel, smell or touch the ingredients, while older children might help to weigh and measure. Although this is predominantly adult-led, the children can be involved in making decisions, pretending to be bakers in a shop and clearing away at the end.

Often the range of ages means that older children support younger children in their play – they act as role models and encourage interactions. There are even more opportunities for these kinds of experiences during school holiday periods.

These children are different ages but they are having fun, interacting and communicating.

Child-initiated play could include role play and small-world play. You can support children to take the initiative in learning and encourage them to make their own choices in their play by ensuring that resources are accessible, appropriate and not overwhelming.

Opportunities for children to make choices

Home-based care can provide opportunities for decision making and spontaneity by making sure that activities are accessible. In fact, simple play can be supported by using everyday activities. Consider the activities in Figure 17.1, which can take place as part of a daily routine.

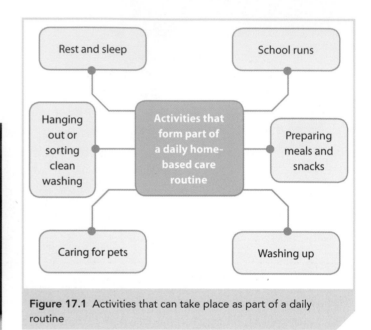

Figure 17.1 Activities that can take place as part of a daily routine

With a bit of thought, it is easy to see how each of these routines can support children's learning. For example, engaging children in preparing their own meals and snacks supports hand–eye coordination, measuring and weighing supports early mathematical concepts, and conversation during any activity supports the development of communication skills.

Acknowledging the value of play

Be realistic about how long everyday routines and activities take, especially with young children. Children flourish in a relaxed, unhurried atmosphere where they are able to return to activities if they wish. Children can sometimes be rushed from one thing to another, but it is important to take time to praise and encourage children, asking them to share their experiences and creations.

Assessment practice 17.3 | 3C.P4 | 3C.P5 | 3C.M3

Imagine you are caring for four children aged 9 months and 2, 5 and 9 years in the school holidays.

1 Plan a day that includes two physical play opportunities in a home-based setting. Consider how you will meet the individual play needs of all children and ensure that children of all ages can join in. Your plan could include the activity, resources needed, links to festivals/special events and links to the curricula.

2 Consider the role of observation in helping you to identify individual children's needs. Create a spider diagram that shows why observation is important.

3 Next, analyse the role of the adult in providing appropriate play experiences for children of mixed ages in a home-based environment.

Reflect

Claire is a nanny caring for two children, one aged 18 months and one aged 6 years. The 6-year-old has created a model out of junk and is very proud of this. How can Claire show she values this child's work? Think about the following:

- How was the child encouraged, and were they able to make decisions?

- How can the child keep this work safe to share with parents later?

- How might Claire use this activity to inform future planning?

D Understand how to meet the personal, social and emotional needs of children in a home-based environment

Children flourish when they feel secure and valued. This learning aim focuses on the uniqueness of each child and the role of the home-based carer in providing an inclusive environment where parents and practitioners work in partnership.

Meeting the needs of individual children in a group setting

Practitioners working in home-based childcare are expected to have a knowledge and understanding of child development from birth to the teenage years. Unlike other types of childcare, where you might specialise in working with babies or 2-year-olds, in home-based childcare you would need to provide care across the ages. Therefore, it is important to have a good knowledge and understanding of children's

development beyond the early years. Home-based practitioners care for disabled children and children from a wide range of social and cultural backgrounds, and need to ensure that the unique needs of individual children are met.

This can be achieved by ensuring that all children are welcomed and valued and given equal chances. Children should be encouraged to share their story. What is it that makes them unique? Encourage parents' involvement by asking them to provide photographs and stories from home. Ensure that the resources available reflect the diversity of today's society.

Through your observations of children and knowledge of child development you will be able to identify, plan and implement enjoyable learning experiences.

Forming secure relationships with children

We all know how important first impressions are. Imagine you are a child walking into a setting for the first time. How might you feel?

First meeting

Home-based practitioners can do many things to support and develop relationships with the children they care for. The first meeting is important. This gives the parents and child a chance to meet the carer and, in the case of a registered childminder, the carer's home and family. It also gives the home-based practitioner the opportunity to find out more about the child and their family. This meeting should be fairly relaxed and a pleasurable experience, with toys available for the child to play with.

As we have already covered, some home-based practitioners like to produce a welcome pack that includes information about their service and any policies they may have. This enables parents to have something to take away and remember them by, especially if they are visiting several providers.

Other home-based practitioners provide a welcome pack for the child with some photos of themselves and their setting, and a space for the child to write about themselves, or draw a picture.

Settling in

It is important to allow time to get to know the child and to be able to support them in this transition. For children who have not been separated from their parents before, this may take time and sensitivity. As the key person, the home-based practitioner will be able to support this change by providing reassurance and allowing the child to feel safe. They may need to reassure parents that a close emotional relationship with the child will not undermine the child's feelings for them.

Settling-in visits will allow the parent to visit with the child and stay for short periods, gradually getting to the stage where the child is happy to stay in the setting on their own. This will be arranged according to the child's needs. Children should also be encouraged to bring along comfort items to make them feel secure.

The impact of new relationships

For home-based practitioners working in their own home, they may also need to prepare their own family for life caring for other children. The following ideas can help to support them in this.

- Ensuring that their own children have a safe private place for their own possessions.

- The childminder's own children will witness their parent spending time with and caring for other children in their home, and this may cause jealousy, depending on their age. It is important for the childminder to set aside time for their own children. Older children may like to take responsibility for roles within the home.

- It is also recommended as far as possible that home-based practitioners attend important events in their own child's life such as sports days or school plays.

Home-based practitioners should help children settle in to their home and build a relationship with parents.

Listening to and consulting children

Home-based practitioners have a duty to protect and promote children's rights. Rights are the basic needs that we all have to be able to live a healthy and secure life. This includes access to food and clean water, healthcare, education, play and leisure, and somewhere safe to live. Children have the right to be listened to and make their own decisions.

The United Nations Convention on the Rights of the Child (UNCRC) was drawn up in 1989 and approved in 1991. It is made up of 54 Articles that state that children under 18 have their own rights. Although the Convention itself is not legislation, its implementation has been achieved through policies and Acts such as the Children Act 2004.

Of the 54 Articles, the 7 Articles listed in Table 17.2 are most relevant to home-based practitioners.

In order to provide good-quality home-based care, all planning needs to include the thoughts and decisions of the children being cared for. By actively listening to children and involving them in decision making, we can support them to become independent learners and problem solvers.

We need to consider the age and stage of the child, and think about how we can ensure that even those children whose speech is developing are able to have a voice.

Respecting and valuing children's contributions

Children have the right to feel valued and respected. This ensures that they feel good about themselves, helps build self-esteem and enables children to feel in control. There are many ways in which you can support this in the home-based setting.

Table 17.2 Articles from the United Nations Convention on the Rights of the Child (UNCRC) relating to home-based childcare

Article number	Article aims
Article 2	Children have the right to be protected from all forms of discrimination.
Article 3	The best interests of the child must be the primary consideration in all activities and actions concerning children.
Article 7	The child shall have full opportunity to play and recreation, which should be directed to the same purposes as education – society and the public authorities shall endeavour to promote the enjoyment of this right (note this comes from the 1959 Declaration of the Rights of the Child).
Article 12	A child has the right to express his or her views freely and that view is to be given appropriate weight in accordance with the child's age or maturity.
Article 13	A child has the right to freedom of expression and exchange of information regardless of frontiers.
Article 16	Children have a right to privacy.
Article 28	A child has the right to education with a view to achieving this right progressively on the basis of equal opportunities.

Source: © (1989) United Nations. Reprinted with the permission of the United Nations.

How can home-based practitioners support children to make decisions and have their voices heard? Here are some ideas.

- Allow choices, such as at snack time and story time.
- Ask them what clothes they might need to put on if it is raining.
- Allow children to choose where to play and offer a wide range of resources for them to choose from.
- Seek children's views on the care that is provided to them in the setting.
- Think about using different methods for children of different ages and stages of development.

The Mosaic approach

There is a large amount of research about the benefits of listening to children. One area you might wish to explore further is the Mosaic approach. This approach gives practitioners the opportunity to see the world through the children's eyes. By giving children cameras, videos and maps, you can begin to explore their world and gain a deeper understanding of their learning and the connections being made.

Listening to children promotes their emotional development, self-esteem, self-confidence and well-being by helping them to:

- learn how to trust others
- learn how to make and maintain strong relationships
- learn how to share
- begin to understand that their views and opinions can make a difference
- learn how to empathise with others.

Meeting the emotional health needs of children

We live in a multicultural society in which different languages, religions and cultures affect our interactions and communication. Like all practitioners, home-based child carers must avoid making assumptions about the families they work with. Children look to us to reassure them that we respect and value their families and where they have come from.

First impressions are important. How does a child know they are welcomed and valued? Welcome packs for both parents and children can be helpful here.

It is important to respect different ethnic and cultural backgrounds by finding out how families wish to be addressed. The resources and activities provided must reflect the diversity in our society and any notices displayed could be in different languages.

It is useful to gather as much information about individual children as possible and remember that parents are the most important people in children's lives. Encourage children to feel proud of their individuality and share their experiences. Do not be afraid to ask or find out more about the families using the home-based setting.

Managing transition

The term 'transition' relates to the passing from one place or stage to another. What should not be underestimated is the emotional impact this can have on children. Children can experience many transitions in their early lives, such as starting preschool or moving house, as well as daily transitions as they move from one activity to another. Home-based practitioners are well placed to support children's emotional health by actively listening, working closely with parents, and preparing the child as far as possible for the transition. This preparation might be through role play, visits, use of resources such as books and giving children as much notice as possible of any change so that they feel in control.

Books are useful in helping children to prepare for transitions.

Managing behaviour

Home-based practitioners have an important role to play in supporting children to behave in an acceptable way. They work closely with parents to understand and provide continuity when managing behaviour.

Research

Refer to either Ofsted in England or CSSIW in Wales for the regulatory requirements in your home country relating to managing behaviour.

If you work as a home-based practitioner you are likely to be caring for children of different ages from varying backgrounds. All families will have their own ideas about how children should behave. It is your job to provide a safe and fair environment in which children are aware of consistent boundaries, are valued and have the opportunity to be in control of situations some of the time.

Children can be affected by many outside influences that may change the way they behave, such as the arrival of a new baby. Effective communication with the child's parents allows us to support children during these times.

Supporting and promoting positive behaviour

It is important to establish a set of ground rules that will help support positive behaviour. These rules are based on the need to keep children safe. Consider any unwritten rules already in place, for example, everyone taking their shoes off indoors. These rules can then be developed further, involving the children and parents where possible, and explaining why the rules are important. Children very quickly learn what is acceptable in different environments. Figure 17.2 shows an example of what these 'ground rules' might look like.

Consider how to promote positive behaviour, remembering the uniqueness of each child and adapting the approach to meet each individual child's age and stage of development.

OUR GOLDEN RULES

1. Hang up your coat
2. Take your shoes off
3. Share all the toys
4. Be kind to one another
5. Don't jump on the furniture
6. Remember your manners
7. Tidy up your mess
8. Eat and drink at the table
9. Wash your hands before food and after going to the toilet
10. Help each other

Figure 17.2 An example of rules that may be applied in a setting

If you have children of your own, you will need to consider how you will promote positive behaviour strategies with them as well. Do you need to examine how you currently manage their behaviour?

To ensure the smooth running of your setting, your house rules and boundaries will need to apply to your own children too.

Reflect

What can you remember about how you were treated as a child by your teachers or parents? Do you think this influences how you approach behaviour management now?

Theory into practice

To help promote positive behaviour, remember the following points.

- Think about the tone and message you are sending out. Try to use positive language. For example, rather than 'don't do that' try 'let's do this'.
- Give plenty of praise.
- Use methods of distraction.
- Be consistent.
- Try to separate the behaviour from the child. Remember, you are unhappy about the behaviour, not the child.
- Be a positive role model – children learn by copying others.
- Explain to children why certain behaviour is unacceptable.
- Allow children the opportunity to make decisions and have responsibilities.

The importance of inclusion

In order for all children to reach their potential they need to be fully included, respected and given meaningful opportunities to learn and develop. In order for a setting to be truly inclusive, home-based practitioners need to share with parents their policies and practices, and involve them in key decision making.

Registered home-based child carers have a personal responsibility under the Equalities Act 2010 to anticipate the individual needs of all children and families who use their service. This requires them to think about not only their attitudes, but also the environment, resources and equipment they provide, and any paperwork they hand out.

Reflect

First impressions are really important. The way in which a home-based practitioner welcomes families into their home will instantly demonstrate their commitment to the children they care for.

The environment should be welcoming and accessible for children and their families, and this can be achieved by considering the layout. There should be space for children to move around, a table to sit at for mealtimes and activity times, a place for children to be calm and quiet and a garden or access to outdoor play daily. Children's artwork could be displayed on the walls, and there should be a place for children to hang their coats.

The resources provided should cover the ages and stages of development of the children being cared for. These should be stored so that children can select them for themselves. All resources should be freely available to both boys and girls.

The paperwork that is provided for families, such as a welcome pack, policies and newsletters, should be written clearly. Consideration should be given to families with a specific requirement or whose first language is not English.

Available support

Home-based childcare can be very isolating, so it is important to find out about the local support available to you. Many local authorities will provide training and resources to support inclusive practice. There are also area SENCOs (Special Educational Needs Coordinators) who can provide advice regarding children with disabilities and/or special educational needs. Children's centres will have access to specialist services, for example, speech and language support, health visitors and paediatricians. PACEY provides factsheets and training to support members.

Theory into practice

Imagine you are asked to care for a child whose mother is visually impaired. What might you need to do to ensure that the setting is accessible? Think about the layout of the setting and any paperwork you might need to share.

Now consider a child whose first language is Polish. What might you need to do to support their language development? Where might you go for support?

Early identification of needs

Working closely with individual children allows home-based practitioners to observe their progress. They will have an understanding of children's development and be able to recognise that children develop at different rates. Through their observations they may recognise that a child needs to focus on a particular area of learning and can plan in partnership with their parents the steps that will help them to achieve this.

It is important to approach this sensitively with parents, as they may feel that their parenting skills are being judged. Think about how you would like to be approached if it was your child. If the message being delivered is particularly difficult, ensure that you:

- consider the timing – do not try to do it as the parent is rushing off to work, and instead set aside time without interruptions
- explain what you have noticed and ask if the parent has noticed this too
- remember to depersonalise things where possible and focus on what the child can do rather than what they cannot do.

Develop an awareness of other professionals and services or resources in your area that you could direct parents to, and be willing to work with other professionals to support the child's development. For instance, a speech therapist may be able to suggest activities that you can carry out in your setting.

If a parent has difficulty in recognising that their child has a need, it is important that the home-based practitioner continues to work sensitively with them and provide support. They may be able to provide information and resources, and explain the benefits of working closely with them. The home-based practitioner will carry on observing and planning for that child's particular needs while the parents recognise their child's progress.

Link

Go to Unit 1 in Student Book 1 to find more information about John Bowlby and his theory.

Challenging discrimination and stereotypes

Children are influenced by adults at home, in the media and in their local communities. Home-based practitioners are well placed to be role models for inclusive practice. They can help children have positive attitudes towards diversity by taking the time to explain the similarities and differences of people around them. They are able to offer a wide range of resources and learning experiences that will encourage children to respect others.

Challenging discriminatory remarks that children may make is important in order to help them develop an understanding and awareness of others. An explanation that their actions are unfair should be given alongside pointing out anything that is untrue, helping the child to learn from the situation. Discriminatory behaviour should never be ignored and the victim should always be reassured to maintain their self-esteem.

We all have a role to play in challenging stereotypes and ensuring that children have access to a range of resources and materials that show both genders in different roles, such as female fire-fighters and male nurses. Children should also be able to select the toys they wish to play with by themselves and have access to cars, dolls, dressing-up props and so on, regardless of gender.

E Understand the role of parents and other agencies as partners in home-based childcare

Parents know their children best, and their knowledge of their child is crucial to the home-based practitioner in enabling them to support and plan appropriate activities effectively. This section explores the key benefits of effective partnership working with both parents and other professionals.

▌Working with parents

Many parents see home-based practitioners as experts in their field and look to them for advice and support. Although this may be true, home-based practitioners must recognise that parents are experts in knowing their own children. When parents and home-based practitioners work closely together, children's outcomes are improved. There are many reasons why it is important to work closely with parents. Table 17.3 lists some of them.

Table 17.3 Benefits of working with parents

Areas where you may work with parents	Benefits
Policies and procedures	Policies and procedures are working documents that should be shared, discussed, monitored and reviewed. Parents need to be shown and to agree to the home-based practitioner's policies and procedures. Taking time to do this will mean that parents have all the required information about the service provided as well as an awareness of the regulatory requirements. They should have the opportunity to feedback about the service, which in turn informs the setting's practice.
Managing behaviour	Children benefit from clear and consistent boundaries. Sharing your house rules and policies ensures that families know what is expected. It is important to be aware of parents' own behaviour strategies, while also recognising your home nation's regulatory requirements (Ofsted/CSSIW).
Sharing information	In order to provide the best service for families you will need to establish a relationship based on trust, which allows you to share information about daily routines and events that may affect how the child is feeling or behaving. With permission it may also be useful to share information with other professionals working with the child, such as a teacher or health visitor, to support any specific needs. This ensures a consistent approach across settings.
Signposting to other agencies	Parents may look to you for advice and support that you are not able to provide. In this case it would be beneficial if you had built up an understanding and knowledge of services that could provide further support, such as links with your local children's centre.
Involving parents in children's learning and development	Children develop at different rates and while they are with you, you will observe this. You can share this with parents through your daily conversations. This allows parents to see all the stages their child passes through and gives them the chance to tell you about what they have been doing at home. For example, potty training will be most effective when parents and home-based practitioners are in agreement about the process and regularly update each other on progress.

Working with other agencies

Working closely with the child's parents is important. Children are also likely to come into contact with a range of other **universal services** and/or specific services as they grow and develop. This might be the health visitor when the child is young, when specific advice may have been given about a child's dietary needs, or the reception teacher as the home-based practitioner supports parents in preparing their child to start school.

Multi-agency working allows different services to come together to support the **holistic** needs of families. All of those involved can work together to identify needs, agree where to begin, plan which service or professionals may be involved and then implement the work, ensuring that the needs of the child and the families are at the centre of it.

Supporting families to access their local children's centre can provide a vital link, as children's centres are able to offer access to a wide range of services for families with children under 5 years. They are often able to signpost voluntary organisations such as Home Start, which is able to provide a volunteer to support families in their own homes, or give access to bereavement networks.

Links with home learning

We have previously seen how the home-based practitioner can share information about the child's progress with the parents. The use of learning journals and daily diaries gives parents the opportunity to feed back about the child's progress and developments at home. By sharing children's progress with parents and emphasising to parents the value of play, home-based practitioners are able to make links between what happens in the setting and at home.

There are also real benefits for children when parents share home learning experiences with the home-based practitioner. The practitioner is then able to extend the learning opportunities in their setting, allowing the child to make connections in a range of situations that help to reinforce positive experiences.

Sharing home learning experiences

Aaron is 4 years old and he spent the weekend at his grandparents' house, by the sea in Southend. Aaron's grandmother took some photographs of Aaron holding a bucket with a crab inside.

When Aaron got home, his parents talked about his weekend and stuck the photograph into Aaron's diary. Aaron took the diary to Lisa, his home-based child carer, the following Monday. Lisa sat down with Aaron and the other children in her care and talked about the seaside. She remembered that

she had a collection of shells and showed these to the children. This led to a whole week of activities based around the sea, including sand and water play, ice-cream tasting and making hats to wear in the sun.

1 Why is it important to extend Aaron's weekend learning experience?

2 How might you encourage parents to share information in this way?

Professionalism

Home-based practitioners will be expected to act professionally at all times, and there will be occasions when they will be observed going about their daily routine. Consider, if you were a parent, what you would like to see for your child.

Home-based practitioners are given a large amount of information about the families they work with. This can include personal details about the family, medical needs, photographs and so on. It is important that this is not shared or discussed or posted on social networking sites.

Establishing links with other settings

Developing networks

Home-based practitioners are working alone so it is important that they network with others to share good practice and develop effective partnerships. This might be other home-based practitioners, or the local preschool or nursery. Some areas may have childminding groups or networks to join. Many children's centres hold stay-and-play sessions, or opportunities specifically aimed at home-based practitioners.

Supporting transitions

Home-based practitioners will have gained a huge amount of information about the child's likes and

dislikes and will have recorded their achievements and progress. With the parents' permission it is beneficial to share the child's progress with their next setting. This will support both the child and the setting in understanding what has been learned to enable them to plan for the future.

For many children who attend the home-based setting as well as nursery or school, good communication means that planning ideas can be shared which can extend their learning. This avoids children having to repeat topics and gives them the chance to develop ideas and interests further.

Importance of boundaries when working with parents

The nature of home-based childcare means that practitioners can become very attached to the families they work with. Parents sometimes see the practitioner as a friend who can support not only their child's needs but also their entire family. This could lead to parents persistently collecting their children late, forgetting to pay or phoning at weekends.

It is important that home-based practitioners remain professional and clear about the service being provided. Figure 17.3 gives you some ideas about how to do this.

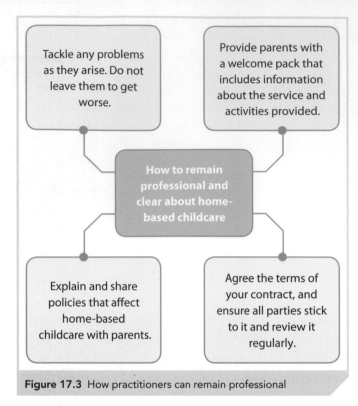

Figure 17.3 How practitioners can remain professional

When working with other professionals to support the needs of families, remember to ensure that you have parental permission to share information. If you are invited to meetings, ensure you are prepared, and feel confident that your contribution to the child's well-being is equally important as that of other professionals.

Respecting different cultures and ethnicities

The regulatory body for your home nation will have specific requirements to ensure that you provide opportunities that meet the needs of all children. You will be required to show that you respect individual families' cultures and ethnicities.

Here are some ideas for ensuring this.

- Be a good role model, and think about what you say.
- Ask families to share information about their cultures with you.
- Support children to recognise their uniqueness.
- Plan activities about where children have come from, who is in their family and what they enjoy doing.

- Encourage children to recognise and respect differences.
- Challenge discrimination.

Further reading and resources

Websites

The Early Years Foundation Stage: www.gov.uk/dfe

Care and Social Services Inspectorate Wales (CSSIW): www.cssiw.org.uk

Scotland, Care Inspectorate: www.scswis.com

Ireland, Department of Children and Youth Affairs: www.dcya.gov.ie

Welsh Government: www.wales.gov.uk

Food Standards Agency: www.food.gov.uk

Ofsted: www.ofsted.gov.uk

Professional Association for Childcare and Early Years: www.pacey.org.uk

Ready for work?

Vicky Jenkins Home-based practitioner

I have always worked with children, firstly caring for my younger brothers and sisters and then as a room leader in a day nursery. I had my own daughter a year ago and decided that I wanted to spend time at home with her while still having the opportunity to earn some money.

I thought I knew all about caring for children, child development, keeping them safe and healthy and how to provide lots of great activities. This was until I spoke to my neighbour Gill, who is a registered childminder. She suggested I come round for coffee and see how it works in her home.

I was really surprised at the amount of resources she had, and the age range of the children she was caring for that day. She did an amazing job of juggling three different routines. She had a baby that needed bottle feeding, a 2-year-old she was potty training and a 3-year-old who was learning to put his shoes and coat on for preschool.

It really opened my eyes to the skills and knowledge needed to work in a home-based setting. There is no one to help you – you have to be extremely organised and allow plenty of time to get anywhere.

Completing the course and having Gill to share ideas with has given me the best start in my childminding career and I am learning all the time.

Skills for practice

Practise doing the following things related to working with children in home-based environments.

- Select resources and activities that can be adapted for children at various stages of development.

- Take opportunities to discuss the children's day with parents or carers and promote the importance of working in partnership with parents.

- Plan an activity involving children in your care, assessing the potential risks in the environment. Consider the differences between a home-based environment and a group setting.

Have a look at the Professional Association for Childcare and Early Years (PACEY) website for further ideas. You can access this website by going to www.pearsonhotlinks.co.uk and searching for the ISBN of this title: 9781447970972.

Introduction

When working with children, you will need to have some knowledge and understanding about what is meant by 'additional needs', and their impact on a child's development and learning. You will also need to be able to work with parents and carers alongside other professionals and agencies both within and outside the setting in order to ensure that all children are included as much as possible in all activities. As part of your role you will work with others to plan and carry out specialised learning programmes, taking into account the needs of individual children. As well as knowing about legislation and the assessment process, this includes being aware of the support organisations and networks available for children and their families.

Assessment: You will be assessed by a series of assignments set by your teacher/tutor.

Learning aims

In this unit you will:

A understand additional needs of children

B understand provision to support children with additional needs in early years settings

C understand the role of adults working with children with additional needs.

> I have always wanted to work with children who have special educational needs and I learned so much on my placement. In the setting where I was working I was able to work closely with a child who had cerebral palsy and it enabled me to gain first-hand experience of the kinds of issues she faced as well as the support that is available. It was also useful to talk to colleagues about their experiences so that I was able to get a wider view.
>
> Christian, *a learner on an early years course*

Working With Children Who Have Additional Needs

This table shows you what you must do in order to achieve a **Pass**, **Merit** or **Distinction** grade, and where you can find activities to help you.

Assessment criteria

Pass	Merit	Distinction
Learning aim A: Understand additional needs of children		
3A.P1 English Describe additional needs of children and the factors that may cause them. **Assessment practice 19.1**	**3A.M1** Analyse how the additional needs of children could impact on children and their families. **Assessment practice 19.4**	
3A.P2 Explain the effects of discrimination on children with additional needs. **Assessment practice 19.2**		
3A.P3 Explain how families may be affected by the additional needs of a child. **Assessment practice 19.4**		
Learning aim B: Understand provision to support children with additional needs in early years settings		
3B.P4 Explain how the social model of disability has influenced provision for children with additional needs. **Assessment practice 19.3**	**3B.M2** Discuss the impact of inclusive education on children with additional needs. **Assessment practice 19.3**	**3B.D1** Evaluate the extent to which effective assessment supports inclusive provision for children with additional needs. **Assessment practice 19.5**
3B.P5 I&CT Describe the process for identifying and providing support for children with additional needs. **Assessment practice 19.4**	**3B.M3** Analyse the role of assessment in providing support for children with additional needs. **Assessment practice 19.5**	
3B.P6 Explain the role of parental involvement in the assessment of children with additional needs. **Assessment practice 19.4**		
3B.P7 Explain the role of professionals who may be involved in supporting children with additional needs in an early years setting. **Assessment practice 19.4** **Assessment practice 19.5**		

continued

Assessment criteria (*continued*)

Pass	Merit	Distinction
Learning aim C: Understand the role of adults working with children with additional needs		
3C.P8 Explain how adults can work to support children with additional needs in the development of confidence and self-esteem. **Assessment practice 19.6**	**3C.M4** Analyse the role of the adult in implementing a plan drawn up to support a child with additional needs. **Assessment practice 19.6**	**3C.D2** Evaluate collaborative and partnership working when supporting children with additional needs. **Assessment practice 19.6** **Assessment practice 19.7**
3C.P9 Explain how adults use individual education plans to support children with additional needs. **Assessment practice 19.6** **Assessment practice 19.7**		
3C.P10 Explain how to work with parents when supporting children with additional needs. **Assessment practice 19.6**		

English	English Functional Skills signposting	I&CT	Information and Communication Technology Functional Skills signposting

How you will be assessed

This unit will be assessed by a series of internally assessed tasks set by your teacher/ tutor. Throughout this unit you will find assessment practice activities that will help you work towards your assessment. Completing these activities will not mean that you have achieved a particular grade, but you will have carried out useful research or preparation that will be relevant when it comes to your final assignment.

In order for you to achieve the tasks in your assignment, it is important that you check you have met all of the Pass grading criteria. You can do this as you work your way through the assignment.

If you are hoping to gain a Merit or Distinction, you should also make sure that you present the information in your assignment in the style that is required by the relevant assessment criterion. For example, Merit criteria will require you to discuss and analyse, and Distinction criteria will require you to assess and evaluate.

The assignment set by your teacher/tutor will consist of a number of tasks designed to meet the criteria in the assessment criteria table. This is likely to consist of a written assignment, including items such as:

- a good practice guide
- a response to a case study
- a written article.

Getting started

What do you understand by the term 'additional needs'? Discuss with a partner or a group and come up with your own definition.

A Understand additional needs of children

When working with children it is important for you to have a clear understanding of what is meant by the term additional needs. In the past this has also been known as **special educational needs** (SEN).

> **Key term**
>
> **Special educational needs** – used to describe children who have a learning difficulty that calls for special educational provision to be made for them – children who learn differently from most children of the same age, and who may need different or extra help from that given to others.

The Special Educational Needs and Disability (SEND) Code of Practice 2014 states the following.

> 'A child or young person has SEN if they have a learning difficulty or disability which calls for special educational provision to be made for him or her.
>
> A child of compulsory school age or a young person has a learning difficulty or disability if he or she:
>
> - has a significantly greater difficulty in learning than the majority of others of the same age, or
>
> - has a disability which prevents or hinders him or her from making use of facilities of a kind generally provided for others of the same age in mainstream schools or mainstream post-16 institutions'

Source: Special Educational Needs and Disability Code of Practice, 2014.

The Code of Practice was revised in 2014 so that it covered children and young people up to the age of 25.

You will need to know how to work with colleagues, parents and outside agencies to provide additional educational support for these children. As a starting point you should look at different areas of need that children may have.

> **Activity**
>
> Which of the following children might cause you concern? Briefly outline the reasons why.
>
> - A 2-year-old child cries regularly and cannot be pacified.
> - A 3-year-old child has not yet started to speak.
> - A 4-year-old child does not hold a pencil correctly.
> - A 6-year-old child displays aggressive behaviour towards children and adults.

Areas of additional need

Additional needs are often divided into different areas, although children may have needs in more than one of these and be affected in a number of different ways. This will also affect different areas of a child's development. You will always need to approach each child differently and get to know them in order to provide the best possible support.

Physical needs

Children are defined as having additional needs if they have a disability that prevents or hinders them from making use of educational facilities of a kind generally provided for children of the same age. In other words, disability is considered an additional need only if it stops the child from participating in the day-to-day activities that are enjoyed by others. Many children who have a physical disability will be independent and able to participate without support.

Josh is 5 years old and uses a wheelchair. He has recently moved into Year 1 in his mainstream school. The school environment has been adapted to accommodate wheelchair users, as this is now a legal requirement. Josh manages well and is able to go out to play, get himself to the main hall and move around the classroom independently.

Discuss the following in groups.

* Will Josh need any kind of special treatment?
* If so, what?

Children who have disabilities will need varying levels of support and you will need to work alongside others to make individual provision for them.

However, a child with physical needs may not necessarily have a disability. Their needs may include mobility issues such as a medical condition or they may need additional support in order to carry out routine tasks such as changing for PE or toileting. Some children may also need support to develop their **fine motor skills** so that they are able to carry out activities such as cutting or threading.

Key term

Fine motor skills – control of the smaller muscles, such as those in the fingers, to carry out activities such as threading, using a knife and fork, or holding a pencil.

Sensory needs

Children who have sensory needs may need different levels of support from others in the class. Sensory needs may mean that the child has an impairment that is visual or auditory. In other words, they may have difficulty in seeing or hearing, and this may be temporary or permanent. For example, if a child suffers from regular colds, their hearing might be affected on a regular basis. When working with very young children, you should be aware that these kinds of sensory needs may not yet have been recognised. Look out for signs that a child is having difficulty in these areas.

Case study

Hearing problems?

Nilaya has recently started in your nursery. She does not seem to be listening when adults are talking and often seems to be in her own world. Her records do not show that she has any kind of impairment.

1 Should you have any concerns?
2 If so, what should you do?

Communication needs

Children who have communication needs will have difficulty in the areas of speaking and listening and the processes involved in deciphering information. They may also find it hard to understand and respond to non-verbal communication.

Communication and language are crucial to learning and development as they are linked to what we are thinking. Language lets us store information in an organised way. If children have difficulties communicating, they are at a disadvantage because they will be less able to organise what they are thinking or less able to express themselves. They may also find it harder to form relationships with others. As a result, they may become frustrated or feel isolated. Very young children in particular will not have the experience to be able to recognise the reason for their feelings and this could lead to behavioural problems. In more extreme cases, children may not speak at all.

Figure 19.1 shows some of the causes of communication difficulties and delay.

Reflect

What do you understand by the terms verbal communication and non-verbal communication? Discuss all the different ways in which we can communicate with one another.

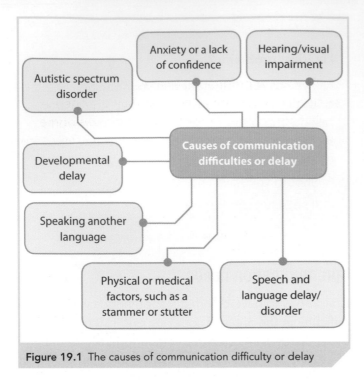

Figure 19.1 The causes of communication difficulty or delay

Learning disabilities

A learning disability will mean that a child has difficulty processing and understanding information. Children who have learning disabilities may need extra support in different areas. For example, with:

- language, memory and reasoning skills
- **sequencing** and organisational skills
- understanding and working with numbers
- problem solving
- coordination and development of physical skills.

Learning disabilities may be global or specific. In other words, they may affect all or only part of a child's learning. For example, a child who has dyslexia has a specific learning difficulty, as it may only affect one area of their learning. A child who has moderate, severe or profound learning difficulties may be affected in all areas of their learning (physical, social, emotional and intellectual).

Key term

Sequencing – being able to put events or pictures into the correct order.

Long-term conditions

If children are suffering from long-term or life-limiting conditions or illnesses, they will need to have additional support of some kind. It is rare for these children to be in a mainstream nursery or school, but at some point in your career you are likely to work with them. These conditions may be caused by different factors and have varying effects on the child. The kinds of conditions may include cystic fibrosis, Duchenne muscular dystrophy, child cancers and other conditions that may be progressive and affect children over many years.

Behavioural or emotional needs

Behaviour, emotional and social difficulty (BESD) describes children with a range of behavioural problems that may delay learning and other areas of development. This is because they may find it hard to focus on what they are doing or are disruptive to others around them. They may also be withdrawn or reluctant to join in with activities with others.

Factors that may lead to additional needs

There are a range of factors that may lead to additional needs in children.

Genetic

Children may have inherited a genetic condition or illness that means they have additional needs. These may vary in the impact they have on the child and in how they affect learning. For example, a condition such as Fragile X syndrome or muscular dystrophy may have more of an effect on a child's learning and development than a stammer or cleft palate. Some conditions may also have a genetic component but are not necessarily caused by genetic factors – these include epilepsy or cerebral palsy. There are also studies that have shown that conditions such as autistic spectrum disorder (ASD) have a genetic link, although research is still being carried out, and this condition is more often considered developmental.

Developmental disorders

Developmental disorders will occur at some stage in a child's development up to the age of 18, and are likely to prevent the child from developing normally in one or more areas. Children may suffer from a developmental condition or disorder that has not been picked up in the early years as they have not yet been required to carry out complex tasks. The most high-profile developmental disorders are ADHD (attention-deficit hyperactivity disorder) and ASD, although Down's syndrome and Tourette's syndrome are also considered to be developmental.

Environmental

Additional needs that are environmental may be caused by situations such as those occurring within the home or in domestic circumstances. Social or emotional factors may affect the child in this way. An example of this is neglect, where children are not given sufficient care and attention to thrive. Another is where children are asylum seekers and have been forced to move away from their home country. Conditions within the home such as violence, alcoholism, drugs or other social issues may affect a child's development and make it hard for them to learn.

Accidents

You may work with a child whose additional needs are the result of an accident. These needs might be physical or emotional depending on the nature and severity of the trauma, and how the child has been affected.

Assessment practice 19.1
3A.P1

Design a booklet for staff outlining the different areas of additional needs and factors that may cause them, and giving examples of how children with additional needs may need to be supported in the setting.

Emotional health and well-being needs

For children to progress in all areas of their development, it is important that they experience consistency in care, a loving and supportive home, and positive relationships with others. In cases where these basic needs are not met, children may be affected in a negative way. Children who experience a lack of interest from adults or who are subjected to domestic violence or abuse are likely to develop behavioural, emotional and social difficulties and possibly mental illness later in life.

Children's physical and emotional health are also interrelated – where a child has physical needs such as a disability or long-term medical condition, their ability to build relationships with others may be affected if they have long periods of time away from the setting, or are unable to join in easily with games and play activities with their friends. This may be even more difficult if children also have a sensory impairment or communication difficulties.

When children have a delay in their emotional health, they may also have less resilience to **transitions**. This will affect their ability to deal with difficult situations and to build friendships.

Key term

Transitions – the changes that happen in all children's lives, such as starting school or personal changes such as a family break-up.

Families might also have different views on the expectations for children's behaviour and you may notice that some parents are stricter with their children than others. While this will not necessarily have a negative impact, problems may arise if there are mixed messages between the setting and home, or if boundaries for behaviour are not consistent.

In all of these cases, children with emotional health and well-being needs will require additional positive attention from others in order to support their development.

The impact of additional needs on the child and their family

If you are working with children who have additional needs, you will need to have an awareness of how their needs affect them and those closest to them. Some children who have conditions that limit them physically may manage well, whereas others may become frustrated or even bad-tempered.

Even if this is not always apparent, it can come out in other ways, and young children in particular may not be able to express how they are feeling. As you are working with these children and get to know them, you will be able to pick up on when they are particularly affected.

As well as the condition itself, other factors may affect the child and how they cope on a day-to-day basis. Figure 19.2 outlines these factors.

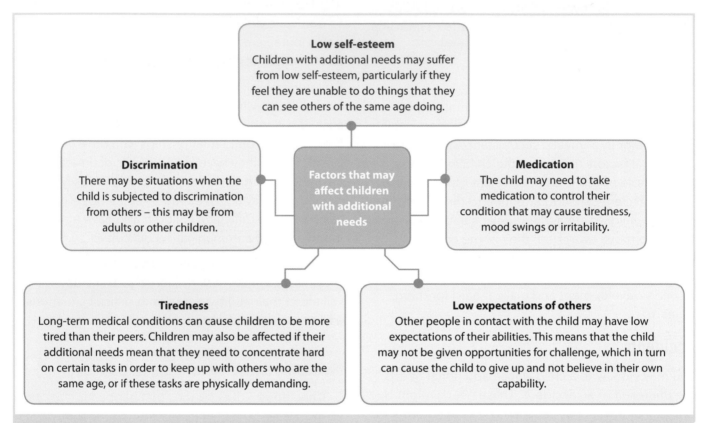

Low self-esteem
Children with additional needs may suffer from low self-esteem, particularly if they feel they are unable to do things that they can see others of the same age doing.

Discrimination
There may be situations when the child is subjected to discrimination from others – this may be from adults or other children.

Factors that may affect children with additional needs

Medication
The child may need to take medication to control their condition that may cause tiredness, mood swings or irritability.

Tiredness
Long-term medical conditions can cause children to be more tired than their peers. Children may also be affected if their additional needs mean that they need to concentrate hard on certain tasks in order to keep up with others who are the same age, or if these tasks are physically demanding.

Low expectations of others
Other people in contact with the child may have low expectations of their abilities. This means that the child may not be given opportunities for challenge, which in turn can cause the child to give up and not believe in their own capability.

Figure 19.2 Factors that may affect a child with additional needs

Assessment practice 19.2

3A.P2

Children may face discrimination in different forms.

Consider whether the following are examples of discrimination.

1 The parent of a child with additional needs tends to be over-protective and limits the activities that they allow the child to do.

2 A setting does not include all children in all activities.

3 A parent complains to the setting that a child with disabilities is not in the right school.

4 A setting does not train its staff on how to manage the needs of all children.

5 Another child speaking within earshot of the child with additional needs says that they cannot play because they are not like everyone else.

6 A child with global learning delay has peers who consistently leave them out of games and activities in the setting.

• How might you deal with each situation?

• How might a child with additional needs be affected in each case?

Depending on the needs of the child, the impact on their family will also vary. For example, if the child has always had a disability or long-term medical condition, they may have had time to come to terms with this and with the fact that they may need additional support and financial help. However, in some cases the daily pressures of caring for their child may mean that parents or carers become tired or find their needs difficult to manage. Siblings may

It is important to work alongside parents to offer them support and advice.

also be affected if parents or carers are required to spend a lot of time with a child with additional needs. In this situation, the setting will need to work alongside parents and give support and advice or refer them to other sources of support.

Where the child's needs have been recently diagnosed, or have arisen suddenly due to an accident or environmental factor, families may need urgent support from outside agencies to enable them to cope. This could be because their needs are emotional, financial or practical.

Research

Special Families is a website that provides information and advice for families of children with additional needs. You can access this website by going to www.pearsonhotlinks. co.uk and searching for the ISBN of this title: 9781447970972.

What other support can you find that is available to these families? How easy is it to access the support?

B Understand provision to support children with additional needs in early years settings

Provision to support children with additional needs has changed a great deal over the last 20 years. In particular, since the introduction of the 2001 Code of Practice children and their parents in both early years and school settings have been far more involved in the kinds of decisions that will have an impact on the provision that is required. There have also been changes in legislation that have impacted on the provision made by schools and early years settings. This section outlines some of these changes and their impact.

Impact of models of disability on legislation and provision

In the past, there have been many unhelpful labels given to children who have additional needs.

The danger of doing this is that we are more likely to focus on the child's disability or condition first, rather than looking at them as an individual. In the past, the medical model of disability has been used more frequently than the social model (see Table 19.1). The kind of language that has been used with the medical model has promoted the attitude that people with disabilities or additional needs must be corrected in some way to be brought in line with everybody else. This has sometimes led to unhelpful labelling of children in terms of their disabilities rather than their potential. The social model of disability values the person and celebrates diversity, and calls on society to make changes to the way in which it views those who have additional needs and disabilities. Table 19.1 outlines the medical and social models of disability.

Table 19.1 The medical and social models of disability

Medical model of disability	Social model of disability
Child is faulty	Child is valued
Diagnosis	Strengths and needs defined by self and others
Labelling	Identify barriers and develop solutions
Impairment becomes focus of attention	Outcome-based programme designed
Segregation and alternative services	Training for parents and professionals
Ordinary needs put on hold	Relationships nurtured
Re-entry if 'normal' enough OR permanent exclusion	Diversity welcomed, child is included
Society remains unchanged	Society evolves

Source: © World of Inclusion (www.worldofinclusion.com) and Richard Rieser.

Legislation for children with additional needs has been affected by these changes, with the introduction of the Disability Discrimination Act 2005 to encompass schools and educational establishments and to reduce the reliance on the medical model. This has now been replaced by the Equality Act 2010, which encompasses all existing equality legislation including the Race Relations Act and the Sex Discrimination Act. In addition, all newly built schools and educational establishments must be accessible and have provision for people with disabilities to include ramps, handrails and disabled toilets.

Reflect

The social model of disability states that it is attitudes within society that are the barriers to inclusion, and not the person's disability. How much do you agree with this? What types of barrier might these be?

Assessment practice 19.3   3B.P4 | 3B.M2

Research and write a report on the emergence of the social model of disability and inclusive education, and how they have changed the way in which children with additional needs are included in mainstream schools. Refer to legislation, regulations and initiatives.

Provision for people with disabilities should be made in schools and educational establishments.

Legislation and initiatives for children with additional needs

Legislation and guidelines have been changing gradually since the Education Act of 1970, which transferred the responsibility for special education from the health service to local authorities. Since this time a key change started, following the Warnock Report of 1978 in which Mary Warnock carried out a study of the needs of children with special educational needs. In her report she called for changes to specialist provision and sought the inclusion of children with additional needs in mainstream schools.

Following the Education Act of 1981, the first Special Educational Needs Code of Practice was introduced in 1996, which set out practical guidance for local authorities in providing for children with special educational needs. Finally, the Special Educational Needs and Disability Act 2001 gave a stronger right to children with special educational needs to be educated in mainstream schools, and also a right for early years providers to request support for those children who could be identified as having additional needs at an earlier age. The contribution of Parent Partnerships, and child participation in matters that involved them, were also given a high priority.

This piece of legislation is a working document for those who are working with children who have additional needs. It sets out clearly the requirements of schools and early years settings, and gives straightforward information on their roles as well as that of local authorities. The new Special Educational Needs and Disability (SEND) Code of Practice came into effect from September 2014.

The Children Act 2004 is also a key piece of legislation, as it is closely linked to Every Child Matters (since renamed Helping Children Achieve More), which set out to change children's services and to improve multi-agency working. This aims to ensure that all organisations and agencies involved with children between birth and 19 years should work together to ensure that children have the support they need to stay safe, be healthy, enjoy and achieve, make a positive contribution, and achieve economic well-being.

Aiming High for Disabled Children (AHDC) is a programme set up by the government in 2007 to transform services for children with disabilities and to make them a priority, as well as supporting their families.

Research

Find out about legislation and initiatives that are interconnected with the area of special educational needs. You may look at, for example, the Education Act 2011, the Children Act 2004 and the Helping Children Achieve More government initiative.

- Why is it important to know about these?
- How much do they affect your practice on a day-to-day basis?

Identifying and providing support and the involvement of parents

Since the introduction of the SEN Code of Practice in 2001, children in schools and early years settings have been through the same assessment process. Before this, the process did not start until the child was in school and, due to the length of the process, this would often mean that support was not given for some time. Due to the importance of early diagnosis and the implementation of support at the earliest possible stage, the process needs to be started as soon as possible. Unless a child has already been given a diagnosis, for example, if they have a medical condition or a disability, nurseries are often the first places to identify developmental difficulties. Parents should also be involved from the earliest stages as they know their children the best and are their child's first educators.

You may have been asked in your setting to observe and monitor a child whom staff or parents have identified as a concern due to their progress. This may be in one or more areas of their development. If a child has been monitored and targeted by staff over time and progress is still not being made, the setting may decide to put them at the first stage of intervention. In a nursery setting, this is called Early Years Action, and in a school, School Action.

Stages of identifying and providing support

Early Years/School Action

At this stage, staff will speak to parents and discuss the child's progress. The Special Educational Needs Coordinator (SENCO) will be involved and if it is decided that the child may need additional help to make progress, they will move to the next stage. Parents will be invited to contribute any new information – in some cases this may be from health professionals or other agencies. Early Years or School Action means that the setting is putting in additional resources such as extra adult support, or additional materials or equipment, in order to help the child to progress. The strategies that are to be put in place are then recorded on an **individual education plan** (IEP) in the form of three or four targets. The IEP will be discussed with the parents and the child, and will be reviewed.

Link

Go to Unit 9, Section A in Student Book 1 to find more information about implementing an IEP.

Key terms

Individual education plan – targets and planned implementation strategies for children who have special educational needs.

Statement of Special Educational Needs – this means that the local authority will assess the child to decide whether it is necessary for them to have an additional adult to support them in school. If so, the local authority will then produce a statement that sets out what is needed for the child to access the curriculum fully.

Activity

Speak to your SENCO and find out how many children in your setting are at each stage of intervention.

Early Years/School Action Plus

If progress is not made over time, and staff and parents still have concerns about the child, they may be moved to the next stage of intervention, which is known as Early Years or School Action Plus. At this stage, there will be involvement by outside agencies, who will give the setting advice and support in devising targets for the IEP.

Requests for a Statutory Assessment

At this stage, some children may still have made little or no progress and will be noticeably behind their peers in one or more areas of their development. The SENCO will speak to the parents and discuss making a request for a Statutory (Multidisciplinary) Assessment. This means that they will have to submit a request to the local authority for additional support for the child. The request will need to provide evidence of the steps that the setting has made to support the child, and include reports from all the professionals involved, as well as the setting and the child's parents. If the Statutory Assessment is successful, the child will be allocated a number of hours of individual provision each week and given a **Statement of Special Educational Needs**. They will need to continue to be monitored and have an IEP, with regular reviews in order to check whether the provision continues to be needed.

Theory into practice

Looking at the Special Educational Needs and Disability Code of Practice 2014, find out about the Statutory Assessment of children who are under compulsory school age. Does it differ in any way from that for school-age children?

Parental involvement

The Special Educational Needs and Disability Code of Practice 2014 emphasises the importance of involving parents at each stage of the assessment process. Parents should be informed about what is taking place and be invited to contribute by writing reports and speaking to professionals. This is because in most cases they have expert knowledge of their child and the closest relationship with them.

Parents should have copies of IEPs and be involved in their reviews. In some cases, the process may alarm parents, particularly if they had not been previously aware of their child's additional needs. They will need to be given as much information as possible by early years settings and schools about the process. Health authorities and NHS trusts are also required to inform parents about additional voluntary organisations that may be able to give support or advice.

Assessment practice 19.4
3A.P3 | 3A.M1 | 3B.P5
3B.P6 | 3B.P7

A child has been admitted to your setting and, after a period of intervention, has needed to have a full Statutory Assessment.

- Using case studies, write a report about the child, describing in detail the different stages of the assessment and the role of any professionals involved.

- You will need to include the involvement of parents at each stage of the assessment and explain why this is important.

- How might the child and family be affected if they were not aware of any issues before, and what could you put in place to support them?

Professionals involved in supporting children with additional needs

You will find that you are often required to liaise with other professionals when supporting children with additional needs. This is so that you can work together to support the child in the best possible way. Meetings may take place within or outside the setting, depending on the role of the professionals and the nature of the support. As a result of a full Statutory Assessment, a range of professionals may become involved in supporting children. These may include an educational psychologist, occupational therapist, a speech therapist, a physiotherapist, a health visitor and a portage worker.

Link

Go to Units 5 and 6 in Student Book 1 for more information about the support provided by other professionals.

Activity

Investigate the role that each of the professionals in Units 5 and 6, Student Book 1 has in supporting the needs of identified children.

Research

Find out more about portage by visiting the website for the National Portage Association. You can access this website by going to www.pearsonhotlinks.co.uk and searching for the ISBN of this title: 9781447970972.

Assessment practice 19.5
3B.P7 | 3B.M3 | 3B.D1

Helena is 3 years old and has just started in nursery. She is an only child of very young parents and it is clear from her lack of physical and social skills that she needs some additional help.

1 Why is it important to organise some kind of assessment of Helena's needs as soon as possible?

2 What professionals might be involved in the assessment process for Helena and what would their role be?

3 How does effective assessment support inclusive practice for children with additional needs?

The role of organisations that support parents

Parent Partnership services were set up as part of the Special Educational Needs Code of Practice in 2001 (revised in 2014). They are designed to support parents who have children with additional needs and ensure that they have access to information, advice and support. This may be through the assessment process in order to gain additional support in the child's setting, but they may also refer parents to other agencies.

Parent Partnership services will be made available by local authorities, which are responsible for making sure that schools and early years settings know how to access the service.

There are also a number of voluntary organisations and charities that support parents of children with additional needs. These may be specific to a particular condition, for example, the Down's Syndrome Association, which offers advice and support groups for new parents.

Research

Find out about Parent Partnership services in your own area. How are they publicised and made available to parents? To help you, visit the website for the National Parent Partnership Network. You can access this website by going to www.pearsonhotlinks.co.uk and searching for the ISBN of this title: 9781447970972.

C Understand the role of adults working with children with additional needs

All adults working with children will need to have a good understanding of their role and how it fits in with others' roles in order to best support the children with whom they work. If you are working with or supporting children who have additional needs, you are likely to be working with a wide range of other professionals from both within and outside the setting. This section will look at how these different roles fit together and the importance of multi-agency working.

Ensuring inclusive practice

The Special Educational Needs Code of Practice 2001 (revised in 2014) was introduced in part to strengthen the right of children with additional needs to a mainstream education. However, you may find that these children still face barriers to their learning and that other people focus on what they are not, rather than what they are. It is important that you are able to support and empower children who have additional needs, in particular if they lack confidence or have a poor self-image. Barriers to learning may include the following.

- Organisational barriers

These may be due to school policies, lack of staff training or lack of diversity within the school curriculum. Your school or setting should have an up-to-date equal opportunities or inclusion policy that sets out its priorities for developing inclusion. It should also ensure that all staff working with children who have additional needs are fully trained and able to do so with the full support of the setting.

- Physical barriers

There should be no reason for a child who has a disability or special educational needs not to be able to gain access to educational facilities. If you are working with a child who has a disability or additional needs, make sure all staff are aware that provision must allow every child to participate. This may mean that adaptations need to be made to the environment or that additional resources and equipment are purchased.

- Barriers in the attitudes of others

This barrier can be one of the most challenging to overcome, as it is hard to change the opinions and attitudes of others. You should always remember that the needs of the child come first and to stand up for the rights of the children you support. You may need to challenge discrimination within your setting if the views of parents or other staff are intolerant or prejudiced.

- Barriers in their own confidence and self-image

Some children who have additional needs are lacking in confidence or have a poor self-image.

This may be for a number of reasons, including reduced opportunities, lack of support and encouragement, or simply not believing in themselves. It is important that you encourage and empower these children as much as you can. This includes providing an environment that celebrates diversity and gives encouragement to all children by identifying their strengths and needs, and working with them to help them to achieve their goals through person-centred planning. You might ask questions such as those outlined in Figure 19.3.

Activity

How would you challenge the attitudes of others if they were prejudiced against children with additional needs? Carry out a role-play activity with your group in which you challenge the opinions of others showing prejudice.

Reflect

Nick Vujicic is a motivational speaker who was born without arms and legs. Visit his website, 'Life without Limbs', by going to www.pearsonhotlinks. co.uk and searching for the ISBN of this title: 9781447970972 to find out more about his inspirational story. Think about how we can encourage children to have a similar positive attitude and self-image.

Planning for individual needs and reviewing progress

Planning for individual needs

When you are working with a child who has additional needs, it is important that you are clear about the stage at which they are working according to the SEND Code of Practice 2014.

You will need to know whether they are being monitored due to initial concerns, or whether they are on Early Years Action or Action Plus and have been given an IEP with personalised targets. IEPs are designed to give children additional provision to ensure that they are able to access the curriculum. Although lesson plans should always include differentiated activities for all, children who have an IEP will have additional targets to work on according to their needs.

Depending on whether outside agencies are involved, some of these targets may focus on their specific needs and may include speech and language, physiotherapy or behavioural targets. In addition to this, work may still need to be adapted or changed and additional resources and/ or equipment used in order to facilitate children's learning. You will need to be able to monitor the child's progress at all times and intervene if necessary in order to ensure that they are able to meet the learning intention.

My needs are…

My dreams are…

My strengths are…

The help I need from you is…

Figure 19.3 A person-centred approach to planning

Ask if you can have access to copies of any IEPs that have been devised for children in your setting. Are all of the staff aware of the needs of these children?

Assessing and reviewing progress

All IEPs will need to have a review date so that the child, their parents and those working with them are able to meet and discuss the child's progress. This will mean that they will need to document whether the targets have been met or whether they are still ongoing. They will then need to set new targets together as well as a new review date.

Once a year, children who have an Assessment Statement will also have an annual review, which all professionals working with the child, as well as the child and their parents, will be invited to attend and to contribute reports to. The minutes of this meeting must then be submitted to the local authority, which will take the child's needs into consideration and decide whether they still need additional support. This is important, as children's needs will change over time, and the child may have made significant progress due to the support given.

Reflect

Do you and those you work with:

- have high expectations of all children?
- celebrate diversity?
- ensure that all children participate in all areas of the curriculum?

It is important that you develop positive attitudes towards all the children you work with and challenge or support them appropriately.

Amara has cerebral palsy and has been in your setting for a few weeks. It is clear that she has very low self-esteem. She is extremely quiet with her peers and with adults, and often does not even try to carry out activities, saying that she 'can't do anything'.

She interacts with one or two other children when they are together but does not put her ideas forward in group activities or when the children are on the carpet. You and your team leader are about to devise an IEP for Amara at the stage of Early Years Action along with the SENCO.

1 What kinds of targets might you put in place to support Amara and help to develop her confidence, and how would you involve her parents?

2 Why is it important for all adults in the setting to be aware of Amara's needs? How can you work as a team in order to empower her and to encourage her to focus on her strengths?

3 How would you implement the IEP and assess its impact with your colleagues and any outside agencies, and what would you do to ensure that Amara continued to make progress?

Collaborating with other professionals

When supporting children with additional needs you will need to be able to collaborate with other professionals. This includes not only formal but also informal opportunities to talk about children's progress. You should work together in the best interests of the child and draw on one another's expertise in order to provide support. In early years settings and schools, this may start with your room leader, nursery manager or class teacher, as well as your SENCO. You may also need to work with others who are based externally. Together, you are likely to have meetings, sometimes known as multi-agency meetings or team-around-the-child meetings, in order to ensure that all of you have a joined-up approach to working with the child.

A joined-up approach is important, particularly in the early identification of additional needs, as it encourages professionals who work with these children to work cooperatively to share information.

Research

Find out a bit more about the CAF by visiting the website for Children's Workforce Matters. You can access this website by going to www.pearsonhotlinks.co.uk and searching for the ISBN of this title: 9781447970972. You can also visit your own local authority website for guidance on the CAF in your area.

The Special Educational Needs Coordinator (SENCO)

The SENCO is responsible for managing and monitoring the provision for those with special educational needs within a school or early years setting.

Link

Go to Units 5 and 6 in Student Book 1 to find more information about the role of the SENCO.

Working in partnership with parents

The Warnock Report into special educational needs provision in 1978 stated that for children under 5 years old, there should be 'greater recognition and involvement of parents, wherever possible, as the main educators of their children during the earliest years'. It is during the early years that children learn and develop most rapidly, and it is through their parents that they will develop many of their attitudes to learning. Parents should be encouraged to

communicate with the setting as much as possible, by both formal and informal means.

There are many ways in which settings can work in partnership with parents, including:

- informal events
- providing information in leaflets and newsletters
- encouraging parents to be involved in the day-to-day running of the setting
- having an open-door policy to discuss any issues
- inviting parents to contribute to IEPs, ongoing assessments and reviews.

It is important for children, and especially those who have special educational needs, that their parents are encouraged to be involved in the setting and feel able to discuss their child's needs with staff. Parents who feel excluded or are not confident enough to communicate with the setting may unwittingly start to build barriers between home and the setting.

Reflect

Your setting has a high proportion of parents who speak English as an additional language. What could the setting do in order to encourage them to liaise with staff and to become involved in the activities of the setting? What advantages will this bring?

Assessment practice 19.7   3C.P9 | 3C.D2

Write a report about how settings should work in partnership with parents to support children who have additional needs. Give examples of the kinds of formal and informal opportunities that may arise for adults in the setting to speak with parents about their children, and evaluate the impact of positive relationships between the setting and the family.

Following policies and procedures and providing for personal care

Schools and early years settings are required to have a number of different policies in place to ensure that all staff work together and follow the same procedures. As a result of this, settings are required to have a policy for children with additional needs, or a Special Educational Needs Policy. There will also be an Equal Opportunities Policy and an Inclusion Policy. You and other staff in the setting will need to ensure that you are aware of the correct procedures to follow when working with children who have additional needs. These may also include gaining information about children's individual needs and some health and safety aspects when using equipment or being asked to lift or restrain children. If you are asked to use physical restraint for any reason, you must make sure that you are following your setting's and the local authority's guidelines.

Theory into practice

How many of the following key policies have you read?

- Safeguarding/Child Protection Policy
- Health and Safety Policy
- Equal Opportunities/Inclusion Policy
- Special Educational Needs Policy
- Confidentiality Policy
- If you work in a school, the Early Years Policy

You will also need to check the setting's policy if you are asked to carry out any personal care for children, such as helping with toileting. Although all adults working with children are required to have a Disclosure and Barring Service (DBS) check, you may be vulnerable if you are not aware of correct procedures and carry them out incorrectly or do not maintain hygenic practice. In most cases, adults are advised not to be alone with children at any time. However, this case may be an exception. You will also need to be sensitive to the needs of the child and allow them to carry out as much as they can independently to empower them.

Confidentiality and privacy are also important when working with children who have additional needs. You should not speak about any issues concerning a child or their family outside the setting, to ensure that their privacy is respected.

Activity

Find out about your setting's policies for managing restraint, and what to do if you need to do this.

Further reading and resources

Hodkinson, A. and Vickerman, P. (2009) *Key Issues in Special Educational Needs and Inclusion*, London: SAGE Publications Ltd.

Porter, L. (2002) *Educating Young Children with Special Needs*, London: SAGE Publications Ltd.

Special Educational Needs and Disability: Code of Practice, Department for Education, 2014.

The Warnock Report (1978) Special Educational Needs: Report of the Committee of Enquiry into the Education of Handicapped Children and Young People, London: Her Majesty's Stationery Office.

Wall, K. (2010) *Special Needs and the Early Years: A Practitioner's Guide*, London: SAGE Publications Ltd.

Websites

Portage: www.portage.org.uk

National Association of Special Educational Needs: www.nasen.org.uk

SEN magazine: www.senmagazine.co.uk

Many charities such as Barnardo's, Sense, Mencap and the Hope Centre also provide support and assistance through their work and on their websites.

Ready for work?

Soriya Gupta Nursery worker

I have been working at the nursery for three years. I have worked with quite a few children who have had additional needs, from speech and language difficulties to Down's Syndrome and also two autistic children. It's really important to have a good understanding of how children with additional needs are looked after in different early years settings and to have a good working knowledge of the Code of Practice. This is important, as it gives us a clear document to work from alongside our own policies and procedures.

We also need to understand the whole assessment process and be able to carry out observations so that we can feedback to colleagues and parents, and be part of a whole-team approach to managing the child's needs. I have been sent on a couple of training courses on additional needs which were run through the local authority and these have given me a really good insight into the kinds of issues to look out for and also a source of additional advice if needed.

I have also had the opportunity to work with a few other professionals, including my area SENCO, the speech and language therapists, and both occupational therapists and physiotherapists. This has been really interesting for me as I have learned a lot more about what their roles involve, and it has been great to be involved in meetings with them along with parents and really feel that I am making a difference to these children.

Skills for practice

Effective relationships with children – supporting a child with additional needs

- Get to know as much as you can about the child from parents and other staff in the setting.
- Form a relationship with the child by finding out about them and their interests.
- Make a point of saying hello and talking to them each day.
- Find out about any additional equipment or resource they may need and learn to use it too.
- Make sure you are aware of their targets and IEP.
- Work with them on different areas of the curriculum – both indoor and outdoor – and support them where needed.

Professional relationships with adults

- Show that you can work as part of a team by supporting others in your setting.
- Be organised and prepared each day when you come to the setting. If working with a child who has additional needs, you may need to bring additional resources.
- If you are working as part of a team around a particular child, remember to keep channels of communication open and be approachable.
- Keep up to date with contact details of other agencies and individuals with whom you are working to support the child.
- Develop and nurture good relationships with parents and carers, and remain approachable and easy to contact on a daily basis.

Introduction

Imagine the scene: a toddler comes over to you with a plastic cup. They stand and pretend to drink from it, then they offer it to you. This is typical of imaginative play in young children. It shows that the child has reached a level of cognitive development that allows them to use symbols in their play. From this type of play most children go on to play together cooperatively and create quite complex pretend worlds. Children often play with small figures too, in what is known as small-world play.

In this unit, you will learn about the different types of imaginative play and how they support children's learning and development. It also covers how to plan for imaginative play, including how to set up and maintain the resources used. Finally, it looks at ways in which we can support children when they are engaged in imaginative play and the importance of challenging gender stereotyping.

Assessment: You will be assessed by a series of assignments set by your teacher/tutor.

Learning aims

In this unit you will:

A   understand the importance of imaginative play for children

B1   understand planning for imaginative play

B2   understand the role of the adult in imaginative play.

Our children love role play. It is a major focus for our work and we always have a home corner and a shop as standard provision. In our setting, role play is used to cover many aspects of the curriculum, but particularly communication and language. It is surprising how much chatter comes from the role-play areas and just how imaginative young children can be. My all-time favourite was when we created a Chinese takeaway, which we started off by ordering a takeaway from a local business. It was great fun.

Debbie, *a preschool practitioner*

Supporting Children's Imaginative Play

BTEC
Assessment Zone

This table shows you what you must do in order to achieve a **Pass**, **Merit** or **Distinction** grade, and where you can find activities to help you.

Assessment criteria		
Pass	**Merit**	**Distinction**
Learning aim A: Understand the importance of imaginative play for children		
3A.P1 Explain ways in which imaginative play supports learning. **Assessment practice 21.1**	**3A.M1** Analyse the contribution of imaginative play to children's learning and development. **Assessment practice 21.1**	**3A.D1** Evaluate how imaginative play can impact on outcomes for children. **Assessment practice 21.1**
3A.P2 **I&CT** Review the benefits of imaginative play for children's social, emotional and cultural development. **Assessment practice 21.1**		
Learning aim B1: Understand planning for imaginative play **Learning aim B2: Understand the role of the adult in imaginative play**		
3B1.P3 Explain the role of observations in supporting planning and extending children's imaginative play. **Assessment practice 21.2**	**3B1.M2** Analyse the role of the adult in planning for imaginative play. **Assessment practice 21.2**	**3B.D2** Evaluate the contribution of adults to effective imaginative play in an early years setting. **Assessment practice 21.2**
3B1.P4 **English** Explain how to provide resources in an early years setting to support: • domestic play • fantasy play • superhero play • small-world play. **Assessment practice 21.2**		
3B1.P5 Describe ways of using indoor and outdoor environments in an early years setting to support imaginative play. **Assessment practice 21.2**		
3B2.P6 Explain how adults in an early years setting can support and extend children's imaginative play. **Assessment practice 21.2**	**3B2.M3** Analyse the role of the adult as a play partner in children's imaginative play in an early years setting, using examples. **Assessment practice 21.2**	
3B2.P7 Explain why it is important for adults to challenge stereotypes in imaginative play. **Assessment practice 21.2**		

English English Functional Skills signposting	**I&CT** Information and Communication Technology Functional Skills signposting

How you will be assessed

This unit will be assessed by a series of internally assessed tasks set by your teacher/tutor. Throughout this unit you will find assessment practice activities that will help you work towards your assessment. Completing these activities will not mean that you have achieved a particular grade, but you will have carried out useful research or preparation that will be relevant when it comes to your final assignment.

In order for you to achieve the tasks in your assignment, it is important that you check you have met all of the Pass grading criteria. You can do this as you work your way through the assignment.

If you are hoping to gain a Merit or Distinction, you should also make sure that you present the information in your assignment in the style that is required by the relevant assessment criterion. For example, Merit criteria will require you to analyse and Distinction criteria will require you to evaluate.

The assignment set by your teacher/tutor will consist of a number of tasks designed to meet the criteria in the assessment criteria table. This is likely to consist of a written assignment but may also include activities such as:

- a presentation for parents
- case studies and observations
- a leaflet.

Getting started

Have you ever seen a toddler talking intently on a toy phone? Or two 4-year-old children sitting pretending to have dinner? In these moments children are in their own worlds and are enjoying their play. By the end of this unit, you should know why children enjoy this type of play and how it helps their development.

A Understand the importance of imaginative play for children

Imaginative play has not always been recognised as important in children's learning and development, and in the past was often seen as 'just play'. Today its importance is recognised and provision is made for it in early years settings. In this section, we consider why imaginative play is so important for children.

Definition of imaginative play

There are many definitions of imaginative play, but the idea of suspending belief in reality and moving into a pretend world is often talked about in this context. At 18 months, most children begin to take objects and pretend to do something with them. At first the actions are quite simple and are based on what the child has directly seen or experienced, but later children develop the ability to imagine things that they have not directly encountered. By 4 years old, children are often creating quite complex imaginary scenes and are able to fully immerse themselves in them. Interestingly, if you ask children about what they are doing, they will often tell you that they are pretending, before quickly slipping back into character or into their imaginary world. This makes imaginative play a **symbolic action** as well as a creative one.

Key term

Symbolic action – a gesture that is representative of a real action.

Features of different types of imaginative play

There are different types of imaginative play that you may observe children engaging in. It is useful to understand the features of each type so that you can provide for it.

Domestic play

This is often provided by settings in the form of a home corner, as children are pretending to be in a home. They pretend to prepare meals, iron or care for a baby. Much domestic play is based on children's own observations of adults and their own experiences of domestic life. It is often a feature of young children's imaginative play, but remains popular with older children. Interestingly, children will often use domestic play in role-play areas that were designed for fantasy play. For instance, you may see two children in a space rocket making a cup of tea.

Fantasy play

Children engaged in fantasy play are basing their play on situations that they have not encountered personally, but have some knowledge of. This knowledge may come from stories, hearing about others' experiences or seeing photographs. They may, for example, pretend to be in a hospital or working in a shop. This type of play requires that children are imagining a situation rather than recreating something that they have experienced.

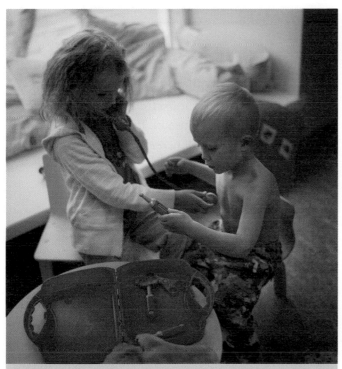

What type of imaginative play are these two children taking part in?

Superhero play

As the term implies, this type of play is about children pretending to be 'heroes' and is often influenced by television, cartoons and small-world figures such as Action Man. This type of play is often very exciting for children and usually involves plenty of noise and movement. It is often associated with boys, but many girls will also enjoy this type of play. Superhero play often poses a dilemma for settings as many children will 'arm' themselves with a pretend gun and may pretend to kill or hurt the 'baddies'. Some settings have clear policies about restricting how children engage in this type of play, whereas others take a more relaxed point of view. It is interesting that this type of play can also divide parents too.

Research

Find out more about superhero play.

1 Talk to staff in your setting and find out about the setting's policy on superhero play.

2 Talk to parents and see whether they allow toy guns at home.

Small-world play

In small-world play, children play with small figures and objects such as farm animals, play people and cars. Children move these around and build stories around them. Many children will make noises for different objects or pretend to talk for the different figures. Most of the play happens on the floor or at low tables. Figure 21.1 shows the many different types of small-world toys that children may use.

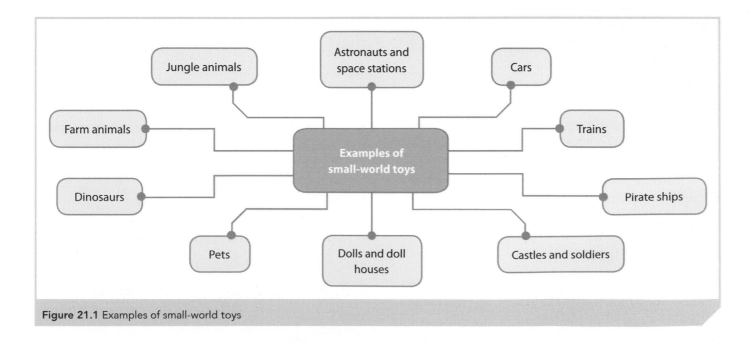

Figure 21.1 Examples of small-world toys

Benefits of imaginative play for development

Imaginative play is a major part of children's emotional and social development. This is one reason why it is often used therapeutically with children who have experienced a trauma. We will now look at some of the specific benefits of imaginative play.

Self-expression

While children are pretending, they are free of restrictions and can express whatever they wish. This kind of play is usually a child-initiated activity and, while it may be supported by adults, children can take on whatever role they wish. They may want to act out being a baby, or being angry or strong. This freedom allows for great self-expression.

Exploring feelings and empathy

As children's role play develops, they increasingly try to 'be' different people. They may take on the role of a tired mother, angry older brother or naughty child. Playing out these roles helps children to explore new feelings in a safe way. They know that they can stop 'being' this role at any time. By playing out different roles, children also get a glimpse of what it is like to be someone else. This in turn can help children develop empathy.

Exercising choice

Young children spend significant amounts of their time being told what to do or having limitations placed on their activity. In role play, children can choose to be whomever they want or act in any way that they wish. In small-world play, children are in control of the figures, cars and animals. They can decide who goes where and what happens to them. Having this choice, even in a pretend world, is liberating for children.

Cooperation, negotiation and resolving conflicts

From around 3 years, most children start to engage in some imaginative play alongside others. Two or three children may play together in the home corner or with small-world toys. As imaginative play is exciting and pleasurable, there is a real incentive for children to find ways of cooperating and thus learning the skills of negotiation and conflict resolution. This is interesting to listen to, particularly as children become older. Usually their imaginative play becomes more complex and so the need for organisation becomes greater. It is not uncommon for children to begin their play by deciding who should do what and what will happen during the action.

Theory into practice

Observe a group of children engaged in role play or small-world play.

Listen to their conversation and consider whether they are showing the skills associated with cooperation.

Importance of imaginative play in supporting creativity

Imaginative play is part of creativity, as it is an expression of the child's imagination. In the National Curriculum it is known as drama. By pretending, children are learning another way of expressing themselves and their experiences. Through imaginative play, children also learn to think creatively by, for example, taking their own initiative or problem solving as they work out how to use resources in their play.

Interestingly, children often use imaginative play as a starting point for other creative activities. They may, for example, decide that their play people need a shelter and so make something using junk modelling. From around 5 years old, children may also pretend to be dancers or actors and extend this to put on a show.

How imaginative play supports learning

Imaginative play can help children's cognitive and language development. The extent to which this happens can depend on the richness of the props and the ways in which adults plan and support children's play.

Extending thinking and problem solving

In imaginative play, children incorporate experiences or information into their play. This helps them to extend their thinking and so is a good way of supporting their cognitive development. Through play, children can explore problem solving in a practical way. An example of this is the way that many children, when they are outdoors, will start gathering items to make a den or look for items that they can pretend to cook with.

Exploring mathematical concepts

Children will often put into practice the mathematical concepts they have. They may, for example, count out 'biscuits' for baby or set a timer to act as parking meter. Some settings will also help children to explore mathematical concepts further by ensuring mathematical equipment such as scales, tape measures and real money are provided as props. A pretend carpet shop or a Chinese takeaway might be set up.

By playing shops, this child is learning to count and to recognise the value of coins and notes.

Using technology

As technology is increasingly being used in today's world, so this is reflected in children's imaginative play. Some small-world toys have technology built into them, for example, programmable robots and dinosaurs. Within role play, equipment such as toy cash registers and microwaves are also built with lifelike sounds that help children to use these technologies. In some settings, children have access

to walkie-talkies, which they can incorporate into their play. Although not everyone is a fan of such gadgets, children using them do gain knowledge of technology.

Exploring and selecting materials

As with other types of child-initiated play, children are able to access and choose materials freely. What is interesting to note is the way that children are good improvisers and will often choose things from all over the setting to improve their play. This means that if children need play food, for example, they are likely to go to the dough table or over to the sand tray. Wherever possible, it is good practice to take a relaxed view of this, because through exploring and selecting materials, children are learning about their properties and are also being creative.

Developing language and literacy

Imaginative play is a great incentive for children to talk and communicate; especially when they are engaged in role play. This is one of the reasons why most early years settings will make provision for imaginative play. It is also why many settings will use role play as a way of developing children's vocabulary by setting out a new role-play experience such as 'at the garden centre' and then starting off the play by joining in. This allows children to hear new vocabulary and expressions in context.

Settings also find that children will often enjoy writing or mark making during role play. This is usually encouraged as part of the play, and so a child who is pretending to be a traffic warden may be given a clipboard and a pen so that they can write out and give 'tickets' to other children.

Supporting imaginative play to value ideas and interests

As you will see later in this unit, adults have an important role in supporting imaginative play. Key to this is the interest and value they place on it. By providing resources, being interested in what children do and giving children sufficient time, adults give children a clear message that this type of play is important. This can help children to explore more intricate and complex ideas and concepts through their play. Imaginative play also provides opportunities for children to explore their own ideas and interests freely as there is no right or wrong way to play. This helps children try out new roles and props and be adventurous, for example, by taking on the role of a superhero or a villain.

Bridging the gap between home and the early years setting

Children who have a home culture that is very different to the culture within the setting are likely to find an outlet in imaginative play. Using different types of imaginative play, they will probably play out their experiences in each of the cultures and try to make sense of the differences. For example, children whose family members take off their shoes before entering the home might remove their shoes, but later on, after seeing other children not doing this, might change their own play. Imaginative play can also help children to understand the differences between families, as they may play alongside others who do things differently. It is helpful for settings to make sure that children have props for domestic play that reflect all of the children's home cultures. This allows children to reflect and build on their own home experiences, and also broadens their knowledge of other children's experiences.

Research

Observe a group of children engaged in domestic play.

- Are resources provided that will allow children to reflect their home experiences?
- Does their play reflect their experiences in their home?

Assessment practice 21.1   3A.P1 | 3A.P2 | 3A.M1 | 3A.D1

You have been asked by a curriculum review panel to give your thoughts on the benefits of imaginative play in the form of an evaluation. Your writing should include:

- the key features of different types of imaginative play
- how imaginative play can support children's learning and emotional, social and cultural development
- the role of imaginative play in outcomes for children.

B1   Understand planning for imaginative play

It is important that adults support imaginative play by providing opportunities for it to occur. In this section, we look at practical ways in which you can plan and set up a range of opportunities.

The role of observation in planning for imaginative play

Adults have a key role to play in observing children during imaginative play. Observations will help you understand children's interests, and also help you plan further opportunities for them. This can in turn help to extend children's learning and enjoyment.

Young children often have favourite types of imaginative play that they return to repeatedly over a period of time. It can be useful to know what

particular children and groups of children enjoy doing, so you can make sure that this is provided for in the setting. Parents may help you with this, as often children engage in imaginative play at home too.

As part of observing children's play, think about the following questions.

How popular is this area?

Some areas of role play or types of small-world play go through phases of popularity with children. If this is the case, you might think about increasing the provision for them. For instance, if the home corner is very popular, you might create another 'home' in another part of the setting. This is because many imaginative play activities have a critical mass in terms of how many children can share the same story.

What is the story?

Most imaginative play develops a storyline. For instance, children may start saying that they are building the strongest train track because a dinosaur is going to come down and break it up. It is worth listening to the children and working out what the story is because this can help you develop it further by, for example, putting out new resources.

Who plays together?

From around 3 years old, children start to develop friendship and play preferences. It is worth looking at who seems to enjoy imaginative play together. This can help with planning if, for example, the setting has times when groups come together.

Setting up resources for imaginative play

Most settings have at least one designated area that is always a role-play area. This is likely to include a home corner, sometimes a shop and an area for dressing up. In addition, it is good practice for settings to have a role-play area outdoors, and this should also be well resourced.

Setting up for role play

A good starting point is to base the setting on what you know children enjoy doing, what you have observed and any additional planning you have carried out. You can also talk to children about what equipment they would like to have out. Many settings are well resourced and this means that selections need to be made about what to put out in a session. If everything is put out at once, this can lead to a very messy and unrewarding play area for children. Do not be afraid of selecting particular resources and putting others away, but allowing children to access them if they want to.

It is good practice to give children the opportunity to engage in mark-making activities so, wherever possible, you should incorporate writing materials such as a shopping list into a kitchen corner or a price list into a shop corner.

Setting up a home corner

Domestic play is always a favourite with children and it is helpful if this area is attractive and well resourced.

This gives the children some play prompts. Within the home corner, you can sometimes give different focuses, such as 'kitchen' or 'bedroom'. This is very useful as a way of extending children's play and vocabulary.

Remember the following tips.

- Make sure the home corner area is clean.
- Take out any inappropriate toys or props that have found their way in from previous sessions.
- Try to make the area as realistic as possible – for instance, put things in cupboards and drawers, lay the table or dress the baby doll.

How could this home corner be made more realistic for these children?

Dressing-up clothes

In some settings, clothes are on a rail, while in others, they may be in a basket. Remember the following tips.

- Sort through the props, checking that they are clean and complete.
- Remove any items that are not looking attractive or need repair.
- Lay out outfits and props such as bags, belts and shoes attractively – perhaps on hangers or on tables.

Setting up small-world play

It can be helpful to put out some small-world play items for children. This gives them a starting point if they need it. A good tip is to combine sensory materials with small-world play. For example, you may put cars or diggers in a builder's tray that has gravel in the bottom of it or put farm animals in a tray of turf.

Maintaining areas

If children are enjoying their play and are very focused, try not to interfere as this may spoil their flow and concentration. This may mean that you need to do some discreet tidying-up of objects that have been discarded during children's play. You may also need to be ready to set things up again, once a child or group of children have changed their focus. This is important because, during a session, other children may want to engage in small-world play or role play and are more likely to do this if the area looks attractive. It is also important to keep observing children so that you can add resources to facilitate their play further.

Fantasy play

Fantasy play covers many scenarios, many of which the children will invent for themselves. This type of play is also often inspired by stories, books and visits. It is helpful if the props that are provided are 'real-life' ones as this will often make it easier for children to extend their play. Interestingly, children are quite resourceful and so, while it is useful to have some authentic props, they do not need every single detail to be accurate. For example, children will be happy putting their 'cupcakes' into a cardboard box that acts as the 'oven'.

Table 21.1 gives a few examples of the types of fantasy play that children may take part in, along with the types of resources that might be needed.

Superhero play

As superhero play can become quite boisterous, it is important to consider this when thinking about what resources you will provide for children. Some settings have clear policies about superhero play, especially with regard to whether or not children can have or make toy guns. It is therefore important to make sure that any resources you use are in line with the setting's approach to superhero play. In general terms, it can be useful to provide potential superheroes with some form of identification – this might mean a cape, badge or belt. As superheroes are likely to need some form of communication device, a toy phone can also come in handy. Interestingly, many settings will prevent superhero play from becoming destructive or very aggressive by providing resources that prompt superheroes to be kind and thoughtful. They may, for example, have a 'mission board' on which calls for help can be written, for example, 'a cat has gone missing' or 'someone needs help with their shopping'. Appropriate props are then provided so that these rescue missions can be enacted.

> **Reflect**
>
> In the past month, what types of imaginative play have children taken part in? Are there any different role-play scenarios you could set up for children? What resources would you need?

Table 21.1 Types of fantasy play and resources

Type of fantasy play	Resources required
Hairdresser	Aprons, curlers, combs, brushes, mirrors, empty bottles for pretend shampoo, toy scissors, magazines for the waiting room
Shoe shop	Shoe boxes, measuring tape, selection of shoes, cash register, money, stools for sitting on
Hospital	Charts on clipboards, beds, stethoscope, uniform, bandages, crutches, pushchair to act as a wheelchair
Birthday party	Plates, birthday cake (made of dough with sticks for candles), pass the parcel, wrapped presents, birthday cards
Petrol station	Pumps (cardboard boxes with a tube or hosepipe sticking out), car wash (sponges, soapy water in buckets), cash register, sign

Using books and stories as a stimulus

Books and stories are often great starting points for children's imaginative play, especially for developing fantasy play. A story or images in a book can act as starting points for the creation of new role-play areas. For instance, following the story of Goldilocks and the Three Bears, a role-play area might be set up that recreates the three bears' house, along with three beds, three chairs and three bowls and spoons. Children may then recreate the story that they have heard and use the actual words in the story. Using books and stories for imaginative play is usually more successful with children who have good levels of language development and so you may find that you see this on placement with children aged 3 years and over. Using books and stories as a stimulus is also a good way of building children's vocabulary.

Many children will also need an adult to support their play, even when they are familiar with the story. They may need the adult to join in or to help them create the space and props.

Using space and the outdoor environment

It is very interesting to observe children as they engage in imaginative play. In this way, we can often work out how best to provide the right type of space for their play.

Small-world play

Some small-world play requires that children are able to spread out, often on the floor. This is particularly true when children are engaged with train sets, cars and also play animals. To provide for this type of play, you should make sure that the floor area is comfortable – this might mean a rug on carpet, or soft grass or matting if outdoors. It is also important to provide a space that is out of the way of other children to avoid elaborate plans or play being trampled on. Children often like to have objects they will require during the play close to hand.

Some types of small-world play, such as playing with dolls' houses, pirate ships and castles, benefit from a low surface in addition to some floor space. A low

table, bench or even a chair can work well for this. In some settings, children enjoy putting items up on shelves or windowsills and then moving the characters around them on the floor.

Theory into practice

Observe children who are engaged in small-world play.

- Where are they playing, and what do they need for their play?
- Are there any difficulties with the location of their play?

Role play requiring large amounts of space

Some types of pretend play require plenty of room to move around in. This is often because movement is an integral part of their play. A good example of this would be children who are pretending to be fire-fighters and need to jump on their vehicles

Children need enough space to move around during their play – set up play outdoors.

(likely to be some form of wheeled toy) to get to the fire quickly. Without the possibility of this movement, much of the enjoyment and purpose of their play would be lost.

While some settings do have plenty of indoor space, this is usually quite rare, so this is one reason why it is important to provide role-play opportunities outdoors. Sometimes, this type of play may not work alongside the other play activities that are offered in the setting, so it is important to observe carefully what is happening in the play area and, if necessary, gently guide the children to a more suitable place where they can carry on playing, but in harmony with the others.

Role play requiring confined spaces

When children are pretending to be indoors they often like small spaces to play in. This means that if they are in the outdoor area, but are playing shop, they might choose an area next to a fence and may move objects to enclose this space. It is also interesting that when children are pretending to be indoors, they like a roof over them and for the space to be quite cramped. This means that you may need to provide more than one area of this nature if there are several children who want to role play. It also means that when organising play outdoors, you will need to create some cosy corners for children in the same way that you might indoors.

B2 Understand the role of the adult in imaginative play

While many children will happily play without adults being involved, we also know that imaginative play can be enriched by us providing resources, ideas and joining in at times. In this section, we look at the role of the adult in supporting and developing children's imaginative play.

Observing children engaged in imaginative play

One of the key ways in which we can support children's imaginative play is to observe them as they are playing. This can be done either discreetly, from the sidelines, or as we are joining in with them. Through this observation we can gain information that will help us to provide further opportunities for them. For example, we may put out additional resources connecting their play to stories and other games, or take them on visits. For instance, if a child seems very interested in playing shop, we might give them more 'stock' or plan a visit to a small shop to extend the play.

Communication and language

Observing play will also help us to assess children's development in areas such as communication and language. As most children talk while they are

engaged in imaginative play, you might consider recording their speech or at least listening to it. You may, for example, notice that a child rarely talks to other children despite being very engaged with the play. This may be because they do not have sufficient language to express themselves and so you may need to look for additional activities or ways of encouraging the child to talk.

Social and emotional development

We may also spot how children's social skills are developing, as imaginative play usually brings children together. From observing children, we may assess the stage of their social development and play. We may also notice children who are consistently submissive to others and so need to develop a little more confidence. Imaginative play is also an expression of children's emotional states, and so we may look out for children who are showing feelings of anger. This could mean that we need to look for additional activities to help them express themselves.

Child protection and imaginative play

Some children who have been subjected to abuse may replay it through their play. It is important to look out for this and consider what might have influenced their play. If you see children who are playing out scenes that seem unusual or inappropriate given their age, you should pass on this information to the person in your setting with responsibility for safeguarding. Look out for unusual sexual knowledge or very detailed enactments of violence.

Link

Go to Unit 8 in Student Book 1 for more information on child protection and safeguarding.

Assessing effectiveness of provision

By watching children, especially the complexity of their play and how engaged they are in their play, we can use this as a tool to reflect on our provision for imaginative play. It may be that the resources, layout or props need refreshing or changing, or that we need to be more involved in their play.

Asking focused, open-ended questions

It is quite a skill to know when and how to ask questions of children as they are engaged in imaginative play. You could try talking to children about what they are doing when they are taking a break or want you to help them in some way. The key is to be genuinely interested in what children are doing and to ask questions about what is happening and why. By asking children about their play, you can learn about what is of interest to them and use this to plan further play experiences. This can help children to think about what they are doing. Sensitive questioning also helps children extend their thinking and problem-solving abilities, for example, asking them what might happen next. Sensitive questioning may also develop children's vocabulary, as you recast and expand children's explanations and thoughts.

Case study

Asking questions

Owen saw that a group of children were playing intensely in a den that they had made earlier in the day. It was nearly snack time and Owen asked the group if they would like to have a snack in the den. They were very keen, but he reminded them that they would still need to wash their hands. He went with them indoors and while they were washing their hands, he asked them about their play. They were happy to talk to him and when they were back inside the den, they showed him what they were doing.

He asked them what the rules of their game were. The children thought about this for a while, and then started to articulate their very complex rules.

1 How did Owen talk to the children without interrupting the flow of their play?
2 How did this approach help the children to feel that their play was valued?
3 How did their conversation help the children to articulate their play?

Supporting and extending thinking and learning by becoming a role-play partner

From an early age, children love sensitive play partners. We may pretend to be on the telephone with an 18-month-old child, or to be enjoying a cup of tea that they have handed to us. Joining in with children's role play can help them gain skills and is a good way of supporting their development. It does require sensitivity and skill, as children must still have ownership of their play and the play has to remain enjoyable.

Joining children in role play is often used in settings when a new role-play area has been created. In this way, children are able to hear the vocabulary and expressions as well as observe any skills or actions that are usually associated with this scenario. An adult may, for example, play the part of a vet and ask a child who has brought in a pet (cuddly toy) to the surgery whether the pet has been off its food and whether it has been vaccinated. The adult may then 'examine' the pet using a stethoscope before suggesting that it may need some medicine. By seeing the adult in role, the children can later use the same script and know what to do.

In the same way, an adult who is playing the part of an assistant in a shoe shop might ask a 'customer' about what kind of shoes they are looking for. This would provide an opportunity to naturally introduce words associated with shoes such as 'lace-ups' or 'boots'.

Why is it a good idea for us to join children in role play?

How to explore and extend ideas using drawing, writing and ICT

Imaginative play can be used as a wonderful starting point for children to explore and develop other ideas and skills. Children, for example, who are pretending to be a superhero, may be prompted by an adult to create a map that helps them find their way to a rescue. This would involve drawing or using a computer and so would help the child gain further skills. The following are three examples of how easy it is to help children to develop their interest and skills in drawing, mark making/writing and Information and Communication Technology (ICT).

- Role-play area: hospital
  - Children might go online with an adult and print out medical charts.
  - Children may draw pictures or make cards and then make 'get well' cards for patients.

- Superhero play
  - Children might draw maps to help them 'fly' to where they need to go.
  - Children may write out the story of what happens.
  - Children could draw and paint props to support the play.
- Small-world play: trains
  - Children might make tickets.
  - Children may write signs for stations or notices to the driver.
  - Children could look at different types of trains on the internet.

The importance of challenging gender stereotyping

From around 3 years, most children start to explore gender as a concept – what it means to be a little boy or a little girl. This starts to show in their imaginative play as they may start to restrict themselves to certain roles. They may also make comments to other children about what they can and cannot do. While the exploration of gender concept is usual, it is important that you do not encourage and support the narrowing of gender roles that have traditionally existed in our society. Early attitudes and understanding about what men and women can and cannot do can sometimes become restrictive and may later subconsciously affect a child's choices. It is therefore important to find ways to challenge gender stereotyping.

You can do this in a variety of ways.

Using photographs and images

Photographs and images are very powerful for young children. Look out for photographs of men doing tasks that have traditionally been associated with women, such as cooking, looking after children and nursing. In the same way, look out for images of women in jobs such as fire-fighting, plumbing or decorating.

Using resources

Look at the resources that are put out and consider whether they contribute to gender bias. While many girls love wearing princess-type dresses, consider whether these should be available all the time. It is also worth looking out for 'real' props as these are often more interesting than toys and are more likely to appeal to both boys and girls. Think also about the colour of toys and resources, as some colours such as pink, purple and blue send out a message to children about who the toys are for. This can be limiting.

Visitors and outings

Any real-life experience, as we have already seen, can enrich role play. If children are engaged by what they have seen or who they have met, this can help them to expand their concept of gender.

Joining in play

You can join in role play, as we saw earlier. Wherever possible, try to make sure that you engage in role play that is not traditionally associated with your gender.

Challenging comments

It is important to challenge children's comments or actions if they seem to be discriminatory. This needs to be done very sensitively, because children are often expressing views that they have either heard or have based on their experience to date – so, if in their household, they only see a women ironing, they may come to the conclusion that boys 'aren't allowed' to iron. Explaining that this is not necessarily the case is important.

▌Helping parents understand the value of imaginative play

Most parents will recognise that their child enjoys imaginative play, but not all will be aware of the many benefits that this type of play offers. It can be helpful to show parents that it is valuable, through the ways that we observe and talk about it.

Can you see here how gender stereotypes are being challenged?

In some settings, posters are put up by the home corner that indicate the benefits children gain from this type of play, so that when parents collect their children or visit on open days, they can find out more. This approach works well, but parents may also like a more personal approach and will need to know how imaginative play is supporting their child's development. They may also be interested in understanding how imaginative play is likely to change as their child develops. Many settings will do this with parents by sharing observations with them, in particular **learning journeys** and photographs or film clips or by holding information evenings.

Key term

Learning journey – a way of assessing and planning for children's development using a narrative approach that can easily be shared and constructed with parents and children.

Learning journeys

Many settings use learning journeys as a way of sharing information with parents. Learning journeys usually comprise an observation that includes a photograph, and practitioners explore with parents what the next steps for the child might be at home or in the setting. As children are likely to engage in this type of play at home, it can be a good idea to find out how the child usually plays and incorporate this into the planning for the child. While sharing the child's learning journey, you can also talk to the parents about what the child is gaining and how you may help the child develop further.

Photographs and film clips

Most parents love watching their children in action. Using photographs and film clips, you can talk to the parents about the child's imagination, speech and social development. It can also be useful to refer back to previous photographs and film clips so that parents can see the development that has taken place.

Link

Go to Unit 9 in Student Book 1 for more information on the different types of observation methods.

Assessment practice 21.2

3B1.P3 | 3B1.P4 | 3B1.P5 | 3B1.M2 | 3B2.P6 | 3B2.P7 | 3B2.M3 | 3B.D2

An international early years group is interested in sharing perspectives on children's play. You have been asked to write an article that explains how imaginative play is valued and supported by early years practitioners. Your article should include comments about:

- the importance of observing and planning for children's imaginative play
- how play may be resourced and provided for indoors and outdoors to support the different types of role play

- the role of the adults in planning for imaginative play
- the role of the adult as a play partner in imaginative play
- how adults can support and extend play
- challenging gender stereotyping in role play.

You should conclude your article by evaluating the contribution of adults to effective imaginative play in an early years setting.

▌ Further reading and resources

Cummings, A. and Featherstone, S. (2009) *Role Play in the Early Years*, London: A&C Black Publishers Ltd.

Duffy, B. (2006) *Supporting Creativity and Imagination in the Early Years* (2nd ed.), Maidenhead: Open University Press.

Featherstone, S. (2013) *The Little Book of Role Play*, London: Featherstone Education, Bloomsbury Publishing plc.

Harries, J. (2013) *Role Play (Play in the EYFS)*, London: Practical Pre-School Books.

Ready for work?

Justin Gerrard Teaching assistant

In the reception class we use imaginative play as a tool, primarily for children's language and literacy development. Within the room, we have a role-play area that is always a home and then, in addition, we usually set up two other areas. For the next couple of weeks, we have a shoe shop and a train! Outdoors, we have limited space, but we have a small playhouse that the children transform into anything from a spaceship to a café. We base the areas both on children's interests and the topic or book that we are reading. We think that this strikes a balance, as this way there is plenty of child-initiated play going on, but we are also creating opportunities to develop language and to support the topic.

I think that getting the role-play area up and running is absolutely key, as it is one of the most popular play activities that we have here. Children never seem to tire of pretending, and so often we can use this as a starting point for other areas of the curriculum. When the children turned the playhouse into a café, we made menus with them, took them out to the local café and also talked about healthy eating. We also worked with the children on a price list and it helped the children talk about and recognise coins. It is important, though, that these areas are maintained and set up nicely. I have been in other settings where role play is less of a priority and it shows in terms of the quality of interaction and the time that children spend there.

Skills for practice

Support outdoor play and learning: Setting up a carwash

This is a great activity for outdoors. Children love anything to do with water and so with a little preparation, this can be a great activity.

- Start by finding out whether any children are allergic to washing-up liquid, as a little bit of this in lots of water is needed.

- Look out for buckets, sponges and aprons.

- Find a space where children can bring their bikes or other wheeled toys.

- Create a sign and put out a table and a cash register.

- Get into character and ask if any children want to have their bikes washed.

- Tell them the price and ask if they would like a 'full valet service with polish' or the 'basic'.

- Explain that one service is cheaper than the other and give the prices.

- Let any child who wants to come and 'work' with you join in.

- When you feel that the role play is established, step back, but continue to supervise discreetly.

Introduction

During the past 50 years, the number of children who play out in the street or unsupervised in parks has reduced significantly. Outdoors used to be the main area for play, and older children would look after babies and young children. Today, it is rare to find children playing outside unsupervised. There are many reasons for this, but it is now recognised that we need to give children more opportunities to be outdoors as part of early years provision. While health and exercise are important, there are other reasons too, including children's psychological well-being. This is why there is such a focus in early years curricula on ensuring that all children spend time outdoors every day. This unit looks at the importance of children spending time outdoors and ways in which this might be done. It also looks at the role of the adult in promoting the development of children outdoors.

Assessment: You will be assessed by a series of assignments set by your teacher/tutor.

Learning aims

In this unit you will:

A   understand the importance of the outdoors to development and learning

B1   understand the features of effective outdoor provision

B2   understand the role of the adult in promoting development outdoors.

> We have just had a focus on outdoor play in the nursery. We observed children as they were playing, spoke to them about what they would like to do and use during play, and have now transformed our outdoor area. It has been working brilliantly and the children are getting so much from it. We have all noticed the way that children seem to be more engaged in their play and talk to each other, and there is this wonderful buzz about the place. Parents have also noticed a difference and we are planning to work with a group of parents to set up a children's garden project.
>
> Steve, *a nursery practitioner*

Promoting Children's Development Outdoors

25

BTEC
Assessment Zone

This table shows what you must do in order to achieve a **Pass**, **Merit** or **Distinction** grade, and where you can find activities to help you.

Assessment criteria		
Pass	**Merit**	**Distinction**
Learning aim A: Understand the importance of the outdoors to development and learning		
3A.P1 English I&CT Explain the benefits of outdoor play to children's learning and development. **Assessment practice 25.1**	**3A.M1** Analyse how outdoor provision supports the needs of children in an early years setting. **Assessment practice 25.1**	**3A.D1** Evaluate the extent to which outdoor learning environments in early years settings could impact on outcomes for children. **Assessment practice 25.1**
3A.P2 Describe how approaches to outdoor learning and play are applied in practice. **Assessment practice 25.1**		
3A.P3 Explain the relationship between indoor and outdoor environments in promoting children's learning and development. **Assessment practice 25.1**		
Learning aim B1: Understand the features of effective outdoor provision **Learning aim B2: Understand the role of the adult in promoting development outdoors**		
3B1.P4 Describe the physical features of effective early years outdoor provision. **Assessment practice 25.2**	**3B1.M2** Analyse how effective outdoor provision can contribute to children's development and learning. **Assessment practice 25.2**	**3B.D2** Evaluate the extent to which adults in early years settings contribute to children's learning and development outdoors. **Assessment practice 25.3**
3B1.P5 Explain the importance of flexible resources in outdoor provision in an early years setting. **Assessment practice 25.2**		
3B1.P6 Research resources for outdoor provision in an early years setting that will encourage children's creativity and imagination. **Assessment practice 25.2**		

continued

Assessment criteria *(continued)*

Pass	Merit	Distinction
3B2.P7 Explain why it is important for adults in an early years setting to have positive attitudes to outdoor learning. **Assessment practice 25.3**	**3B2.M3** Discuss, using examples, how adults can best promote the development of children of different ages outdoors. **Assessment practice 25.3**	
3B2.P8 Explain how to support child-initiated experiences outdoors in an early years setting. **Assessment practice 25.3**		
3B2.P9 Describe how the weather and seasons can be used to support learning and development outdoors in an early years setting. **Assessment practice 25.3**		

English	English Functional Skills signposting	I&CT	Information and Communication Technology Functional Skills signposting

How you will be assessed

This unit will be assessed by a series of internally assessed tasks set by your teacher/tutor. Throughout this unit you will find assessment practice activities that will help you work towards your assessment. Completing these activities will not mean that you have achieved a particular grade, but you will have carried out useful research or preparation that will be relevant when it comes to your final assignment.

In order for you to carry out the tasks in your assignment, it is important that you check you have met all of the Pass grading criteria. You can do this as you work your way through the assignment.

If you are hoping to gain a Merit or Distinction, you should also make sure that you present the information in your assignment in the style that is required by the relevant assessment criterion. For example, Merit criteria will require you to discuss and analyse, and Distinction criteria will require you to evaluate.

The assignment set by your teacher/tutor will consist of a number of tasks designed to meet the criteria in the assessment criteria table. This is likely to consist of a written assignment but may also include activities such as:

- case studies
- a presentation
- training materials.

A Understand the importance of the outdoors to development and learning

Outdoor learning is now a major part of the curricula in the United Kingdom (UK). In this section, we look at how it supports children's development and learning.

The positive impact on well-being

It is now recognised that young children can become stressed and also depressed. We know that being outdoors and taking part in physical exercise can reduce anxiety and thus help stress and depression, and promote resilience. This is because during exercise, endorphins, which are chemicals that affect the brain, are released by the pituitary gland, improving our self-esteem and making us feel positive. In addition, children benefit from opportunities to engage in child-initiated play, which is known to support children's self-esteem and perseverance.

Link

Go to Unit 2 in Student Book 1 to find more information about child-initiated play.

Encouraging healthy lifestyles

Years ago, it was normal to see children playing outdoors. Today, for a variety of reasons, including fears over safety, digital entertainment and less available time, fewer children spend time outdoors. This is of great concern, as by spending time outdoors, children gain positive attitudes towards walking, running and enjoying nature. By taking exercise without realising it, they are also learning how to deal with stress. Spending time outdoors is therefore good for children's all-round health.

Positive attitudes towards being outdoors gained in childhood can also influence our attitudes towards walking and taking exercise later in life. The UK has an increasingly overweight population, so this is currently extremely relevant.

Supporting physical development

Encouraging children to enjoy the outdoors is an ideal way to support development, especially in spaces such as woodlands, fields and beaches. Such places have in-built natural challenges, such as uneven surfaces and slopes. These require children to balance and develop stamina. Even in outdoor spaces specifically designed for children they can gain physical skills, as they may use wheeled toys, run and climb. Any vigorous activity will build stamina and strengthen bones. Figure 25.1 shows how development can be supported by outdoor activity.

Benefits of outdoor play on social and emotional development

As well as it helping to prevent stress and anxiety, children are more likely to concentrate during child-initiated play outdoors. There are other skills that children can gain by being outdoors too. They will have opportunities to play with other children and so develop their negotiation and cooperation skills. Children also benefit psychologically from the ability to be noisy and make large movements, and this is one reason why many adults, when thinking about their childhood, use the word 'freedom'. Children get

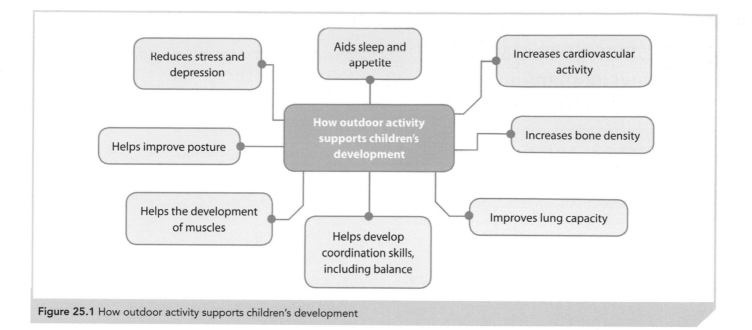

Figure 25.1 How outdoor activity supports children's development

excited about playing outdoors and if you provide them challenges, they will also be encouraged to develop self-confidence.

Link

Go to Unit 3 in Student Book 1 to find more information about promoting children's physical development.

Opportunities for cognitive development

Children benefit from stimulating environments. By visiting a range of places such as parks, beaches and woodlands, as well as playing in outdoor spaces, they are more likely to learn new concepts and also develop new vocabulary. When children are outdoors, they also have the opportunity to notice things that are new or of interest, be creative and solve problems, and this allows them to find out more about the natural world or scientific concepts. Interestingly, many of these learning opportunities are likely to be spontaneous, such as a child noticing a snail on the climbing frame or a gutter leaking because it is raining hard.

As you will see later in this unit, it is important that adults look for and plan opportunities to support children's learning and development. They may, for example, encourage children to design a mural or make decisions about what should be planted in a gardening area.

Offering experiences through activity or movement

Being outdoors can give children plenty of first-hand opportunities such as watering plants or washing windows. In some settings that use a **Forest School approach**, children may also (under supervision) experience some real-world activities such as fire lighting and cooking on an open fire. Such experiences are not only exciting for children, but also memorable, and so support their learning. Being outdoors in a stimulating environment seems to give children more chance of 'learning by doing' and is one reason why outdoor play is considered so important.

Key term

Forest School approach – where settings are spending time outdoors, usually in woodlands, and carry out activities typically used in Scandinavian countries.

The value of different environments to learning and development

There was a time when many adults, including parents, associated children being outdoors with play, and being indoors with work and learning. Since the introduction of the early years curricula in the UK, this thinking has been challenged. The term 'outdoor classroom' is widely used, which suggests that learning and development take place outdoors as well. To support this change in thinking, activities and resources are now used outdoors that allow children to develop skills and knowledge in all parts of the curriculum. For example there are now mark-making tables and role-play opportunities outdoors, not just equipment to promote physical development.

Complementing and extending indoor provision

The current trend in early years is to make sure that the outdoor provision looks at all aspects of the curricula. Thus, children may be engaged in playing hopscotch and rolling dice or drawing pictures of

items that they have gathered during a walk. There are also some activities that can start indoors and then continue to be developed outdoors. Table 25.1 shows examples of these.

Importance of free access to outdoor provision

The ideal in early years is to allow children to move from inside to outside and vice versa. This allows them to follow their play ideas without needing to ask permission or have a break.

Table 25.1 Activities that can start indoors and finish outdoors

Activity	Tasks	Link to the curricula
Making kites	Making them indoors and then taking them out to fly	• Understanding of concepts such as flight • Problem solving • Design
Sending balloon messages	Messages are written indoors, but are attached to balloons and let go of outdoors	• Early literacy and mark making • Cooperation • Concepts such as flight and distance
Story telling	Stories such as Jack and the Beanstalk are told indoors, but children can then role play them outdoors	• Communication and language • Negotiation • Turn taking • Imagination
Water and sand play	Children can play with water and sand indoors, but then do so again on a larger scale outdoors	• Volume and capacity • Exploring concepts such as density by observing which items float or sink

This concept is sometimes called 'free flow'. An example of this might be where two 3-year-old children begin indoors and pretend to go shopping. They get dressed and then go outdoors where they use the wheeled toys to 'drive to the shops'. Then they realise that they have not written a shopping list and one of them suggests that they should go indoors to write one. In this example, children can go from one place to another in support of their child-initiated play. The advantage of this style of access is that children's play becomes more meaningful and incorporates many different skills. It is also likely to be of a longer duration and so helps children to concentrate and persevere.

Approaches to outdoor play and learning in curricula

It is important to understand how the outdoors is included in the curriculum framework in the country where you are working. In the EYFS, for example, there is a welfare requirement that children are given opportunities to play outdoors every day, even when it is not dry and sunny. In the Welsh Foundation Phase, it is also clear that play and learning should take place both in and out of doors.

Research

Read the early years curriculum framework for the country in which you wish to work.

Find out what the expectations are for outdoor play and learning.

Other approaches to outdoor play and learning

During this course, you have already looked at the approaches of Froebel, Steiner and Montessori. Each of these pioneers felt that the outdoors was significant in children's learning and development. While Froebel and Steiner stressed the importance of children learning about nature and also being imaginative, Montessori set up a garden for children so that they could plant seeds and watch plants grow as part of their 'practical life' skills.

In the UK, the Forest School approach has also become popular, influenced by Forest Schools in

Denmark and Sweden. The idea is that children spend time in woodlands, learning about nature and gaining practical skills such as making fires and shelters, as well as story telling. Forest Schools are very popular with both children and their parents, and they seem to help children to gain in confidence and enjoy physical activity. As many settings do not have access to woodlands, dedicated centres have been set up (some by the Forestry Commission) to allow regular visits from settings.

Link

Go to Unit 2 in Student Book 1 to find more information about how different philosophies approach the provision of play opportunities.

Research

Find out more about Forest Schools in your area.

If possible, visit a Forest School or talk to staff in your setting to find out about Forest School training.

You can also read more by visiting a page dedicated to Forest Schools on the Directgov website. You can access this page by going to www.pearsonhotlinks.co.uk and searching for the ISBN of this title: 9781447970972.

Assessment practice 25.1   3AP1 | 3AP2 | 3AP3 | 3AM1 | 3AD1

You have been asked to write a policy for your setting about outdoor play and learning. As part of the policy process, you have to outline the benefits of outdoor play and learning to children. This needs to be sufficiently detailed so that new staff can understand the rationale behind the policy. Your policy should provide:

- information about the benefits to children's development, learning and well-being
- information on why children should have good access to the outdoors and how this is applied in practice
- ways in which the indoor and outdoor environment can be used together to promote children's learning and development.

B1 Understand the features of effective outdoor provision

The idea of having children play in and out of doors is quite simple, but in reality there are a lot of practical challenges that need to be overcome. This section looks at the features of effective outdoor provision and how these features can help overcome some of the challenges while supporting children's development.

Integrated indoor–outdoor early years provision

Wherever possible, early years settings are encouraged to find ways of enabling free-flow play, allowing children to go outdoors whenever they wish. To facilitate this, many settings have installed patio-type doors or have even moved their location. The latter is particularly true of reception classes in some schools that have been moved closer to outdoor areas. Some settings have also created smaller, fenced-off areas within the outdoor space to allow children to come and go without an adult always needing to be outdoors.

Integrated provision does throw up some practical issues that most early years settings have to work through. This includes whether or not an adult always has to go outside with the children, how to prevent the indoor space becoming cold and how to monitor where the children are in case of evacuation.

Theory into practice

Find out how children access the outdoor space in your setting. If your placement has patio doors or easy access, find out the following:

- Does an adult always have to be outside with the children?
- How do they monitor which children are indoors and which are outdoors?
- How do they manage the coats and shoes?
- How do they keep the indoor space warm?

Providing shade and shelter

It is important that outdoor provision has both shade and shelter if it is to be used in all weathers.

Shade

There should be some shaded areas for children, particularly in the summer months when it is important to keep children out of the sun because of the risk of dehydration and skin cancer. Figure 25.2 shows the many approaches that settings can use to create shade.

Shelter

As well as shade, you also need to think about some shelter for children. Many of the ideas for creating shade will also create some shelter, but in addition, some settings will also install tents and teepees – this can be a good activity in itself.

Different surfaces and levels

To support children's learning, it is helpful to provide as many different surfaces and levels as possible. A range of surfaces may include gravel, bark chippings, tarmac, soil and grass. A variety of surfaces gives children, especially babies, the opportunity to feel and experience different textures. It is also helpful for children to experience different levels. This helps develop their gross motor movement and balance skills. Toddlers particularly like climbing and standing on low structures or running down slopes. A variety of levels also makes an outdoor environment look more visually interesting. The following can be used by settings to enable children to experience different levels:

- steps
- ramps
- climbing frames
- raised beds or grassy areas
- treehouses
- low walls
- logs
- grassy mounds
- car tyres.

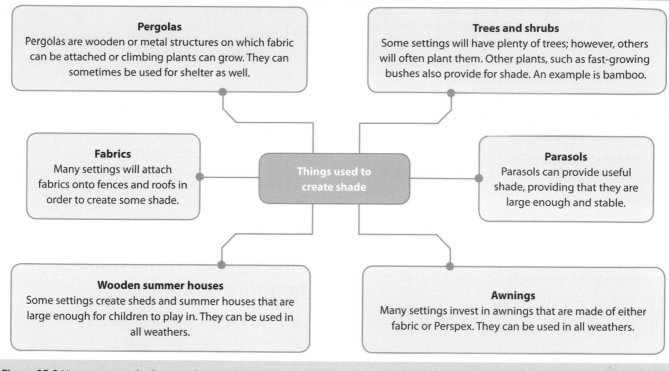

Pergolas
Pergolas are wooden or metal structures on which fabric can be attached or climbing plants can grow. They can sometimes be used for shelter as well.

Trees and shrubs
Some settings will have plenty of trees; however, others will often plant them. Other plants, such as fast-growing bushes also provide for shade. An example is bamboo.

Fabrics
Many settings will attach fabrics onto fences and roofs in order to create some shade.

Things used to create shade

Parasols
Parasols can provide useful shade, providing that they are large enough and stable.

Wooden summer houses
Some settings create sheds and summer houses that are large enough for children to play in. They can be used in all weathers.

Awnings
Many settings invest in awnings that are made of either fabric or Perspex. They can be used in all weathers.

Figure 25.2 How to create shade in outdoor areas

This child is being shaded by fabric that has been used to make a den.

Activity

With the permission of your placement supervisor, take a photograph of the outdoor environment when there are not any children in it. With other learners on your course, compare photographs and look to see how different early years settings manage:

- shade and shelter
- surfaces
- levels.

Independent access to resources

It is good practice for children to be able to access resources independently. This is important, as children may wish to add to their play or have clear play preferences, and by being able to freely access materials they gain independence. In many early years settings, storage both indoors and out is a big issue. If storage is poor and difficult to access, there is a likelihood that fewer resources will be put out or that there is insufficient variation in what is put out. It is important for children to be involved in the setting up and putting away of resources. Settings have different approaches to this challenge, as we will now see.

Use of sheds

Ideally, these need to have double doors for easy access, a ramp for accessing wheeled toys and a range of shelves. Sheds can also double up as play areas and for shade if they are carefully arranged.

Storage boxes and bins

Plastic storage boxes and bins are often used for smaller items that are not valuable.

They can be left outdoors and children can access them easily. Different-coloured boxes are useful as they can help children to remember what might be inside, for example, a red box contains balls, while a blue box contains items for water play.

Car ports

Some settings store wheeled toys in specific covered areas similar to car ports, and encourage children to 'park' the toys they have been using. This keeps the wheeled toys from becoming wet, although this approach will not prevent rust.

Tarpaulin sheets

Some settings will use tarpaulin sheets to cover materials and resources. This can be effective, although if it has rained, care has to be taken when removing them.

Appropriate clothing and protection

The current trend is that all children should have outdoor access all year round, not just on fine, sunny days. This means that settings have to create outdoor environments that will allow children to be outside in all weathers, hence the need for different surfaces and the provision of shelter. In addition, settings will need to make sure that children are wearing suitable clothes. In some settings, outdoor clothing is provided and settings will often buy all-in-one suits, wellingtons and rain capes as well as gloves, socks and hats. In other settings, parents are expected to provide these items for the children. However, it is quite common for settings also to keep some spare clothing just in case a child comes unprepared. Here are some simple lists of outdoor clothing that should be available for different weather types.

Clothing for sunny weather

- Long-sleeved T-shirts
- Sunglasses
- Sunhats

Note: Although not an item of clothing, sunscreen should be applied according to parents' wishes.

Clothing for rainy weather

- Wellingtons
- Rain capes/all-in-ones/waterproofs
- Umbrellas

Clothing for cold weather

- Warm socks
- Wellingtons or outdoor shoes
- Hats, gloves and scarves
- Fleeces or additional layers
- Coats/anoraks/padded all-in-ones

Making use of the special features outdoors

The main features of the outdoors that provide children with different learning experiences are the available space and the changing weather. It is important that these features are well utilised when creating outdoor environments. Many settings do this in the following ways.

Exploring the weather

Many settings will provide specific activities and resources that will help children to explore the weather. There may be thermometers, windmills and kites, as well as heat-sensitive strips. In addition, settings may also use naturally occurring opportunities, such as drawing children's attention to a layer of ice in a gutter or the way in which the ground has become hard and dry.

Using the available space

Additional space should mean that children can engage in noisier and potentially bigger activities. Many settings will put up sound walls or will have large digging areas and places where children can run or use sit-and-ride toys.

Flexible and versatile provision

Some of the best outdoor spaces for children are very flexible and versatile. This means that every time the children go outdoors, they can potentially find new things to do or new ways of playing.

Open-ended resources

One way in which settings can provide flexible and versatile provision is to give children open-ended resources that they can use in a variety of ways. Car tyres are a good example of this. Children can use them as stepping stones, as seats and also as part of obstacle courses. They can also be lined and used as planters or as makeshift containers for sand and gravel. Figure 25.3 shows other popular resources that are used in settings.

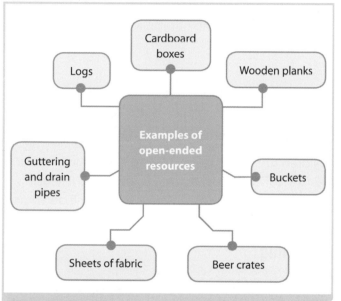

Figure 25.3 Examples of open-ended resources

Buckets are a good open-ended resource. What other activities could you use buckets for?

Supporting inclusion

As well as providing open-ended resources, settings also need to be aware of how they will support inclusion and enable all children, regardless of age, disability, medical condition or gender, access to the outdoors. This requires settings to be thoughtful when carrying out any large-scale building work such as putting in doors, ramps and fixed apparatus, to meet the needs of children with mobility needs or visual impairments, for example. Once in position, this apparatus cannot easily be changed. When steps are built or a new level added, there should always be a ramp fitted. It is also important to understand that over time there may be a range of children with different needs. Creating a large, open area may suit a child in a wheelchair, but it could be too open for a child with emotional and behavioural needs who would benefit from a cosier area. This is a good argument for not having too many static resources such as climbing frames that cannot be moved or adjusted to suit different children's needs.

As well as thinking about the physical needs of children, it is also important that the outdoor space is appealing to all children. Close observation of the activities that children are choosing or avoiding is important here.

Resources for different types of play

In most early years settings, the outdoor provision is characterised by a number of resources that will support children's play and development. The aim in most early years curricula is to ensure that children can cover each of the areas of learning both indoors and outdoors, so for example most early years settings will have areas for mark making outdoors.

Natural materials

There is a wide range of materials that can be provided outdoors for children to explore. Each material provides children with a different tactile experience and a range of possibilities that can be incorporated into children's play. In addition, as most children love 'mixing', it is usual to find children bringing together different materials in a bucket or in the digging area. Most settings will provide natural materials in a variety of ways, for example, in water and sand trays, buckets, builders' trays, inside tyres, and also directly on the ground, such as soil, bark chippings, leaves, gravel, stones and straw.

Materials for construction and den play

Children love building things outdoors. This could be anything from a hideout or den using fabrics, tarpaulin, cardboard boxes, bamboo sticks and metal frames or rods, through to using wooden or plastic blocks and beer crates to create a ship.

What have this group of children used to create their den?

Encouraging creative and imaginative play

The outdoors can provide opportunities for children to paint, make marks and be creative. It can also be a place where children can engage in extended role play by, for example, using a wheeled toy or bike to 'go to the shops' before going to a playhouse or den to 'unload the shopping'. Some settings will also create areas such as petrol stations, shops and garden centres to develop children's role play outdoors. These opportunities also allow children to engage in physical play. Other common ways that early years settings can provide for children's creative and imaginative play are by:

- creating mark-making boards
- painting walls
- making tents
- providing role-play props, such as bags, spoons and items from the home
- providing real objects for children to explore, such as crates, tubing and brushes
- providing sand and water trays
- providing opportunities to dig and explore mud, leaves and gravel.

Resources for experiencing the natural world

Young children are often fascinated by nature. Resources to encourage this include magnifying sheets, bug boxes, wormeries and equipment for growing things such as plant pots, trowels and watering cans.

Theory into practice

Make a list of ways in which your setting supports the following types of play:

- creative and imaginative
- exploration of the natural world
- construction.

Resources to support real-world experiences

Children of all ages enjoy feeling grown-up and like being involved in real activities. They also like using real tools and resources. Many settings will do some or all of the following with children to support this.

Gardening

Children love digging and planting. Ideally, children need to experience using real tools or ones that are still effective but have been designed for smaller hands.

Hanging out the washing

This has been a traditional activity that children have been involved in for hundreds of years. Children can pass you pegs, hand up washing and even peg up smaller items for themselves.

Sweeping and clearing

Most outdoor spaces will need sweeping and clearing at times. It may be that leaves have blown in or the odd weed is appearing. Involving children in these tasks and using tools such as yard brushes can be very popular.

Washing

Most early years settings will encourage children to wash windows, wheeled toys and other items. Buckets, sponges and soapy water are the main resources for this activity.

You have been asked to look at the resources and overall provision required for a stimulating outdoor environment in a nursery that has children from 0 to 5 years and an after-school club taking children up to 8 years. Your brief is to prepare a presentation that looks at the types of resources that will support children's learning and development and features that support excellent outdoor provision.

Your presentation must include:

- the importance of provision to children's overall development and learning
- the physical features of effective outdoor provision
- the importance of flexible resources and examples of resources that will support children's creativity and imagination.

B2 Understand the role of the adult in promoting development outdoors

Most children love being outdoors, so it is essential that adults working with them enjoy being outside too and that they understand how to support children's learning and development.

▌Having a positive attitude

If adults find being outside a chore, it shows in the way that they are not always properly dressed for the occasion and how they look for reasons to bring children back inside. This is a shame, because children pick up on the way that adults feel by noticing their facial expressions, movements and tone of voice. A positive attitude gives children permission to play and explore, but an adult who is not keen on being outdoors often prevents children from settling down to play. One of the reasons why adults often do not have a positive attitude is that they become bored. This is strange, because there are plenty of things that adults could be doing that will be interesting and helpful. When the adult is busy, children will either want to see what they are doing and join in or will go off happily and start playing themselves. Here is a list of things that adults could be doing outdoors, alongside, of course, supervising and encouraging children's play:

- weeding
- sweeping
- clearing leaves and debris
- planting
- observing children's development, friendships and interests
- supporting children's play
- organising activities for children
- observing nature and drawing interested children's attention to it.

This adult is joining in with a child's play. Make sure you show a positive attitude about playing outdoors.

The need for risk assessment

Safety is often cited as a reason why children cannot play outdoors in challenging and interesting ways. Risk assessments either support this view or are used to reduce the risks to acceptable levels. As part of your work with children, you will need to be aware of the risks of being outdoors, but you should also use common sense and look for ways of counteracting them. Table 25.2 shows the dangers commonly associated with activities outdoors, but also shows how they can be managed. This principle should be reflected in risk assessments.

Behavioural boundaries

Children will need to know what they can and cannot do when outdoors, so adults are required to set some boundaries. These will depend on the age/stage of the children and the outdoor areas. Boundaries should always be set in relation to keeping children safe and this should be based on risk assessments carried out both before and during an activity. As we have seen, it is important that children's learning and development are not hampered by over-zealous adults worried about safety.

Some of the usual boundaries set when children are outdoors are as follows – note how easy it is to understand the rationale behind them.

- Climbing equipment should only be used as intended by the manufacturer.
- Numbers should be limited and turn taking is required for equipment such as slides, climbing frames and wheeled toys.
- Children should go to the adult when they are called.
- When playing outside in public areas, children should remain in sight of an adult and should return promptly when called.
- Certain activities should only be done in dedicated areas to avoid accidents, such as the use of wheeled toys or throwing or kicking objects.

Table 25.2 Dangers associated with being outdoors

Danger	How to manage the risk
Children becoming lost or taken by strangers	<ul><li>Fencing</li><li>Supervision by adults</li><li>High-visibility jackets to be worn by staff and children</li><li>Mobile phone in case of an emergency</li></ul>
Traffic	<ul><li>Supervision by adults</li><li>High-visibility jackets to be worn by staff and children</li></ul>
Stings and bites	<ul><li>First-aid kit available</li><li>Children instructed not to approach dogs or other animals</li><li>Supervision by adults</li><li>Mobile phone in case of an emergency</li></ul>
Falls and accidents	<ul><li>First-aid kit</li><li>Supervision of staff</li><li>Visual risk assessment at the time</li><li>Mobile phone in case of an emergency</li></ul>
Weather	<ul><li>Protective clothing provided</li><li>Sunscreen applied when required</li><li>Adults aware of shelter and shade</li></ul>

Supporting child-initiated experiences

Child-initiated play is important as a way of promoting children's imagination, concentration and self-reliance. Many adults find it easiest to provide this type of play outdoors because there is more space, resources are often used differently and there is more of a sense of freedom. The following are some ways in which adults can support child-initiated play.

Allowing materials to be mixed

Many children want to use a range of materials to construct their own world. They may want to put some sand in a bucket with some water before adding a few stones. This might then become their 'magic soup'. It is important that we do not stop children from mixing materials unless there is a health and safety issue or some other pressing reason.

Not over-supervising children

When children are over-supervised, they tend not to play as well as when they feel that they are 'free'. This means keeping an eye on children, but not patrolling them.

By standing back a little, we effectively give children permission to explore their own world.

Providing interesting and varied materials

Earlier we saw that children need flexible and versatile resources. These will help with child-initiated play as children can use them in a variety of ways and they can symbolise different things every time children play with them – for example, a bucket might be a saucepan, a magic pool or an oven.

Enabling freedom to explore

It is very difficult to give definite guidance about how the outdoor space should be organised, as some settings have relatively small amounts of space and many constraints, while others have whole fields! Ideally, there need to be spaces where children can play slightly away from the gaze of adults. This is why children tend to like huddling in bushes or on steps in doorways. Children also need space to use wheeled toys and it is good to provide a 'reason' for using them, for example, a space where there is a petrol station and shops alongside a path for the wheeled toy. This allows children to develop a story or rationale.

You can see that this setting has enough space outdoors to allow children to play with wheeled toys.

Using natural features

One of the wonderful things about the outdoors is the way that there are plenty of spontaneous learning opportunities to share with children. It is important that we take opportunities to explore what children have noticed or are interested in and draw their attention to things such as buds on trees or the shapes of clouds. With babies and very young children, we may simply talk about what they see and where possible allow them to touch and experience sensations. This might mean encouraging a toddler to splash in a puddle or putting up a mirror that catches the light for babies.

With older children, we can use the weather and seasons as starting points for further exploration. Table 25.3 shows some more examples.

This child has been allowed to explore outdoors and make a snowman. What other play opportunities could children be given on a snowy day?

Table 25.3 Learning about the weather and seasons outdoors

Starting point	How the weather/seasons can be explored
Ice	<ul><li>How ice has formed</li><li>How long it takes to melt</li><li>How it floats on top of water</li></ul>
Snow	<ul><li>Different types of snowflake</li><li>Ways in which snow sometimes settles, but other times hits the ground and melts</li><li>Making snowmen</li></ul>
Rainbows	<ul><li>How rainbows form when there is rain and sunshine at the same time</li><li>Stories with rainbows</li><li>Count the colours in the rainbows</li></ul>
Birds and nests	<ul><li>Different types of birds</li><li>Birds that arrive in spring but are not there in winter</li><li>Nests that birds make</li><li>Putting out bird feeders and making bird food</li></ul>
Clouds	<ul><li>Different types of clouds</li><li>Noting which clouds may indicate rain</li></ul>
Mini-beasts	<ul><li>Wondering what a creature is doing, such as a spider spinning a web, and why</li><li>Learning respect for living things</li><li>Observing how they move</li></ul>
Seasons	<ul><li>Changes to temperature</li><li>Effects on animal and plant life</li><li>Change in amount of light available</li></ul>

Enabling children to return to projects

It is good practice to find ways of allowing children sufficient time and opportunities so that they can follow their interests and their play until they feel they want to stop. This may sometimes pose practical challenges, as it may be time for a session to end – especially when settings are sharing space with other settings. However, it may be possible to take photographs of what the children have been doing (such as building a den) so that we can later help them pick up where they left off.

There are huge benefits for children when we can find ways of enabling them to return to projects. First, it helps children develop patience and perseverance. It also helps them to explore concepts on a deeper level and gain more skills. These days many toys and resources provide instant gratification and do not require children's imagination and input, so it is particularly important that we prioritise giving children sufficient time to develop their projects, with opportunities for thought and making changes.

Involving children in decisions

It is good practice to involve children in decisions that will affect them. This can also be applied to outdoor provision. Many settings, when redesigning or setting up an outdoor space, ask children for their ideas and views. When this is done, the results are usually very positive, as children often know best what they would like to do and use.

We can also involve children on a day-to-day basis by asking them what they would like to do, encouraging them to access resources independently and following their interests. Children are also able to plan for their future activities as well. Younger children may need prompts such as photographs to help them do this.

Using parks and public spaces

Not all settings have a large outdoor area, and using parks and public spaces such as woods, beaches and fields is an ideal way to provide children with more outdoor experiences. As this type of resource counts as an outing it is important that the following things are undertaken:

- risk assessments that look at security issues, health and safety and transport
- gaining parental consent for the outing.

In addition, you will need to follow the guidance or legal requirements set out in your country's early years framework or inspectorate document.

In order to get the best of any provision, it is important to visit the space that you want to use with the children and consider how it might be used. This is in addition to the practical considerations and risk assessments. It may be that a particular space such as a park will be ideal for building a den, using wheeled toys or flying kites. Other spaces, for example, woodlands or beaches, might be better for helping children learn about the natural world.

It is worth taking small groups of children first and also observing how they seem to use the space. This can then help you to see the possibilities and build on children's interests. In this way, you are also involving children in decision making.

The importance of observation for assessment

All of our work in early years should be underpinned by observing children, and using these observations to reflect on our own practice and as a basis for planning activities and resources. There are two areas in which observation is particularly required.

Inclusion

It is essential that we notice whether children are benefiting from and able to access different learning opportunities outdoors. It may be that groups of children are dominating some spaces or resources, or that the types of resources available do not appeal to particular children or groups. In some cases, we may need to re-evaluate our provision to ensure that it can meet a child's particular need, for example, a child with visual impairment or a child with mobility needs. As part of this work, it would also be sensible to involve parents and those who are directly involved in supporting the child, such as physiotherapists.

Challenge

For children to have ongoing learning and development experiences outdoors, they do need to find sufficient challenge and stimulation. What might be suitable and interesting for a child at 2 years may no longer hold any appeal at 4. Observing what children play with, how long they spend with it and how interested they seem can be helpful in this respect. It is also worth looking at what children are attempting to do, which often, for reasons of safety, has to be stopped. This can tell us what level of challenge they really need, given the chance. From this, we can then look for ways of creating it safely.

Link

Go to Unit 9 in Student Book 1 for more information about observations.

Case study

Providing challenge

Lara is working in a day nursery. Many of the children have been there since they were babies and she suspects that some of the older ones have become bored. She makes a note of everything that the 4-year-old children try to do, but are often stopped from doing. She focuses on their actions and after a couple of weeks, she picks out some common themes including climbing, throwing and using slopes. She talks to her manager and suggests that it might be worth looking for activities and resources that will help the children develop these themes. Over the next few weeks, part of the outdoor area is modified. A low wall is created so that children can walk along it and an area is created where children can throw safely. Lara dubs this area the 'range'. The ramp that was out of bounds for the children has been altered so that it is now safe for children to ride down on wheeled toys. The effect on the children is amazing. All the staff note that the older children seem to be playing more purposefully.

1 How did Lara approach the issue of challenge in her setting?

2 How might children benefit if there is sufficient challenge?

3 Explain the importance of observing children and then making changes to the outdoor environment.

Assessment practice 25.3 | 3B2.P7 | 3B2.P8 | 3B2.P9 | 3B2.M3 | 3B.D2

You have been asked to write an article about the role of the adult in supporting children's development through outdoor play and learning for a newsletter that is aimed at local practitioners. As there have been several articles about outdoor play, you will need to make some interesting points about the role of the adult.

Your article should give examples of practice and include ideas around how to use the weather and seasons, the importance of positive adult attitudes and how to support child-initiated play.

You should also provide an overview that evaluates the extent to which adults contribute to children's learning and development through outdoor play.

Further reading and resources

Bilton, H. (2010) *Outdoor Learning in the Early Years: Management and Innovation*, Oxon: Routledge.

Featherstone, S. and Ingham, K. (2001) *The Little Book of Outdoor Play*, Leicestershire: Featherstone Education Ltd.

Garrick, R. (2009) *Playing Outdoors in the Early Years* (2nd ed.), London: Continuum.

Knight, S. (2011) *Risk and Adventure in Early Years Outdoor Play: Learning from Forest Schools*, London: SAGE Publications Ltd.

Ready for work?

Gerard Morris Preschool assistant

I have always been a fan of outdoor play, but recently I have attended Forest School training. I am a complete convert and we are lucky that there is a small area of woodland not far away. We have approached the owner and he has given us permission to use it on a temporary basis with the children. Our first step was to carry out a thorough risk assessment that included how we would work with children to keep them from wandering off and also how to manage the journey there on foot. As everyone in my setting was keen to do this, there were no real obstacles that we could not overcome. We bought some high-visibility vests for the children and also a super buggy for toddlers to sit in. We also involved the parents and arranged a weekly rota so that there would be some additional support. Interestingly, this has been one activity that has really appealed to some of our dads. When we get to the site, we generally try and light a small fire. The children often make some newspaper twists in the setting and then we look for sticks. It is a little like a treasure hunt and children get very excited when they find sticks that are not wet. It is these practical details that children seem to pick up quickly and already many of our 3-year-old children can tell you what a fire does and how it stays alight. There is something special about sitting around a fire and having a story outdoors. We have a special circle of logs that the children sit on. They know that at 'fire time' they must stay seated. We even go out when it is wet and the children love hearing the rain on the leaves and standing in the rain and catching drops on their hands! I would recommend that anyone interested in early years should visit a Forest School.

Skills for practice

Support outdoor play and learning

What should you do if your setting's outdoor area is more suited to older children?

- Babies love swings and this can be a good resource for outdoors.
- Try to install a swing that is quite high up to prevent other children from getting knocked over.
- You could also think about a circle of natural logs that would allow babies to pull themselves up to a standing position and look out on the other children.
- It is important for babies to be taken out in pushchairs for walks. Remember to stop and talk about what the babies are noticing.

Glossary

A

Active learning – the process by which children concentrate and keep on trying if they encounter difficulties, and enjoy their achievements.

Attitudes – the views or opinions of an individual about an issue or topic. These views may be positive or negative.

C

Caste – a system of dividing society into classes or different social groups.

Child poverty – according to the UK government, children and families are deemed to be living in poverty when their reported income is less than 60 per cent of the UK median income before housing costs have been paid.

Coeliac disease – a digestive condition caused by gluten intolerance.

Conventions – using a set of agreed characteristics, e.g. in writing we use full stops, capital letters, commas and sentences.

Correlation – a relationship or connection between two things.

Creating and thinking critically – when children have and develop their own ideas, make links between ideas and develop strategies for doing things.

Curriculum – all of the experiences and learning that are provided by a setting.

D

Data – the information that is produced by your research methods. It covers facts, statistics and perceptions. Data has to be interpreted.

Debriefing – a conversation between a researcher and participant following an experiment to inform the participant about their experience and allowing them to talk about it.

E

Empower – to enable individuals to make choices about their own lives.

Ethics – the values and principles that govern the way a society operates.

Experiential learning – taking meaning from direct experience and hands-on activities.

F

Fine motor skills – control of the smaller muscles, such as those in the fingers, to carry out activities such as threading, using a knife and fork, or holding a pencil.

Fluctuate – to change quickly.

Food allergy – when the body has an abnormal reaction to a food or a component of a food.

Food intolerance – when the body is hypersensitive to a food or a component of food; there is a reaction but the reason for this reaction is not always clear.

Forest School approach – where settings are spending time outdoors, usually in woodlands, and carry out activities typically used in Scandinavian countries.

Formative assessment – assessment that takes place during the learning process, or 'assessment for learning'.

H

Holistic – all the child's needs, to include physical, emotional, social and cognitive.

Hypothesis – an explanation for an observation or scientific problem made using limited evidence as a starting point for further investigation.

I

Individual education plan – targets and planned implementation strategies for children who have special educational needs.

Informed consent – getting agreement from the person involved in the research, ensuring they fully understand what is happening and why.

In need – this refers to children who are unlikely to maintain, or be given the opportunity to maintain, a reasonable standard of health or development, or whose health could be impaired without the support of local authority services. It also includes children who are disabled.

K

Key person – a practitioner designated to take responsibility for a child's emotional well-being by having a strong attachment with them and a good relationship with their parents.

L

Learning journey/learning story – a way of assessing and planning for children's development using a narrative approach that can easily be shared and constructed with parents and children.

Legislation – the act of making laws.

Looked-after children – children who are in residential care, such as foster care or a residential home.

M

Macronutrients – a type of food required in large amounts in the diet.

Metabolism – the term used to describe the chemical processes that take place within the body to maintain life.

Micronutrients – a type of food required in small amounts in the diet.

N

Neuromuscular coordination – the joint operation of different muscles to produce a movement, e.g. raising your arm.

O

Organic – relating to or derived from living matter.

P

Policy – a written statement about what you will do.

Positional language – using terms such as 'on top' or 'to the left'.

Primary research – finding things out (new information) for yourself.

Procedure – an explanation of how you will do something.

Purposeful play – through play, children investigate and experience things, and 'have a go'.

Q

Qualitative research – exploratory research that allows us to go deeper into the research issues. Common methods to collect data include interviews and observations.

Quantitative research – research that tries to quantify the problem and uses statistics to analyse results. Common methods to collect data include questionnaires and surveys.

R

Raw data – data as it is collected, before it has been organised, analysed or interpreted in any way.

Receptive language – language that a child can understand.

Reflective practice – thinking about the way we work in order to make changes, build on strengths and stay up to date with developments.

Regulations – legal requirements that have to be followed.

Reliable – this means that your research will produce similar information to that found by someone else using the same methods with a similar sample.

Respite care – short-term care with the assistance of professional carers.

S

Safeguarding – the act of keeping children safe from harm.

Sample – a section of people or data used in research.

Secondary research – finding things out using material produced by others.

Self-evaluation form – a form that settings fill out on a regular basis showing how they intend to review and improve their provision.

Sequencing – being able to put events or pictures into the correct order.

Significant harm – this is defined in the Children Act 1989 as 'ill treatment or impairment of health or development'.

Solutes – a substance that is dissolved in another substance.

Special educational needs – used to describe children who have a learning difficulty that calls for special educational provision to be made for them – children who learn differently from most children of the same age, and who may need different or extra help from that given to others.

Statement of Special Educational Needs – this means that the local authority will assess the child to decide whether it is necessary for them to have an additional adult to support them in school. If so, the local authority will then produce a statement that sets out what is needed for the child to access the curriculum fully.

Statutory – set down and regulated by law.

Summative assessment – assessment of what the child knows and can do at the end of a period of learning, or 'assessment of learning'.

Symbolic action – a gesture that is representative of a real action.

Synthesis – the combination of separate elements or substances to form a whole.

T

Transitions – the changes that happen in all children's lives, such as starting school or personal changes such as a family break-up.

U

Universal service – a typical service such as the doctor's surgery, school, brownies or scouts.

V

Valid – this means that your research produces information that is well supported, justifiable and trustworthy.

Values – the principles or personal rules or standards that allow people to make decisions and choose between alternatives.

Variable – an element, feature or factor in a research project that is likely to change.

W

Winding – a process to help babies expel any air trapped in their digestive system during feeding.

Index